The AMA Handbook of

Financial Risk Management

The AMA Handbook of

Financial Risk Management

John J. Hampton

AMACOM

American Management Association
New York ★ Atlanta ★ Brussels ★ Chicago ★ Mexico City ★ San Francisco
Shanghai ★ Tokyo ★ Toronto ★ Washington, D.C.

Bulk discounts available. For details visit:
www.amacombooks.org/go/specialsales
Or contact special sales:
Phone: 800-250-5308
Email: specialsls@amanet.org
View all the AMACOM titles at: www.amacombooks.org

Library of Congress Cataloging-in-Publication Data

Hampton, John J., 1942-
    The AMA handbook of financial risk management / John J. Hampton.
        p. cm.
    Includes index.
    ISBN-13: 978-0-8144-1744-7
    ISBN-10: 0-8144-1744-2
    1. Financial risk management. 2. Risk management. I. Title. II. Title: Handbook of financial risk management.
    HD61.H314 2011
    658.15'5—dc22

                              2010048291

About AMA

American Management Association (www.amanet.org) is a world leader in talent development, advancing the skills of individuals to drive business success. Our mission is to support the goals of individuals and organizations through a complete range of products and services, including classroom and virtual seminars, webcasts, webinars, podcasts, conferences, corporate and government solutions, business books and research. AMA's approach to improving performance combines experiential learning—learning through doing—with opportunities for ongoing professional growth at every step of one's career journey.

Printing number

10 9 8 7 6 5 4 3 2 1

To the MBA and MS in Accountancy candidates and the high-quality graduate business instructors at Saint Peter's College

Contents

Preface

Managing financial risks is all about understanding how to reduce a complex business environment to workable concepts and models. Everything starts with risk. If the risk from a business operation is not acceptable, the analyst does not have to know financial management. But how do you know whether the risk is acceptable if you do not gather a few facts, make a few assumptions, and run some numbers that will give you a picture of risk and return?

The AMA Handbook of Financial Risk Management provides the tools for dealing with what are arguably the most important areas of financial decision making. In a broad risk management framework, every decision involves an exposure and an opportunity. This is a lesson from the emerging concept of enterprise risk management. Further, it is a lesson that is fully integrated into this handbook. Yes, we can lose money with every financial decision. We also can pursue success at higher levels than the present.

What are the areas that should receive attention? We can start by categorizing risks. The firm is producing goods or providing services, usually both. If it loses its edge in design or creation, problems arise. Customers must be found or created. Products must be part of extensive distribution systems involving both suppliers of components and the markets for the products. The firm needs adequate capital to maintain its asset base and conduct operations. It must comply with laws, regulations, and directives. It must be prepared for disruptions and changing conditions and have funds for contingencies. All of these factors require the firm to understand its exposures and opportunities and the relationships among them.

Once we have the big picture, we can build models for managing financial risks. We start with balance sheets, income statements, cash flow statements, and other organized accounting information. We build budgets with an eye to the future and to changing conditions that may cause the future to be different, many times quite different, from the past or the present. In profit planning, we establish goals, build measurement tools, and seek ways to achieve leverage that increases the success of operations. These are the day-to-day and year-to-year processes to establish long-term stability for the firm and its business units.

A quite separate set of financial risks arises when the firm must deal with the financing of assets. The first step here is to recognize that money has a time value. When the firm borrows, the meter of interest starts to run. When a firm considers a new operation, it is proposing to tie up capital that could be productive elsewhere. How much should be borrowed? How risky is it to tie up funds?

Financial investment decisions start with the concept of risk and required return. How much profit, and by profit we mean cash, must be returned to justify an investment with this amount of exposure? Do we have a proven market and a competitive product? Is this investment so large compared to our resources that its failure would lead to bankruptcy? What is our appetite for risk? Does this investment match it?

The next step is to build the models that allow us to answer these questions. We need to forecast a cash flow stream. It must consider the original outlay of cash, the inflows from operations, the tax impact of depreciating assets, the cost and timing of debt financing, and the eventual residual value of the investment at some point in the future. Then, the stream must be adjusted to display the likely return on the investment. This return, when compared with the required return, tells us whether a capital budgeting proposal is acceptable from a financial risk perspective.

Finally, firms face decisions that require more conceptual and even theoretical knowledge. The valuation of the firm is one such area. What makes a firm's stock attractive to investors? Should the firm emphasize short-term profits or long-term growth? What are the other determinants of value? The proper use of debt is equally important. Should the firm borrow from short-term or long-term sources? How much debt is too much? How much is too little? Growth decisions are important. Should the firm acquire other businesses? If yes, what are the risks? How much should be paid by each party in a merger or other business combination?

These are the issues that are addressed in this handbook. The chapters explain the concepts and show models. The appendixes to the chapters apply the models to specific areas of decision making. If the reader is not familiar with a concept, he can read the explanation of it before looking at the applications. If the reader has a strong finance background, she may find the applications useful as fully formatted tools for managing financial risks.

Before we begin this journey, I need to thank Mary Sullivan and Miss Lin Jin. As my administrative assistant, Mary lived with this book for a long time. As a proofreader of numbers and an astute observer of finance, Miss Jin showed the skills she will demonstrate when she completes her MBA program at Saint Peter's College. Thanks to both of you.

I also need to thank Bob Nirkind from the American Management Association. As the editor who directed this effort, he got it on track, moved it in the right direction, and made numerous observations to bring it all together. Thank you, Bob.

John J. Hampton,
Litchfield, Connecticut
November 2010

The AMA Handbook of

Financial Risk Management

Introduction

An ancient story from India tells of six blind men who were asked to describe an elephant by feeling different parts of the elephant's body. One man touched a leg and described a pillar. The man who touched a tusk had a different description, and so did the men who felt the tail, trunk, belly, and ear. The story is often used to demonstrate the possibility of different forms of truth depending upon one's perspective or lack thereof.

We should remember this story as we introduce financial risk management to the reader. As we moved into the twenty-first century, we discovered that there are two distinctly different viewpoints on financial risk. These evolved into two definitions of financial risk management:

- *Definition 1.* Financial risk management is the practice of creating economic value in a firm by using financial instruments to manage the firm's exposure to risk.
- *Definition 2.* Financial risk management is the management of business exposures that affect the availability of resources.

In recent years, we have come to recognize that financial risk is emerging as a new concept within the framework of enterprise risk management. To see what is happening, take a look at these definitions. The issue is not simply the availability of resources linked to exposures. Rather, financial risk deals with both exposures and opportunities linked to a firm's appetite for risk.

An example of the new perspective can be seen when we consider insuring homes in tropical areas against what appear to be strengthening hurricanes. A Category 4 or Category 5 hurricane that lingers over Florida for a few days would produce far more damage than could be covered by existing homeowner's and commercial property insurance mechanisms. That is the exposure for insurance companies as well as for the state of Florida, its Department of Insurance, and its emergency services. Is there also an opportunity in such a threatening situation? The answer is no if we restrict our vision, like the Indian blind men, to what is right in front of us.

However, suppose we broaden the view. Insurance companies cannot solve the financial risk problem. With insurance reserves in the hundreds of billions of dollars, they do not have enough capital. And they should not be taking big risks that could lead to their insolvency. The capital markets, on the other hand, have $40 to $60 trillion in capital, and many participants have a strong appetite for risk if it promises a hefty return.

Thus, financial risk managers have developed catastrophe bonds. An insurance company issues a bond at an interest rate above market rates and deposits the proceeds in an escrow account. If a covered catastrophe occurs, the insurer can use the escrow account to pay claims. An example is a $50 million bond that pays 13 percent interest for three years at a time when market interest rates are only 4 percent. If no hurricane strikes Florida, the principal and interest are paid in three years. However, the bond contains a provision that if the issuing insurance company suffers hurricane losses greater than $25 million in Florida during the three-year period, the losses above $25 million will be covered by the bond. If the losses are large enough, the bondholders will receive no money.

Financial risk management as discussed in this handbook has the dual perspective of exposure and opportunity. The hurricane threat carries an upside as well as a downside. We will look for the financial consequences at both ends of the risk-taking decision. The goal is to create a reference book to grab when you need specific knowledge. Specifically, we have provided:

- *A dictionary.* A collection of terms and definitions that are needed for a profession or a discipline.
- *An encyclopedia.* An authoritative examination of the major ideas and concepts in a field of knowledge, inquiry, or problem solving.
- *A cookbook.* A listing of prominent "recipes" with step-by-step directions for applying techniques to achieve results and outcomes.

The various chapters describe key insights and tools for managing risk in financial statements, profits, cash flows, capital investments, the value of the firm, and capital-structure management. At the end of most chapters are financial models that provide a structure for making sense out of the numbers that provide the framework for financial decisions. If you have specific questions, the "how to" analyses provide pathways to answering those questions. These models have been tested for many years by representatives of the Princeton Consulting Group. They clarify, they simplify, and they work.

Part 1 | Introduction to Financial Risk

This handbook serves all three purposes in the emerging field of financial risk management. Achieving these goals is rather a sizable task when we consider all the risks that organizations face. A partial and unstructured list might include the following:

- *Investment risk.* The firm makes an investment. The investment has risks associated with it. We may fail to earn a return or lose the invested capital.
- *Currency risk.* The investment was in a different country from the home country and involves a different currency. We have an exchange-rate exposure.
- *Liquidity risk.* We own securities or other assets that have value. Unfortunately, no one wants to buy them when we are ready to sell.
- *Cash flow risk.* Our activity did not create a sufficient cash flow to pay our obligations, and now we have to abandon it.
- *Debt risk.* We borrowed money, and now we cannot pay the interest and repay the loan balance.
- *Mortgage risk.* We put up an asset as collateral for a loan, and now we might lose it.
- *Credit risk.* We lent someone money who cannot repay it.
- *More credit risk.* We sold goods to another party, and we have not yet received any cash payment for them.
- *Insurable risk.* We took out insurance, but the insurance company became insolvent before it paid for the loss of our assets.
- *Interest-rate risk.* We gambled that interest rates would rise, but they dropped.
- *Valuation risk.* We bought a piece of property at the top of the market, and now it is worth much less.

- *Information technology risk.* We failed to keep up with new developments in computers and telecommunications, and now competitors are taking over our markets.
- *Hedging risk.* We thought the price we paid for raw materials was dropping, but it skyrocketed.

The list could go on and on. One large corporation identifies 2,100 business unit risks and 800 common risks across all business units. This handbook tries to bring some order to the listing by focusing on the nature of individual risks and techniques to deal with the most important financial decisions facing firms. This is the goal of Part 1.

Chapter
1
Categorizing Financial Risks

THE ENTERPRISE RiSK MANAGEMENT FRAMEWORK

Financial risk management is developed within a framework of enterprise risk management. In this section, we discuss that framework.

Enterprise Risk

This is defined as the variability of risks and opportunities when firms conduct business operations. It is a double-edged sword, as it focuses on both an upside and a downside. The focus is:

- *Missed opportunities.* The failure to undertake a business venture when it provides economic value possibilities at an acceptable level of risk
- *Financial losses.* The exposures that arise from business operations that can cause losses to current economic value

Financial risk is a subset of enterprise risk that encompasses the financial consequences, both good and bad, of managing enterprise risk and pursuing opportunities.

Enterprise Risk Management

A modern approach to understanding enterprise risk is to examine it in the context of enterprise risk management (ERM), one of the most popular and misunderstood of today's important business topics. ERM addresses the methods and processes used by organizations to manage risks and seize opportunities related to the achievement of their objectives. ERM encourages organizations to identify relevant events, developments, and circumstances; assess them in terms of likelihood and magnitude of impact; develop a strategy to reduce risk or seize opportunity; and monitor the progress toward objectives. This process is designed to protect enterprises from harm and create value for owners and other stakeholders.

ERM tells us that there is a new world of risk. No longer is risk management largely limited to the isolated silos of production, distribution, marketing, and segmented lines of business or business units. We do not assume that the chief marketing officer is responsible for the financial exposures and opportunities in the marketplace anymore than the chief financial officer is accountable for financial risks. The risk picture is incomplete when it is limited to the individual components of an organization. This realization encourages new approaches to assess an organization's appetite for risk, avoid unacceptable exposures, and seize opportunities.

Business Risk

ERM is rapidly replacing earlier approaches to risk management. Many risk discussions start with the term *business risk*, which has a variety of definitions, including:

- Risk associated with the unique circumstances of a particular industry or competitor in a market
- A situation, the result of either internal conditions or external factors, that may have a negative impact on the profitability of a given company
- The possibility of a destructive shift in the data, assumptions, and analysis that are used in planning for the employment of assets to achieve financial goals

Sometimes the definitions contradict each other. As an example, one definition refers to the possibility of loss inherent in a firm's operations and environment that may impair a firm's ability to achieve adequate returns on its investment. The proponents of this definition go on to define financial risk as exposures arising from the use of debt or the creation of other liabilities. With these definitions, total corporate risk becomes the combination of business risk and financial risk. This contradicts the other definitions, where financial risk is a subset of business risk.

Addressing Financial Risk

Organizations have two ways to address risk. The wrong way is to assume that people can understand hundreds or even thousands of exposures. This is not possible. Risks and opportunities must be organized and accepted at various levels by risk owners. A brief overview of the new ERM includes the following specific features:

- *Upside of risk.* Most people discuss risk as the possibility of loss. This is totally insufficient, as risk also has an upside. A lost opportunity is just as much a financial loss as damage to people and property. This is a key insight. Ask the ancient Chinese warrior Sun Tzu or the fictional *Godfather* character Michael Corleone.
- *Alignment with the business model.* A business model is a framework for achieving goals. Within it, each manager supervises a limited span of subordinates, functions, or subsidiaries. The manager also oversees a limited number of risks and initiatives. ERM encourages us to align the hierarchy of risk categories with the business model.
- *Risk owners.* Just as someone is accountable for revenues, profits, and efficiency in each organizational unit, a single person should be responsible for each category of risk. When questions arise, we should not be dealing with a committee or multiple individuals. We should go directly to the risk owner. However, some risk assessments must be shared. Exposures arising from the culture, the leadership, or even

the reputation of the organization should be assessed using collaboration among key executives and the board.

- *Central risk function.* Although risks cannot be managed centrally, organizations need a central risk function. Its role is to scan for changing conditions from a central vantage point and share the findings with the risk owners. This approach recognizes that risks cross units and responsibilities, and that critical risks and opportunities can easily be missed in the day-to-day operation of a business. In a change from traditional thinking, organizations should consider creating a central risk function that, by itself, does not have any responsibility for risk management. Risk goes with the risk owners. Risks that cross units or responsibilities are identified centrally and dealt with using customized solutions. Just as the internal auditor identifies and reports noncompliant procedures but does not suggest how to correct them, the central risk function identifies and shares its findings.
- *High-tech platform.* ERM encourages the use of new technologies to clarify risks and opportunities. We now have the capability to tie together the whole story of risk from the top to the bottom of the organization. We can show the relationships visually, isolate key factors, and prepare reports on the status of the exposures we face and the opportunities we pursue. Technology is a friend of risk management.

RISK CATEGORIES

Like so many concepts in a complex modern organization, the term *financial risk management* conjures up various responses. What does it mean? Is it limited to financial risks, such as excessive debt or a shortage of cash? Does it cover business interruption, product-liability lawsuits, or natural disasters that affect operations? How does it differ from corporate finance, where the chief financial officer seeks to increase the value of the firm and achieve required returns suitable to the risk of investments? Finally, is financial risk management the sole purview of the CFO? Are production, marketing, administration, and other executives exempt from the discussion?

Financial risk management encompasses the tools that we use in the framework of enterprise risk management. The tools are part of the planning process as firms develop strategies for creating economic value. They assist in decision making as companies assess risk and seize opportunity.

This approach to financial risk is fundamentally different from earlier definitions. Financial risk management recognizes that every business decision has an upside and a downside. Thus, risks are viewed as being in the realm of uncertainty that can have favorable or unfavorable outcomes. Within this framework, managers identify a variety of exposures and opportunities under the umbrella of financial risk.

Categorizing Financial Risks

Enterprise risk management encourages the organizing of risks and opportunities into a hierarchy that matches the business model of an organization. One structure creates the following categories:

- *Production.* The creation of the goods and/or services sold or distributed by the organization
- *Marketing.* Efforts to reach customers or clients or to identify or develop markets for products or services
- *Cash flows.* Management of cash flows from operations, investment of capital, and creation of an appropriate return on invested assets
- *Compliance.* Aligning activities with legal and regulatory requirements and processes
- *Technology.* Dealing with changes in assets and systems that provide information and communications
- *Business disruption.* Preparing for negative events that slow or cease a business's operations and taking steps to return to normal activity

We can illustrate the structuring of risks by stepping down one level below each category.

Production Risk

Assigned to a chief production officer but shared on the high-tech platform, the exposures and opportunities in this area cover risks such as:

- *Design.* Does production coordinate with marketing, finance, legal, and others to develop the right products or services that meet the needs of all parties?
- *Supply.* Does the organization have policies and procedures to mitigate disruption risks with respect to components or inputs?
- *Process.* Is the organization employing the best practices for creating products or services and ensuring that they meet quality and other standards?
- *Efficiency.* Are best practices being used to control costs and improve the productivity of people, assets, and systems?

Production Risk at Phillips, Nokia, and Ericsson. Sometimes the financial consequences of a "relatively small" incident can prove to be quite substantial. An example is what happened after a Phillips N.V. semiconductor fabrication plant in New Mexico was struck by lightning in March 2000. The bolt started a small fire that was quickly extinguished. Nobody was hurt, and damage was quite minor. However, the problem for a few of Phillips's clients, notably Nokia and I.M. Ericsson, was that the plant was the only source of microscopic circuits for their cell phones. In fact, 40 percent of the plant's production went to these two companies. As shown in Figure 1-1, the financial risk in their production area was a lack of redundancy in a channel for components for a key product. Trays of wafers were destroyed, and production was interrupted.

After the fire, Phillips alerted 30 customers that a fire had taken place and production had been stopped. Phillips told the customers that it estimated a one-week time delay to clean up the facility and start production. Nokia ignored the estimate. After demanding to know all details of the incident, Nokia identified the disruption as a critical risk and pulled out all the stops to find alternative suppliers. Nokia was successful. Even though the disruption extended much longer than one week, Nokia experienced virtually no delay in its production and shipping of cell phones.

Ericsson had a very different experience. Lower-level employees did not tell the head of production about the delay for several weeks. By the time Ericsson sought other sources of supply for microchips, Nokia had contracted for all spare capacity.

It was a small incident at another company that created significant financial losses. Phillips experienced losses of between $1 and $3 million after collecting $40 million from business interruption insurance policies. Nokia had minor additional expenses, which were offset by a small rise in market share as it made sales to former Ericsson customers. Ericsson suffered big time, incurring a loss in excess of $2 billion. Within a year, the company was forced to withdraw from the mobile phone market.

Lesson Learned. Financial risk management needs to incorporate production risk exposures and opportunities.

Production Risk Complexity at Dell. A second story shows the complexity of a system used by Dell Computer. It involves Dell, Intel, and Toshiba. Dell used Intel's Pentium processor to power its personal computers in a multistep production process. Toshiba Ceramics grew silicon and sliced it into wafers in Japan. Intel etched the wafers in a semiconductor lab in Oregon and then shipped the etched wafers to be packaged in an assembly plant in Malaysia. The packages were finally shipped to a Dell plant in Ireland, where they were inserted into computers. Such a system had multiple places where a disruption could cause short-term or even long-term financial risk.

Production Risk at Ford Motor. A third story was an actual disruption that occurred at Ford Motor Corporation in the fourth quarter of 2001. Following the September 11 attack on the World Trade Center in New York City, U.S. airports were closed for a short period of time, but U.S. borders were closed for much longer. Ford experienced a 13 percent drop in U.S. production in the fourth quarter because trucks carrying components for automobile and truck manufacturing were stopped at the Mexican and Canadian borders.

Visualizing Production Risk. Some people argue that it is difficult to foresee the kind of production risks that disrupted the businesses of Ericsson and Ford and could have affected Dell. Financial risk management seeks to identify scenarios where such exposures can be recognized and mitigated. Figure 1-1 shows a view in a high-tech platform where the CEO can see all the way down a risk structure to the issue of multiple suppliers. Avoiding sole suppliers for critical components and creating redundancy in a supply chain are examples of financial risk management.

Marketing Risk

The second category of financial risk involves marketing exposures and opportunities. Examples of subrisks are:

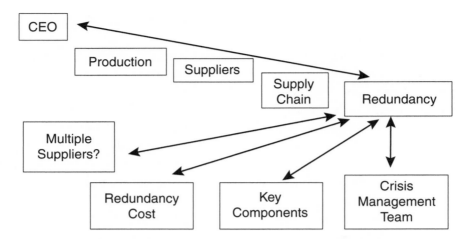

Figure 1-1. Financial Risk Management Solution to Production Risk.

- *Customer needs.* Do we have an understanding of what potential customers will buy based on their real or perceived desires to purchase?
- *Distribution.* Do we have efficient and redundant channels for moving a product or service from creation through a channel to a final customer or client?
- *Volume.* Are we likely to sell sufficient units to justify the original investment of capital and provide an adequate return given the risk undertaken?
- *Pricing.* Do we expect the firm to obtain an adequate price to cover variable and fixed costs, including financing charges, and provide an adequate return on invested capital?

Example: The Upside and Downside of Marketing Risk. As an example of a financial risk management approach to marketing risk, consider a firm that has a choice of two different selling prices that create two different forecasted levels of sales. A quick financial calculation shows the earnings before taxes with each set of data. Once the numbers have been calculated, the decision makers can consider the risk involved with raising the price. Will it scare off buyers? They can also consider the opportunity. Will buyers perceive higher quality so that the higher price produces greater sales? Figure 1-2 shows the data and answers.

Answer: The lower price produces higher earnings before taxes under the original assumptions. With a bad reaction to the higher price, the downside reduces earnings by about one-third. With a positive perception of quality, earnings are expected to jump by more than 60 percent.

Cash Flow Risk

The next subcategory of financial risk management involves having adequate cash to support production, marketing, and other areas of the firm. A number of subcategories can be identified within cash flow risk.

Data	Price 1	Price 2	Downside	Upside
Selling price per unit	$200	$250	$250	$250
Variable cost per unit	$70	$70	$70	$70
Forecasted unit sales	600	400	300	700

Data	Price 1	Price 2	Downside	Upside
Revenues	120,000	100,000	75,000	175,000
Variable costs	42,000	28,000	21,000	49,000
Fixed costs	1,000	1,000	1,000	1,000
Interest	200	200	200	200
Earnings before taxes	76,800	70,800	52,800	124,800
Which is higher?	FIRST			
What is the downside?			-31%	
What is the upside?				63%

Figure 1-2. Forecasting the Earnings Upside and Downside in Market Risk.

Organizational Cash Flows. Cash comes from many sources, and the balancing of cash receipts and disbursements can be a highly technical task. Figure 1-3 shows cash as being at the center of dealings with owners, creditors, production, marketing, and distribution. As can be seen from the figure, other sources and uses of cash can also affect cash flow. A firm may have autonomous subsidiaries, such as Japanese operations or the ownership of an unrelated business. Such an entity can provide cash flow to a parent company or can get into trouble and require cash infusions. Key initiatives are another liquidity concern. A firm can start a project and begin pumping money into it. Or it can discover a new source of cash.

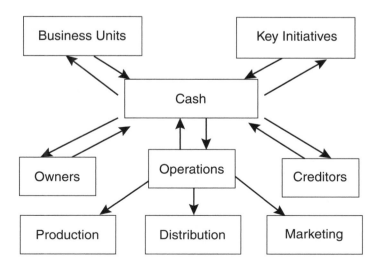

Figure 1-3. Organizational Cash Flows.

Operational Cash Flows. Financial risk management recognizes that investors open businesses with the goal that the firm's primary cash flows will be derived from selling goods or services and that the firm will receive larger cash inflows than the outlays that it experiences. Figure 1-4 shows the liquidity risk from these cash flows. If this picture produces negative cash flows over a period of time, a firm cannot survive.

Key Initiative Cash Flows. The pure operational cash flows are not the full picture of how a firm can get into trouble with its operations. Figure 1-5 adds other operational needs when a firm identifies key initiatives to change or improve operations. A firm may start up a new line of business, open a new operating unit, enter a new market, or seek to turn around a declining business. If it overestimates the cash needs for such initiatives, they can drain cash from operations, and the firm can experience a liquidity crisis.

Capital Structure Cash Flows. Most large corporations use both debt and equity. *Capital structure* is the composition of the debt and equity that a firm uses to finance its

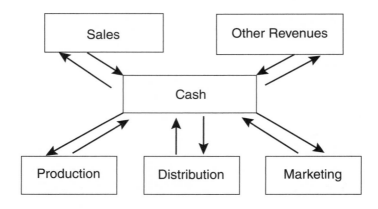

Figure 1-4. Pure Operational Cash Flows.

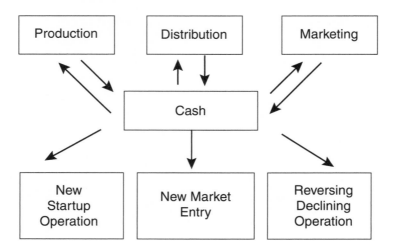

Figure 1-5. Key Initiative Cash Flows.

assets. Figure 1-6 shows cash inflows and outflows from debt sources. Suppliers extend credit when the firm purchases inventory and other items. Financial institutions can lend money. The firm can issue bonds. Liquidity risk arises when capital markets tighten up and debt funding is restricted.

Credit Cash Flows. This liquidity exposure is that a loss of cash might occur when one party fails to make a cash payment as promised. Examples are customers who fail to pay for goods sold on credit terms, borrowers who fail to make payments on loans or mortgages, and insolvent banks, insurance companies, and other financial institutions that fail to release money to individuals and firms that are entitled to receive funds. Figure 1-7 shows the cash flows and possible interruptions as a result of defaults by parties that are obligated to make payments to a firm.

Investment Cash Flows. In addition to their own operations, firms invest funds in new projects and in the securities of and ventures with other parties. Figure 1-8 shows

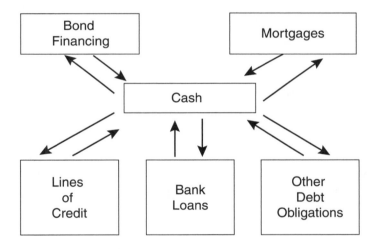

Figure 1-6. Capital Structure Cash Flows.

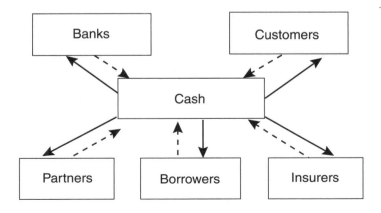

Figure 1-7. Credit Cash Flows.

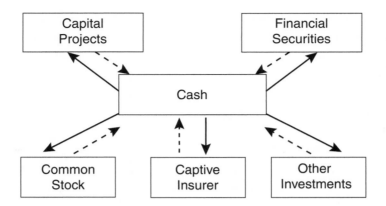

Figure 1-8. Investment Risk.

investments in major projects and the purchase of the common stock or financial securities of other companies. It also shows a captive insurance company, where a firm creates a separate company to insure a portion of its property or liability exposures. Liquidity risk emerges when any of these activities do not meet expectations.

Compliance Risk

Corporations are expected to operate in accordance with legal and regulatory requirements imposed by governments and other bodies. A failure to comply can prove to be quite expensive. Figure 1-9 illustrates cash flows to meet compliance requirements:

- *Financial reporting.* Publicly traded companies must produce accurate financial statements while complying with generally accepted accounting principles and the guidelines of regulators and stock exchanges.

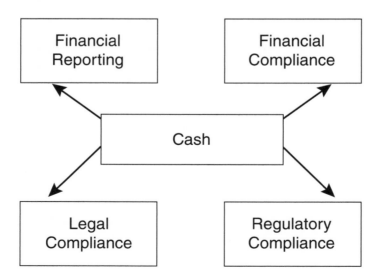

Figure 1-9. Compliance Risk.

- *Regulatory compliance.* In many industries, firms must comply with specific standards for the products they create. Pharmaceuticals and edible products must meet guidelines for purity. Vehicles must meet standards for safety. When an organization lacks internal controls or effective internal audit processes in the production of goods, it can find itself in trouble with government agencies or other regulatory bodies.
- *Financial compliance.* Some companies must comply with regulations concerning their strength and stability. These include banks, insurance companies, and public utilities.
- *Legal compliance.* All companies must conduct business within the laws of the country and/or region in which they operate. The extent of the specific requirements for legal compliance is not widely known. As an example, the state of Florida regulates almost 500 different businesses through a system of licenses, employees, safety, and other regulations.

Technology Risk

The rising importance of technology for the conduct of modern business has raised the profile of technology risk as an area for financial risk management. Figure 1-10 shows areas of such exposure:

- *Business support risk.* An organization faces exposures when it uses technology in its production and marketing. When critical equipment or systems fail, business disruption can be quite expensive.
- *Information systems risk.* Technology connects most companies to the world. Exposures arise when key managers, suppliers, or customers do not receive responsive information on products, markets, and finances.
- *Communications risk.* This exposure deals with linkages among operating units, vendors, customers, and others if information is not exchanged accurately and on a timely basis.

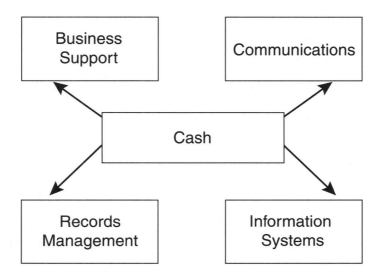

Figure 1-10. Technology Risk.

- *Records management risk.* These exposures endanger the ability to maintain the complete, accurate, and timely records that make up modern information and accounting systems.

Business Disruption Risk

An unexpected disruption of operations is one of the most dangerous areas in financial risk management. What happens if an earthquake destroys a firm's ability to produce goods? What happens if a breakdown in computer systems compromises customers' personal information or causes a leak of confidential business processes? Does the organization have the ability to provide an effective response to an unexpected emergency or crisis? Will a public relations disaster cause serious damage to a firm's reputation or brands? Figure 1-11 shows these financial risks.

FINANCIAL RISK MANAGEMENT

Now we know a number of financial risks and can see how broadly they spread across a company. We are ready to address risk in a broad context. First, we might ask who analyzes risk. Then, we might consider the skills that are needed to do the job.

Who Is the Financial Risk Manager?

Many firms make the mistake of believing that the chief financial officer (CFO) should be the primary manager of financial risk. This is not the case. The board of directors, CEO, and other senior managers and professionals should be involved in assessing business decisions, looking for lost opportunities and downside exposures. In this context, we can identify failures of financial risk management if senior executives do not understand the financial risk. The short answer to the question is: Everybody who contributes to

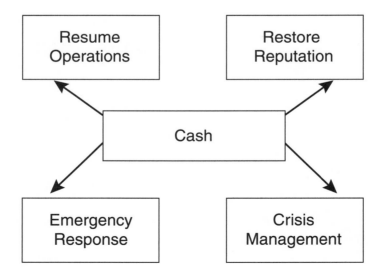

Figure 1-11. Disruption Risk.

the bottom line has to understand the ramifications of failing to understand the financial implications of the risks that he accepts. In this sense, we are all financial risk managers.

Skills for Financial Risk Managers

If financial risk management is within the purview of many managers and professionals in the firm, what is the knowledge needed to understand financial risk within the framework of enterprise risk management? One such list is:

- *Accounting, cash flow, and budgeting risks.* If accounting is a mystery, a fog settles over the process of planning, budgeting, and decision making. In practice, accounting decisions rarely drive business decisions, but firms often become bogged down in the effects of a decision on reported earnings or the balance sheet. A greater danger is that they can make bad decisions about risk. Even though financial risk occurs primarily because of cash shortfalls and liquidity problems, such exposure can be detected from the balance sheet, income statement, and cash flow statement prepared by the firm's accounting department. It is critical to understand these reports.

- *Analyzing operating risks.* The CFO has an advantage in that she knows appropriate techniques to measure whether a firm has sufficient cash flow or adequate profits. However, the CFO should not be the only person with such knowledge. Every key manager should understand the right ways and wrong ways to create budgets. To do this, they need skills in profit planning, leverage, return on investment, and other financial tools.

- *Risk and return.* The framework of risk and return is fully developed, easy to grasp, and essential for long-term business operations. What is our appetite for risk? What opportunities match that appetite? How do we decide whether to do business or avoid business? What is the role of the time value of money? Understanding the relationship of risk and return sets the foundation for analyzing financial decisions.

- *Capital budgeting.* Should we expand our current operations? Should we invest in the development of new products? Do we have opportunities in other markets? All these questions involve the investment of capital. All decision makers should understand how to create a cash flow stream and determine the likely return from investments of capital.

- *Value of a firm.* We know that our firm has value, but how much value? What factors should be considered when we seek to enhance the market price of our common stock or make a decision on purchasing the stock or assets of other companies? Further, we know that the value of the firm is affected by the risk of adding debt to the capital structure. If we borrow at 6 percent and finance assets that earn 10 percent, we increase our return to the owners of a business. But how much should we borrow? When is debt a good choice? When does it get too risky? How do we value business combinations? These topics should not be left to the corporate planning department. They should involve managers and professionals throughout the organization.

CONCLUSION

The breadth of financial risks and the skills needed to manage them are constant challenges for modern corporations, particularly those that operate in an expanding global economy. And who does operate in such a world today? The next section of this book addresses the skills of interpreting financial statements, analyzing operating risks, understanding the interrelationship of risk and return, developing a capital budget, and recognizing drivers of valuation of the firm.

Part 2 | Accounting, Cash Flow, and Budget Exposures

Enterprise risk is not owned by the finance and accounting departments, but they do make many of the rules, and we must understand what they do. In the three chapters in Part II, we establish a foundation in three areas:

- *Risks from financial accounting*. In this chapter, we engage the accountant on his own turf. Accounting is the language of business. If we know the assumptions and theories that lead to financial statements, we can also understand the value and limitations of using accounting data to understand risk and opportunity. This is particularly important because businesses manage their operations using accounting data. They prepare financial statements such as balance sheets and income statements. Can we rely on these statements? Do they show us risk?
- *Risks in cash flows*. Accounting uses its own systems, but cash flows are the goal of businesses. Can we use the output of the accounting process to understand cash receipts and disbursements? The cash flow statement is an ally of the financial risk manager.
- *Risks in operating budgets*. The blueprint for building the firm in the future is, to a large degree, reflected in its operating budget. What are the risks in revenue forecasts? In expense and cost allocations? How do we spot political and other risks in the budgeting process? These topics are covered in this chapter.

Financial accounting, cash flows, and budgeting are the foundation topics for using financial data to identify financial risks.

Chapter
2

Risks from Financial Accounting

OVERVIEW OF ACCOUNTING

It is widely understood that financial accounting is the system that businesses use to keep records that explain what is happening in their operations. The stated goals of accounting involve identifying individual commercial transactions so that they can be used in the preparation of summarized financial statements that provide significant information about the entity. To a large degree, we accept accounting as being the language of corporations, banks, and other organizations. To an even larger degree, we need to be suspicious of accounting records that hide the risks inherent in the firm's management, marketing, and financial activities.

An understanding of financial accounting is an essential prerequisite for making effective decisions in the area of finance.

ACCOUNTING PRINCIPLES

In the United States and much of the rest of the world, accountants have developed *generally accepted accounting principles (GAAP)* that must be followed in recording transactions and preparing financial statements. The following are some of the most important principles and the accompanying risks.

Business Entity

When accounting transactions are recorded, every business or organization is treated as a separate entity. A sole proprietorship has business records separate from the owner's personal records, just as a corporation has records separate from its shareholders' records. *Financial risk:* Companies can hide liabilities and weak assets in a complex structure.

Going Concern

A going concern is a business that is expected to continue to operate for an indefinite period of time. This principle is followed in preparing accounting records unless there is evidence that the business is experiencing difficulties and may cease operating. *Financial risk:* The records might lag current events or otherwise fail to reveal circumstances that could undermine the business's ability to operate as a going concern.

Going Concern Accounting

Four telecommunications companies have agreed to merge. Each company submitted audited financial statements to an independent appraiser to determine a value. One of the companies owned and operated satellites that carried sensitive and encrypted data between the continents of Africa and South America. Based on its reported profits over a six-year period, the appraisal showed the company to be worth $12 million. It was priced at that amount in the transaction.

Six months after the agreement closed, an underwater cable was completed linking South Africa and Brazil. The company's revenues immediately dropped by 80 percent as customers switched to a faster and even more secure transmission system for data. A few months later, the unit ceased operations.

Lesson learned: Sometimes a going concern is not actually going.

Cost Basis of Assets

All expenses are recorded at actual cost as determined by the amount of cash involved or the market value of the transaction. If a machine is purchased for $100,000, the accounting records reflect this value, even though the firm's management may feel that the machine is "worth" $150,000. *Financial risk:* While the values of assets are static in the accounting system, they may be widely different in the marketplace. This can lead to incorrect decisions when assessing both the liquidity and the profitability of a firm.

Cost Basis of Assets

A bank and an insurance company were discussing a merger through an exchange of stock. Based on the accounting value of the two firms' assets, the bank shareholders should receive 65 percent of the stock and the insurance company owners should receive 35 percent. A public announcement was made. Subsequently, both parties learned that the insurance company's real estate consisted of many commercial and residential complexes in the center of several large and modern cities. The properties had been purchased between 1890 and 1940 and had risen significantly in value. The bank, on the other hand, had assets consisting of relatively short-term loans and mortgages, with an accounting value that approximated their actual value. The deal collapsed when the discrepancy in asset values was discovered.

Lesson learned: Beware of how you view the values of assets that have been recorded using GAAP.

Accrual Basis of Revenues

The economic effects of all transactions are recognized during the time period in which they occur. Under an accrual system, revenues are recognized (accrued) at the point of sale, even though cash may be received later. Similarly, expenses are recognized when the obligations are created, not necessarily when they are paid. Revenues resulting from credit sales that have not yet been paid are recorded as receivables. Expenses that have been incurred but not paid are recorded as payables. In a small percentage of cases, businesses may operate on a cash basis, where transactions are not recognized until the cash is collected or paid. This situation is relatively rare. *Financial risk:* Accrual accounting can be misused or misunderstood. As an example, a sale can be made and recorded near the end of an accounting period. It will increase revenues in the period. Subsequently, there may be a long delay before the sale results in a delivery of a product or service. The sale may even be canceled. As a result, profits will be overstated in the period in which the transaction is recorded.

Accrual of Revenues

A fast food chain has a successful business model using franchising to build stores, process food, and market to consumers. It licenses its name, reputation, equipment, recipes, and marketing efforts to other parties, who operate as the owners of their own businesses. To obtain a franchise, a party must agree to pay $200,000 a year for a minimum period of three years. After that time, the franchising party may renew the contract if it meets the standards of the fast food chain.

Under the accounting rules, the fast food chain records all $600,000 for the three years as soon as the agreement is signed. In a recent year, it sold 80 franchises, bringing in $48 million in reported revenues. One-third of the franchisees went out of business in the first year, with most of them defaulting on the payments owed in years two and three. The company was forced to write down earnings in those years by $28 million and almost went bankrupt itself.

It should be noted that this is an abuse of the Financial Accounting Standards Board Standard 45 Accounting for Franchise Fee Revenue but it does happen.

Lesson learned: If it is not done properly, the system of accruing revenues can be a case of counting chickens before they hatch.

CATEGORIES OF ACCOUNTS

In financial accounting, five categories of accounts may be identified. Each of these is discussed in turn, along with a brief statement of the financial risk associated with it and its subcategories.

Asset Accounts

An asset is any resource that allows a firm to conduct its business. A tangible asset has a physical existence, as in the case of cash or a machine. An intangible asset has no physical existence. Assets are typically divided into three categories:

- *Current assets.* These are assets that will be converted into cash within the current operating cycle or within the next year, whichever is longer, as a result of the ordinary operations of the business.
  Financial risk: Some assets become illiquid. If the firm is counting on them to pay its bills, a default may occur.

- *Fixed assets.* These assets are resources that will be used to generate revenues. The assets will not be converted into cash in the current accounting period unless they are damaged, become obsolete, or are otherwise replaced.
  Financial risk: Nobody knows the real value of physical assets.

- *Intangible assets.* These are resources that do not represent physical property or securities. Their value is derived from the fact that the firm has the right to use them. Examples are trademarks and patents.
  Financial risk: These values can change dramatically in a moment as a result of good news or bad news in the media.

Liability Accounts

A liability is a debt of the business. These are normally divided into three categories:

- *Current liabilities.* These are debts of the firm that must be paid during the current operating cycle or one year, whichever is less.
  Financial risk: Excessive short-term obligations can lead to defaults if they depend upon cash flows that can be interrupted.

- *Long-term liabilities.* These are debts of the firm that will not be paid during the next year in the ordinary course of business.
  Financial risk: Longer-term debt may be less of a liquidity risk than short-term debt, but loan agreements often contain covenants that, if broken, can produce demands for immediate payment.

- *Obligations under capital leases.* Also called a financial lease, a capital lease is a long-term agreement to rent an asset on terms stating that the agreement cannot be canceled by either party.
  Financial risk: The economic consequences of such an agreement are the same as if the company had borrowed money and purchased the asset.

Equity Accounts

Equity is a term used to represent the ownership rights in a company. The term *capital* is used to represent ownership rights in a bank. In a corporation, three major types of equity accounts may be identified:

- *Preferred stock.* This is an equity security that is given a preference over other stock in a corporation with respect to dividends and return of the stockholders' investment if the firm is liquidated.

Financial risk: If cash flow stalls, preferred stockholders can take all or most of the firm's after-tax profits, leaving little or nothing for common shareholders.

- *Common stock and retained earnings.* These accounts represent the residual ownership of a corporation. The common stock account is created to record capital contributed by owners who purchase stock. Retained earnings reflects prior profits that were not distributed to shareholders.
  Financial risk: Common shareholders bear all the operational risk and benefit from most of the business opportunity of financing assets for the firm.

Revenue Accounts

A revenue is an inflow of assets, not limited to cash, in exchange for goods sold or services rendered. Two types of revenue accounts are:

- *Operating revenues.* These are inflows from sales of goods or performance of services in the firm's main operating areas.
  Financial risk: Revenues may be inadequate to cover payments to creditors and create profits for investors.

- *Other income.* This involves inflows from investments or other sources that are not considered part of the firm's normal operations.
  Financial risk: The return may be insufficient to offset inadequate operating revenues.

Expense Accounts

An expense is the consumption of any asset while conducting the business of the firm. It may involve the payment of cash for supplies, labor, or other costs associated with services rendered. It may also involve the wearing out of assets during the process of conducting business. Four types of expense accounts are commonly identified:

- *Cash expenses.* These are costs that must be paid in cash shortly after they are incurred.
  Financial risk: Inadequate cash inflows can lead to default on obligations.

- *Noncash expenses.* These are costs that reflect the decline in the value of assets that are consumed during the course of business.
  Financial risk: Noncash expenses may reflect excessive purchase of assets in earlier periods or an inability to update current assets that are deteriorating in performance or value.

- *Interest charges.* When the firm borrows money, it must pay interest on the debt. The interest payments are an expense of the business.
  Financial risk: High interest rates or excessive borrowing can leave the firm unable to pay the interest due.

- *Taxes other than income taxes.* When firms pay state, local, real estate, sales, and other taxes, it is a cash expense.
  Financial risk: Taxes levied may be excessive compared to operating cash inflows.

Recording Accounting Entries

Accountants use a double-entry system of accounting. One entry involves a debit and the other a credit. In computerized systems, the debit is entered with a positive number and the credit is entered with a minus sign. The plus sign does not mean that a balance is increasing. The minus sign does not mean that a balance is decreasing. They are simply debits and credits.

For the five categories of accounts described above, the debits and credits have the following impacts:

- Asset. A debit increases the balance of an asset account. A credit reduces it.
- Liabilities, Equity, and Revenues. These accounts are sources of assets. They increase with a credit offsetting the debits that show rises in assets. As an example, if a firm borrows $100,000, it records a debit of $100,000 to cash and a credit of $100,000 to a liability account.
- Expenses. A debit increases an expense account, reflecting the fact that the expense must be offset by a credit to an asset or liability account. If it is a cash expense, cash is reduced with a credit. If the expense has not yet been paid, a credit is made to a liability account.

A summary of the accounting structure shows:

- Asset   Increase with debit   Decrease with credit
- Liability   Increase with credit   Decrease with debit
- Capital   Increase with credit   Decrease with debit
- Revenue   Increase with credit   Decrease with debit
- Expense   Increase with debit   Decrease with credit

TRIAL BALANCE

The five categories of accounts are organized into a *trial balance*, which is a list of the current summarized values of all accounting transactions in a period. As an example, suppose a company is started when the owners contribute $2 million and borrow $1 million and put the money in a bank. Suppose further that the company has cash revenues of $4 million and cash expenses of $2.5 million during a period of time. Figure 2-1 shows the trial balance for this company at this moment in time. Note that the cash and expenses

Cash	+$4.5 million
Debt	-1.0 million
Equity	-2.0 million
Revenues	-4.0 million
Expenses	+2.5 million
Balance	**$0.0 million**

Figure 2-1. Trial Balance.

have debit balances, indicated by a plus sign, and the other accounts have credit balances, indicated by a minus sign.

FINANCIAL STATEMENTS

Companies develop many financial statements to present a view of their business operations. Two of the most important are the balance sheet and the income statement. We will cover each of these in turn.

Balance Sheet Equation

A *balance sheet* shows the financial position of a firm as of a specific date, usually the close of the last day in an accounting period. It shows how the resources of the firm (assets) are provided by capital from creditors (liabilities) and owners (equity). It provides a snapshot, if you will, of the firm's financial position after the revenue and expense accounts have been zeroed out at the end of an accounting period, in preparation for the start of a new period. It is created from the final balances in the asset, liability, and equity accounts. As its name implies, the two sides of the balance sheet must balance *at the start and at the end of an accounting period*. This may be expressed as:

Assets = Liabilities + Equity

A comparative balance sheet shows the starting and ending balances for the permanent accounts that are not returned to zero balances. Figure 2-2 shows a comparative balance sheet.

Manipulation of the Balance Sheet

The balance sheet is usually reliable as a report on the status of a company at a particular moment in time. Still, it can be manipulated. The Lehman Brothers 2006 balance sheet shows the dangers of relying completely on accounting data. The story is told separately from the balance sheet.

	Start	End
Cash	$900	$1,275
Equipment	2,600	2,600
Building	2,350	2,350
Total Assets	**$5,850**	**$6,225**
Short-term debt	$350	$350
Mortgage	1,500	1,500
Stock	4,000	4,000
Retained earnings	0	375
Total Liabilities and Equity	**$5,850**	**$6,225**

Figure 2-2. Comparative Balance Sheet.

Lehman Balance Sheet

	IN MILLIONS	November 30, 2006
ASSETS		
Financial instruments owned	$226,596	45%
Securities received as collateral	6,099	1%
Collateralized agreements	219,057	43%
Cash, receivables, and PP&E	43,318	9%
Other assets	5,113	1%
Intangible assets and goodwill	3,362	1%
Total Assets	**$503,545**	**100%**

LIABILITIES AND EQUITY		
Short-term borrowings	$20,638	4%
Financial instruments sold but not yet purchased	125,960	25%
Obligation to return securities received as collateral	6,099	1%
Collateralized financing	170,458	34%
Payables and other accrued liabilities	58,609	12%
Deposits at banks	21,412	4%
Total long-term capital	100,369	20%
Total Liabilities and Equity	**$503,545**	**100%**

Lehman Brothers Balance Sheet Manipulation

Richard Fuld, CEO of Lehman Brothers, addressed the fixed-income division of Lehman Brothers in April 2007. He told the audience that Lehman did not have "a balance problem." Perhaps Mr. Fuld has problems reading balance sheets.

In March 2010 Anton R. Valukas, a court-appointed examiner of e-mails and other records of Lehman Brothers', revealed the hiding of $50 billion of toxic assets on the Lehman Brothers' balance sheet. Using a repurchase agreement, Lehman sold the securities in the last days of a financial reporting quarter and thus replaced them with a viable cash equivalent. Unreported to the public was the fact that Lehman agreed to buy back the securities shortly after the start of the new quarter.

In May 2008, a Lehman senior vice president alerted management to the accounting irregularities. His warning was ignored by Lehman auditors Ernst & Young and was not brought to the attention of the board of directors.

Valukas searched 34 million pages of Lehman Brothers' e-mails and documents. Using search terms such as "stupid," "risk," "concern," "breach," "big trouble," and "too late," he found irregularities and prepared a 2,200-page report. Its conclusion was that Richard Fuld certified misleading financial statements. Subsequently, multiple lawsuits were filed for misconduct by Lehman officers.

The outcome: Lehman mismanaged $613 billion of debt. It would take years to unravel the situation, and creditors and others were lucky if they received 15 percent of the value of their assets.

Columbia Journalism Review, March 12, 2010; *Bloomberg BusinessWeek,* June 11, 2010.

Income Statement Formula

An *income statement* is a report of the firm's activities during a given accounting period, normally one year. Also called the *profit and loss statement* or the *statement of earnings*, it shows the revenues and expenses of a firm, the effect of corporate income taxes, and the net income. The relationships on the income statement can be expressed by the formula:

Revenues - Expenses = Net Income

Figure 2-3 shows the format for an income statement.

Role of Financial Statements

The financial statements developed using accounting transactions allow organizations to understand their business. With respect to the income statement, which reflects the revenue and expense accounts, we have two important uses for the information:

- *Financial reporting.* The accounting department prepares reports for managers so that they can interpret the financial impacts of their actions. Financial reports are also provided to regulators, the government, creditors, investors, and the general public.
- *Budgeting.* Department managers prepare forecasts of future revenues and expenses. Based on the relationship between revenues and expenses, the firm will approve expenditures to be charged against specific accounts. The budget represents both a forecast and, when it is approved, permission to make expenditures.

Revenue and Expense Centers

Revenues and expenses are developed and monitored in centers. Three terms are commonly used:

- *Budget center.* This is a cluster of revenues, expenses, or both where a unit forecasts future financial impacts and can be held accountable for actual results compared to budgeted expectations.
- *Cost center.* This is a cluster of expenses only. The unit is responsible for living within its budgeted numbers, has approval to spend money against specific cost objectives, and can request adjustments to expenses when conditions change.
- *Profit center.* This is a cluster of both revenues and expenses. The unit is responsible for the bottom line, after expenses are deducted from revenues.

Revenues	$3,350
Salaries and wages	-1,100
Administrative expenses	-500
Earnings before interest and taxes (EBIT)	$1,750
Interest expense	-100
Earnings before taxes (EBT)	$1,650
Taxes 25%	-412
Net income after taxes (NIAT)	**$1,238**

Figure 2-3. Income Statement.

CONCLUSION

The process of accounting creates the story of financial risk, which is subsequently expressed in financial statements and reports. An understanding of the balance sheet and income statement, along with a recognition of how accounting data can be misused, is a critical component in assessing the status of an organization.

CHAPTER 2 APPENDIXES

How to Prepare Pro Forma Financial Statements

Pro forma financial statements are prepared for future time periods. The Darwin Medical Clinic started on January 1 and prepared a starting and ending balance sheet and income statement for the first year (000s).

Darwin Used Estimated Starting Data to Begin the Process.

Initial investment in the clinic	$10,000
Medical equipment	$6,500
Bank loan to finance part of the clinic	$25,000
Interest rate on the loan	7.0%
Starting inventory of medical supplies	$2,800
Percent of cash paid for starting inventory	20%
Income tax rate	25%

The Starting Data Were Supported by Assumptions of Activities During the First Year.

Likely revenues from operations	$28,000
Cash expected from funding sources	$21,000
Cash still owed from funding source	$7,000
Medical services expenses	$16,800
Nonmedical services expenses	$8,600
Cash not yet paid for services	$2,540
Ending inventory of supplies	$4,000
Equipment to be purchased during the year	$500
Money owed to suppliers at year end	$5,550
Tax rate	20%
Principal to be repaid on loan during year	$200

The Data and Assumptions Were Used to Calculate a Starting Cash Balance.

Equity investment	$10,000
Purchase medical equipment	-6,500

Bank loan	25,000
Purchase medical supplies	-560
Starting cash	$27,940

The Analyst Completed a Starting Balance Sheet.

Cash	$27,940
Inventory	2,800
Fixed assets	6,500
Total Assets	**$37,240**
Accounts payable	$2,240
Bank loan	25,000
Equity investment	10,000
Total Liabilities and Equity	**$37,240**

Next, an Income Statement for the Year Was Prepared.

Revenues	$28,000
Medical services expenses	-16,800
Nonmedical services expenses	-8,600
Operating income	$2,600
Interest expense	-1,750
Pretax income	$850
Taxes 20%	-170
After-tax income	**$680**

The Financial Statements Were Used to Calculate the Expected Change in Cash.

	Start	Changes	End
Cash	$27,940		
Accounts receivable	0	$7,000	$7,000
Supplies	2,800	1,200	4,000
Fixed assets	6,500	500	7,000
Total Assets	**$37,240**	**$8,700**	**$18,000**

Accounts payable	$2,240	$5,850	$8,090
Bank loan	25,000	-200	24,800
Equity investment	10,000		10,000
Retained earnings	0	680	680
Total Liabilities and Equity	**$37,240**	**$6,330**	**$43,570**

Difference in totals	$25,570
Minus starting cash	-27,940
Change to cash	-$2,370

The Ending Balance Sheet Showed Sufficient Cash.

	Start	Changes	End
Cash	$27,940	-$2,370	$25,570
Accounts receivable	0	7,000	7,000
Supplies	2,800	1,200	4,000
Fixed assets	6,500	500	7,000
Total Assets	**$37,240**	**$6,330**	**$43,570**

	Start	Changes	End
Accounts payable	$2,240	$5,850	$8,090
Bank loan	25,000	-200	24,800
Equity investment	10,000	0	10,000
Retained Earnings	0	680	680
Total Liabilities and Equity	**$37,240**	**$6,330**	**$43,570**

How to Interpret Financial Statements

Four partners started Hawking Corporation and operated it for one year. The following information traces the company's accounting activities from the start of operations to closing the accounting records at the end of the year.

Starting Information for the Company.
The partners bought stock

Shares sold	1,000
Price paid per share	$100
The company purchased machinery	$65,000
The company took out a bank loan	$25,000
Interest rate on the loan	4%
Starting inventory	$28,000
The company paid no cash for its starting inventory	
Income tax rate	25%

Starting Cash Balance.

Sale of stock	$100,000
Purchase equipment	-65,000
Borrow money	25,000

Purchase inventory	0
Starting cash	$60,000

Starting Balance Sheet.

Cash	$60,000
Inventory	28,000
Fixed assets	65,000
Total Assets	**$153,000**

Accounts payable	$28,000
Bank loan	25,000
Common stock	100,000
Total Liabilities and Equity	**$153,000**

Summary Data for the First Year of Operations.

Cash sales during year	$200,000
Credit sales during year	$70,000
Still owed for credit sales at year end	$42,000
Cost of goods sold during year	$168,000
Administrative expenses during year	$86,000
Ending inventory	$40,000
Added to fixed assets during year	$5,000
Still owed to suppliers at year end	$55,500
Tax rate	20%
Principal repaid on loan during year	$2,000

Income Statement for the First Year.

Cash sales	$200,000
Credit sales	70,000
Revenues	$270,000
Cost of goods sold	-168,000
Administrative expenses	-86,000
Operating income	$16,000
Interest expense	-1,000
Pretax income	$15,000
Taxes 20%	-3,000
After-tax income	**$12,000**

Change in Cash During the Year.

	Start	Changes	End
Cash	$60,000	-$21,500	$38,500
Accounts receivable	0	$42,000	$42,000
Inventory	28,000	12,000	40,000
Fixed assets	65,000	5,000	70,000
Total Assets	**$153,000**	**$59,000**	**$152,000**

	Start	Changes	End
Accounts payable	$28,000	$27,500	$55,500
Bank loan	25,000	-2,000	23,000
Common stock	100,000		100,000
Retained earnings	0	12,000	12,000
Total Liabilities and Equity	**$153,000**	**$37,500**	**$190,500**

Difference in totals $38,500
Minus starting cash   -60,000
Change to cash   -$21,500

Ending Balance Sheet.

	Start	Changes	End
Cash	$60,000	-$21,500	$38,500
Accounts receivable	0	42,000	42,000
Inventory	28,000	12,000	40,000
Fixed assets	65,000	5,000	70,000
Total Assets	**$153,000**	**$37,500**	**$190,500**

	Start	Changes	End
Accounts payable	$28,000	$27,500	$55,500
Bank loan	25,000	-2,000	23,000
Common stock	100,000	0	100,000
Retained earnings	0	12,000	12,000
Total Liabilities and Equity	**$153,000**	**$37,500**	**$190,500**

Notes.

Starting cash: $100,000 - 65,000 + 25,000 = 60,000$
During this year has cash: $60,000 + 200,000 + (70,000 - 42,000) = 288,000$
Expenses to be paid during this year:
$(168,000 + 40,000 - 28,000) + 28,000 + 86,000 + 5,000 + 2,000 + 1,000 + 3,000 = 305,000$
At the end of this year the company still owed suppliers   55,500
So the company paid cash $305,000 - 55,500 = 249,500$ during this year
At the end of this year has cash $288,000 - 249,500 = 38,500$

Chapter

3

Managing Operating Cash Flows

Financial managers know that cash is king, but exactly what does that mean? Can a firm regularly report profits on its income statement and still be short on funds? Can it have adequate assets compared to its debts and still have a liquidity crisis? The answer to both of these questions is yes. Thus, we must understand the role played by cash flows, separate from the accounting records of a firm.

THE CASH FLOW STATEMENT

A useful starting point for understanding cash flows is the *cash flow statement*. It is often called by other names, such as the *sources and uses of funds statement*. It shows the movement of funds into the firm's current asset accounts from external sources, such as stockholders and customers. It also shows the movement of funds out of the firm to meet the firm's obligations, retire stock, or pay dividends. The movements are shown for a specific period of time, normally the same time period as that used for the firm's income statement.

The cash flow statement has a structure with three categories of cash flows:

- *Cash from operations*. This is the amount of cash that a company generates from the sale of goods or services. Essentially, it is the net cash revenues from sales to customers minus the cash expenses for materials, labor, marketing, distribution, and other business costs. It is calculated by determining accounting earnings and adjusting them for changes in working capital. It excludes long-term cash flows involving investments, debt, and equity.

- *Cash from investing*. This is the cash received from or expended for long-life assets. The sale of fixed assets is a source of cash from investing. The purchase of fixed assets is a use of cash to invest.

- *Cash from financing*. This is cash received from borrowing or selling stock or expended to pay down loans or repurchase a firm's stock.

Working Capital Pool

A key cash flow concept is the *working capital pool*, which consists of all the current accounts of the firm. *Net working capital* is the difference between current assets and current liabilities. It is used as a measure of liquidity. The firm is expected to hold more liquid assets than it has liquid obligations.

The firm's balance sheet can be used to develop the amount of net working capital. Figure 3-1 shows a starting and ending balance sheet for one year for the Allen Company. Figure 3-2 shows the current accounts on the balance sheet and the calculation of net working capital. Figure 3-3 shows a graphic of a working capital pool with the addition of *marketable securities*, defined as short-term investments that are almost as liquid as cash in normal markets.

Income Statement Inputs to Cash Flow Statement

The income statement provides the following inputs to the cash flow calculation:

- *Revenues.* The total customer obligations to pay for goods and services during an accounting period.
- *Cash expenses.* The cost of providing goods and services that is spent in cash during the period.
- *Noncash expenses.* The costs that are registered in the accounting system but do not involve dispensing cash in the current period.
- *Administrative expenses.* Any cash costs that are not directly involved with the creation or delivery of goods or services.
- *Interest expenses.* The costs associated with borrowing money.
- *Taxes.* The taxes paid on the profits of the business.
- *Cash dividends.* Monies dispensed to owners as their share of the firm's profits.
- *Equity adjustments.* Accounting adjustments that do not affect current-year revenues or expenses. When the equity account is increased, it means that the firm misstated

	January 1	December 31
Cash	$25,500	$71,300
Accounts receivable	10,000	40,000
Inventories	22,500	44,500
Fixed assets	30,000	25,000
Total Assets	**$88,000**	**$180,800**

	January 1	December 31
Payables	$26,000	$35,000
Long-term debt	12,000	67,000
Contributed capital	40,000	62,000
Retained earnings	10,000	16,800
Total Liabilities and Equity	**$88,000**	**$180,800**

Figure 3-1. Allen Company Balance Sheet.

	January 1	December 31
Cash	$25,500	$71,300
Accounts receivable	10,000	40,000
Inventories	22,500	44,500
Total Sources	**$58,000**	**$155,800**
Payables	$26,000	$35,000
Total uses	**$26,000**	**$35,000**
Net working capital	**$32,000**	**$120,800**

Figure 3-2. Allen Company Working Capital Pool.

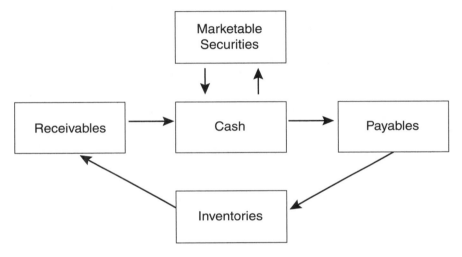

Figure 3-3. Graphic of Working Capital Pool.

a cash disbursement in a prior year. This is a source of funds. When the equity account is adjusted downward, it means that a source of funds in prior years did not materialize as expected.

Figure 3-4 shows the income statement for the Allen Company.

Cash from Operations

The balance sheet changes in the working capital accounts are mixed with the cash flows from the income statement accounts to develop cash from operations. Entries include:

- *Net income.* This is taken directly from the income statement.
- *Noncash expenses adjustment.* This reflects the amount by which net income was reduced by depreciation and other noncash expenses. *Depreciation* is a process of recognizing annual expenses when using a long-term asset. As an example, assume that a firm pays $6 million cash for a machine. That is not an expense. Instead, the tax code allows the machine to be written off over a specified period of time at a rate

Revenues	$120,000
Cash expenses	-55,200
Noncash expenses	-6,000
Cost of sales	$61,200
Gross margin	$58,800
Administrative expenses	-21,600
Operating income	**$37,200**
Interest expense	-1,200
Pretax income	$36,000
Taxes	-9,000
Net income	**$27,000**
Retained earnings change	-6,800
Dividends and adjustments	$20,200

Figure 3-4. Allen Company Income Statement.

specified in the tax code. If the code required a steady reduction in book value over five years, the annual depreciation would be $1.2 million.

- *Current assets adjustment.* This reflects changes in the current assets indicating that cash was freed or used. An increase in a current asset account reflects a use of cash. A decline is a source of cash. The cash account itself is not adjusted.
- *Current liabilities adjustment.* This reflects changes in the current liabilities indicating that cash was freed or used. A decline in a current liability account reflects a use of cash. An increase is a source of cash.

Cash from Investing

The changes in the fixed asset accounts show the cash expended for investments in new long-term assets or the cash received from the sale of existing long-term assets. Obviously, not all the changes in long-term assets involve cash, as some assets have mortgages or otherwise involved borrowing money to finance them. These impacts are included in the next category, which deals with financing the firm.

Cash from Financing

The cash flows involved in financing the firm are divided into three categories:

- *Long-term debt.* A decline in a long-term debt account reflects paying down a liability and is a use of cash. An increase reflects borrowing money and is a source of cash.
- *Contributed capital.* A decline in contributed capital reflects a repurchase of stock and is a use of cash. A rise reflects the sale of stock and is a source of cash.
- *Retained earnings.* When the firm declares cash dividends, the action is a use of cash. Either the dividends are paid or a short-term liability is created. In either case, the retained earnings account is reduced by the amount of the dividend. In addition, any accounting adjustments are posted directly to retained earnings.

Figure 3-5 shows the Allen cash flow statement along with the net change in cash. Figure 3-6 shows a comparison of the net change in cash on both the cash flow statement and the balance sheet.

CASH FLOW EXPOSURES

Building from the categories of cash from operations, investing, and financing, we can focus solely on the cash flows. Figure 3-7 is one representation of the internal and external flow of funds. Note that the flows in 3-7 move from sources to uses of funds.

Working Capital Cash Inflow Risks

The exposures and opportunities are the two sides of a double-edged sword. The financial risk to cash inflows arises from four sources.

Cash flows from operations:	
Net income	$27,000
Current asset adjustment	-52,000
Current debt adjustment	9,000
Operating cash flows	**-$16,000**
Cash flows from investing:	
Investing in fixed assets	$5,000
Investing cash flows	**5,000**
Cash flows from financing:	
Long-term debt	$55,000
Contributed capital	22,000
Dividends and adjustments	-20,200
Financing cash flows	**56,800**
Net change in cash	**$45,800**

Figure 3-5. Allen Company Cash Flow Statement.

From operations	-$16,000
From investing	5,000
From financing	56,800
Net change in cash	**$45,800**
Starting cash	$25,500
Ending cash	71,300
Net change in cash	**$45,800**

Figure 3-6. Allen Company Cash Reconciliation.

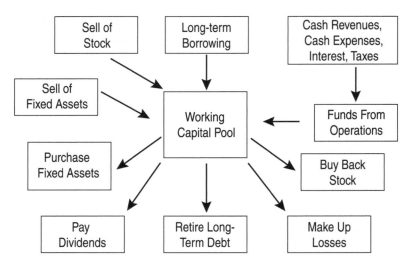

Figure 3-7. Sources and Uses Flowchart.

1. *Sale of stock to funds or individual investors.* A firm can raise capital by issuing additional stock. This is not always easy. In some markets, a firm simply may not to able to find buyers for its stock. Investors may not be interested in the industry in which the firm operates. The firm may have received a bad review from rating agencies with respect to its financial prowess or prospects, thus scaring off investors. The media may have released bad reports on some aspect of the firm's operations.

2. *Long-term borrowing from financial and other institutions.* The firm can issue bonds, take out long-term bank loans, mortgage assets, or otherwise obtain credit to finance fixed assets. The risk of a cutoff of this source of funding depends on multiple factors. The firm's financial position may not be perceived as being highly likely to allow repayment of additional debt obligations. Debt markets may not be sufficiently liquid or may have other constraints that create limits on available funds for lending. The state of the economy can be a factor, as lenders may be conservative in some conditions and thus may be reluctant to lend. Finally, lenders may require collateral to support repayment, and the firm may not have acceptable assets.

3. *Sale of fixed assets.* A firm can always try to sell fixed assets that are no longer needed in its operations. These can range from buildings to equipment. Under some conditions, used assets may produce sizable cash flows. The risk, though, can be large. If a firm is struggling and wants to sell assets after cutting back operations, other firms in the same industry may also be seeking to sell assets. The absence of buyers can endanger this source of cash. At the same time, creativity may be able to help. Many firms have a history of dismantling equipment and shipping it to other countries where it is in demand.

4. *Funds from operations.* For most firms, the cash generated and reflected on the cash flow statement is the primary source of continued financing. This is the best source of funding over the long term, even though it is the source that is most easily disrupted from one year to the next. Some industries, including public

utilities and food stores, seem to have less volatile streams of cash from operations. Others, such as airlines and real estate construction companies, can have
funds from operations that vary widely from one period to another.

Working Capital Cash Outflow Risks

Also shown in Figure 3-7 are the uses of cash. Risks in this area include:

- *Making up losses.* This is the reverse of having funds from operations. The funds
  from operations may even be adequate, but the company may be facing lawsuits,
  uninsured damage to assets, or other losses that have a negative impact on its cash
  position.
- *Buying back stock.* The company can make a conscious choice to buy back its
  common stock. This reduces the number of shares outstanding and can increase
  earnings per share, as net income is divided by fewer shares. At the same time, the
  company can find itself forced to buy back stock to meet obligations, such as stock
  dividends promised to employees. If it pays too much for the stock, it can find itself
  facing liquidity problems.
- *Retiring long-term debt.* As the firm nears the maturity dates for bonds or long-term
  loans, it may not be able to refinance the debt. If it cannot roll over the obligation,
  it must use cash to retire the debt. For a large obligation, this can produce a liquidity crisis.
- *Paying cash dividends.* Shareholders may expect to receive cash payments sharing
  the earnings of the firm. If the firm needs the cash to finance its growth or maintain
  its liquidity position, the board of directors will face a difficult decision. If the firm
  withholds the cash payments, investors may choose to sell their stock, thus lowering
  stock prices. If the company does make the cash payments, it may run short of cash
  and find itself in a difficult liquidity position.
- *Purchasing fixed assets.* Over a period of time, most assets either wear out or become
  obsolete because of technological or other developments. The timing of asset purchases is an important part of financial risk management. If assets are purchased
  before they are needed or if they are bought when prices are high, the cash drain can
  have negative impacts on liquidity. When firms grab opportunities to upgrade their
  asset base at the right time, future cash flow can be increased significantly.

Sources and Uses of Operational Cash

We have already identified funds from operations as the primary source of funds for most
firms over the long term. Figure 3-8 shows the funds as a continuous loop in a complex
business organization. After shareholders and creditors provide funding as external
contributors, the cash flows deal with operations:

- *Fixed assets.* Some assets are purchased. Some are sold. Some are scrapped.
- *Operating expenses.* Cash is needed to cover these expenditures so that the firm can
  produce and market goods and services.

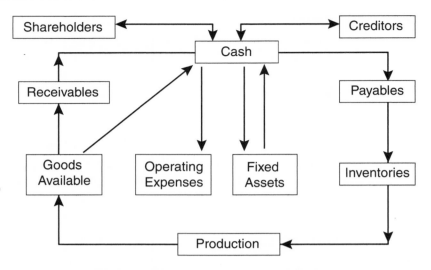

Figure 3-8. Flow of Funds Through a Firm.

- *Operating flows.* This is the loop created when the firm buys components on credit, producing payables; converts raw materials or inputs into inventories or services; makes the goods and services available to the market, generating revenues either in cash or as receivables; and replenishes the cash pool.

CONCLUSION

What does cash flow risk mean at the end of the day? The answer is simple. The crux of cash flow risk is that the most frequent reason that firms collapse is liquidity problems. With an excessive stockpile of cash, often created historically and retained, a firm can operate for an indefinite period of time, even if it is not profitable. It is only when the firm experiences a default as a result of a cash shortage that operations falter, creditors swoop in, and bankruptcy become inevitable.

Managing cash positions and cash is not a small component of financial risk management. For most firms, it is the most critical component. The reason the firm needs profits is certainly to justify the investment of shareholders and the confidence of creditors. In addition, profits create jobs and opportunities for other stakeholders, including employees, suppliers, and customers. Equally important, adequate cash flows prevent the liquidity problems that can eliminate the ability of the firm to continue in operation.

CHAPTER 3 APPENDIXES

How to Convert a Balance Sheet and Income Statement Into a Cash Flow Statement

An investor has a balance sheet and income statement for Magna Limited. She wants to know how the company is doing with its cash flows. She can convert the two financial statements into a cash flow statement using the following process.

Start with the Magna Balance Sheet.

	January 1	December 1
Cash	$10,700	$42,000
Receivables	108,000	114,000
Inventory	240,000	215,000
Fixed assets	173,000	190,000
Total Assets	**$531,700**	**$561,000**
Accounts payable	$11,000	$14,000
Long-term debt	245,000	235,000
Common stock	73,000	82,000
Retained earnings	202,700	230,000
Total Liabilities and Equity	**$531,700**	**$561,000**

Add the Magna Income Statement.

Revenues	$609,950
Wages	-190,000
Cost of goods sold	-185,000
Depreciation	-34,000
Miscellaneous expenses	-135,000
Operating income	$65,950
Interest	19,975
Pretax earnings	$45,975
Taxes	-9,195
After-tax income/loss	**$36,780**
Profits distributed to owners	$14,712

Identify the Sources and Uses of Cash.

1. Any decrease in current assets means that a firm collected receivables, sold inventory, or otherwise brought in cash. An increase causes the company to tie up its cash.

	Change	Source	Use
Receivables	$6,000	$0	-$6,000
Inventory	-25,000	25,000	0

2. Any decrease in net fixed assets means that a firm sold assets and brought in cash. An increase means that the firm used money to buy plant or equipment.

	Change	Source	Use
Fixed assets	$17,000	$0	-$17,000

3. Any increase in any debt means that the firm borrowed money or delayed a payment. A decrease shows that it spent money to reduce a liability. An increase is a source of cash. A decrease is a use of cash.

	Change	Source	Use
Accounts payable	$3,000	$3,000	$0
Long-term debt	-10,000	0	-10,000

4. Any increase in contributed capital means that the owners put more money into the business. A decrease means that the company bought back its stock or otherwise reduced the owners' contribution. An increase is a source of cash. A decrease is a use of cash.

	Change	Source	Use
Common stock	$9,000	$9,000	$0

5. The retained earnings account is somewhat tricky. A change in retained earnings occurs when the accountant adds net income to the account and subtracts cash dividends paid to owners from it. In addition, accountants sometimes post entries directly to retained earnings, adjusting revenues or expenses from prior periods. To see if the accountants made any adjustments, we perform the following calculation:

	Change	Source	Use
Income/loss	$36,780	$36,780	$0
Cash dividends	-14,712	0	-14,712
Expected change	22,068		
Actual change	27,300		
Adjustment	5,232	5,232	0

Make a Cash Flow Statement.

Net income	$36,780
Decrease in receivables	0
Decrease in inventory	25,000
Sale of fixed assets	0
Increase in accounts payable	3,000
Increase in long-term debt	0
Additional contribution by owners	9,000
Adjustment to retained earnings	5,232
Sources of cash	**$79,012**

Net loss	$0
Cash dividends	-14,712
Increase in receivables	-6,000
Increase in inventory	0

Purchase of fixed assets	-17,000
Decrease in accounts payable	0
Decrease in long-term debt	-10,000
Reduction of contribution by owners	0
Adjustment to retained earnings	0
Uses of cash	**-$47,712**
Change in cash during period	**$31,300**

Check to be sure that this is correct:

Starting cash	$10,700
Ending cash	42,000
Change from balance sheet	$31,300
Change from cash flow statement	$31,300
Are they equal?	Yes

How to Calculate the Cash Needed to Start a Business

Larson Medical Products is starting a joint venture to sell microscopes to hospitals, using its existing distribution system. It needs to determine the maximum cash needs of the business prior to the point where cash inflow exceeds cash outflow. It completed the following analysis.

Estimate the Payments for Inventory Over the Planning Period.

	Month 1	Month 2	Month 3	Month 4
Inventory needed	$120,000	$144,000	$172,800	$207,360
Percent paid in				
Current month	15%	15%	10%	10%
Next month	70%	70%	70%	70%
Second month	15%	15%	20%	20%
Amount paid during				
Current month	-$18,000	-$21,600	-$17,280	-$20,736
Prior month		-$84,000	-$100,800	-$120,960
Two months ago			-$18,000	-$21,600
Inventory payments	-$18,000	-$105,600	-$136,080	-$163,296

	Month 5	Month 6	Month 7	Month 8
Inventory needed	$217,728	$228,614	$240,045	$252,047
Percent paid in				
Current month	15%	15%	15%	15%
Next month	60%	60%	70%	70%
Second month	25%	25%	15%	15%

	Month 5	Month 6	Month 7	Month 8
Amount paid during				
Current month	-$32,659	-$34,292	-$36,007	-$37,807
Prior month	-$145,152	-$130,637	-$137,169	-$168,032
Two months ago	-$34,560	-$41,472	-$54,432	-$57,154
Inventory payments	-$212,371	-$206,401	-$227,607	-$262,992

Estimate the Revenues and Collections on Those Revenues.

	Month 1	Month 2	Month 3	Month 4
Revenues	$48,000	$201,600	$311,040	$373,248
Percent collected in				
Current month	10%	10%	10%	10%
Next month	45%	50%	55%	50%
Third month	40%	34%	28%	34%
Never	5%	6%	7%	6%
Cash collected from revenues in				
Current month	$4,800	$20,160	$31,104	$37,325
Next month		$21,600	$100,800	$171,072
Third month			$19,200	$68,544
Total collections	$4,800	$41,760	$151,104	$276,941

	Month 5	Month 6	Month 7	Month 8
Revenues	$413,683	$434,367	$456,086	$478,890
Percent collected in				
Current month	10%	10%	10%	10%
Next month	45%	40%	35%	40%
Third month	40%	45%	50%	45%
Never	5%	5%	5%	5%
Cash collected from revenues in				
Current month	$41,368	$43,437	$45,609	$47,889
Next month	$186,624	$186,157	$173,747	$159,630
Third month	$87,091	$126,904	$165,473	$195,465
Total collections	$315,084	$356,498	$384,829	$402,984

Estimate payments for other expenses.

	Month 1	Month 2	Month 3	Month 4
Wages	-$16,000	-$24,000	-$26,400	-$29,040
Rent and utilities	-$3,000	-$3,000	-$3,000	-$3,000
Insurance	-$1,200	-$1,200	-$1,200	-$1,200

	Month 1	Month 2	Month 3	Month 4
Advertising	-$1,500	-$1,500	-$1,500	-$1,500
Deliveries	-$4,000	-$4,000	-$4,000	-$4,000
Contingency	-$2,000	-$2,000	-$2,000	-$2,000
Other expenses	-$27,700	-$35,700	-$38,100	-$40,740

	Month 5	Month 6	Month 7	Month 8
Wages	-$31,944	-$35,138	-$38,652	-$42,517
Rent and utilities	-$3,300	-$3,300	-$3,300	-$3,300
Insurance	-$1,320	-$1,320	-$1,320	-$1,320
Advertising	-$1,650	-$1,650	-$1,650	-$1,650
Deliveries	-$4,400	-$4,400	-$4,400	-$4,400
Contingency	-$2,200	-$2,200	-$2,200	-$2,200
Other expenses	-$44,814	-$48,008	-$51,522	-$55,387

Estimated Cost of Starting the Business.

	Month 1	Month 2	Month 3	Month 4
Fix up rented space	-$24,000			
Buy two vehicles	-18,000	-$18,000		
Legal/other fees	-2,000	-1,000		
Recruiting personnel	-4,000	-2,000		
Other	-5,000	-2,000	-1,000	
Start-up costs	-$53,000	-$23,000	-$1,000	0

Cash Needed.

	Month 1	Month 2	Month 3	Month 4
Total collections	$4,800	$41,760	$151,104	$276,941
Start-up costs	-$53,000	-$23,000	-$1,000	$0
Inventory payments	-$18,000	-$105,600	-$136,080	-$163,296
Other expenses	-$27,700	-$35,700	-$38,100	-$40,740
Surplus/shortage	-$93,900	-$122,540	-$24,076	$72,905
Cumulative				
Surplus or shortage	-$93,900	-$216,440	-$240,516	-$167,611

	Month 5	Month 6	Month 7	Month 8
Total collections	$315,084	$356,498	$384,829	$402,984
Start-up costs				
Inventory payments	-$212,371	-$206,401	-$227,607	-$262,992
Other expenses	-$44,814	-$48,008	-$51,522	-$55,387

	Month 5	Month 6	Month 7	Month 8
Surplus/shortage	$57,898	$102,089	$105,699	$84,605
Cumulative				
Surplus or shortage	-$109,713	-$7,624	$98,075	$182,680

What Is the Maximum Amount of Cash That Will Be Needed?

Maximum cash needed in	
First Four months	$240,516
Second Four months	$109,713
Maximum Cash Needed	$240,516
Add a second contingency	
Second contingency	15%
Cash with contingency	$276,593
Round it up	$280,000

How to Help a Profitable Firm Avoid Bankruptcy

Sometimes financing arrangements need to be made to avoid a liquidity crisis that can lead to bankruptcy. This is the case for Bentley Products. The company was originally financed with a mixture of debt and equity. Some of the debt securities are nearing maturity, and additional financing must be sought. This analysis shows how to calculate the additional financing needed.

Bentley Forecasts Balance Sheets for the Next Four Years as Follows.

	Year 1	Year 2	Year 3	Year 4
Cash	$17,400	$18,792	$21,047	$22,941
Receivables	108,000	129,600	162,000	191,160
Inventory	225,600	263,952	322,021	408,967
Fixed assets	173,000	221,440	298,944	388,627
Total Assets	**$524,000**	**$633,784**	**$804,012**	**$1,011,696**
Accounts payable	$76,000	$110,200	$149,872	$205,325
Bank loan 1 (one year to maturity)	53,900	0	0	0
Bank loan 2 (two years to maturity)	51,450	51,450	0	0
Mortgage (five years to maturity)	80,850	77,616	73,735	69,311
Long-term note (six years to maturity)	58,800	58,800	58,800	58,800
Additional financing needed	0	128,774	310,874	476,384
Common stock	73,000	74,460	77,438	73,566
Retained earnings	130,000	132,484	133,293	128,309
Total Liabilities and Equity	**$524,000**	**$633,784**	**$804,012**	**$1,011,696**

Bentley Forecasts Income Statements.

	Year 1	Year 2	Year 3	Year 4
Revenues	$570,000	$627,000	$689,700	$758,670
Wages	-190,000	-209,000	-229,900	-252,890
Cost of goods sold	-185,000	-203,500	-223,850	-246,235
Depreciation	-34,000	-37,400	-41,140	-45,254
Miscellaneous expenses	-135,000	-148,500	-163,350	-179,685
Operating income	$26,000	$28,600	$31,460	$34,606
Interest	-20,825	-26,914	-37,690	-51,213
Pretax earnings	$5,175	$1,686	-$6,230	-$16,607
Taxes	-1,035	-337	1,246	3,321
Net income or loss	$4,140	$1,348	-$4,984	-$13,285
Cash dividends	$1,656	$539	-$0	-$0

Bentley Forecasts the Changes in Cash.

	Year 1	Year 2	Year 3	Year 4
Change in receivables	-$20,952	-$21,600	-$32,400	-$29,160
Change in inventory	-40,270	-38,352	-58,069	-86,946
Change in fixed assets	-46,502	-48,440	-77,504	-89,683
Change in accounts payable	32,148	34,200	39,672	55,453
Change in long-term debt	69,491	71,640	126,769	161,086
Change in common stock	1,402	1,460	2,978	-3,872
Change in retained earnings	2,708	2,484	809	-4,984
Change in cash during period	-$1,976	$1,392	$2,255	$1,894

Check to be sure that this is correct.

	Year 2	Year 3	Year 4
Starting cash	$17,400	$18,792	$21,047
Ending cash	18,792	21,047	22,941
Change from balance sheet	$1,392	$2,255	$1,894
Change from cash flow statement	$1,392	$2,255	$1,894
Are they equal?	Yes	Yes	Yes

The following details apply to the long-term debt on the balance sheet:

	Year 1	Year 2	Year 3	Year 4
Bank loan 1	$53,900			
Years remaining	1	OK	Refinance	
Bank loan 2	$51,450	$51,450		
Years remaining	2	OK	OK	Refinance
Mortgage	$80,850	$77,616	$73,735	$69,311

	Year 1	Year 2	Year 3	Year 4
Years remaining	7	OK	OK	OK
Long-term note	$58,800	$58,800	$58,800	$58,800
Years remaining	5	OK	OK	OK
Additional financing needed	$0	$128,774	$310,874	$476,384

Lesson learned: If financial markets are turbulent or if the company risk is perceived as being too high, the company may not be able to refinance its debt. In such a situation, bankruptcy is likely.

How to Distinguish Cash Flows from Profits

Accountants have procedures to differentiate cash and noncash transactions. For example, not all revenues are cash in the current period, and some revenues reported in earlier periods become cash in the current period. Because accountants adjust for cash and non-cash impacts, an accurate cash flow statement is derived from the balance sheet and the income statement.

The steps in developing the cash flow statement are:

- *Determine changes in noncurrent assets.* If an account such as fixed assets increases, it is a use of cash. A decrease is a source of cash.
- *Determine changes in long-term liabilities.* An increase is a source of cash. A decrease is a use of cash.
- *Determine changes in contributed capital.* An increase is a source of cash. A decrease is a use of cash.
- *Determine changes in retained earnings.* This account is affected by three items:
  - *Net income or loss.* Net income is a source of cash. Net loss is a use of cash.
  - *Dividends.* A cash dividend is a use of cash.
  - *Accounting adjustments.* An increase is a source of cash. A decrease is a use of cash. The formula is net income minus dividends plus or minus the adjustment.

The Porter Company has the following balance sheet, net income, and cash dividends. From this information, we can calculate the adjustments to retained earnings and a cash flow statement. Then, we can reconcile the statement with the actual change in cash.

Start with the Porter Company Balance Sheet and Income Data.

	January 1	December 31
Cash	$51,000	$142,600
Accounts receivable	20,000	80,000
Inventories	45,000	89,000
Fixed assets	60,000	50,000
Total assets	$176,000	$361,600
Payables	$52,000	$70,000
Long-term debt	24,000	134,000

	January 1	December 31
Contributed capital	80,000	124,000
Retained earnings	20,000	33,600
Total	$176,000	$361,600
Net income		$35,200
Dividends		-14,080

Calculate Adjustments to Retained Earnings.

Net income	$35,200
Dividends	-14,080
Expected change in retained earnings	$21,120
Actual Change in Retained Earnings	13,600
Adjustments to Retained Earnings	**-$7,520**

Create the Cash Flow Statement.

Cash flows from operations	
Net income	$35,200
Current asset adjustment	-104,000
Current debt adjustment	18,000
Operating cash flows	**-$50,800**
Cash flows from investing	
Investing in fixed assets	$10,000
Investing cash flows	**10,000**
Cash flows from financing	
Long-term debt	$110,000
Contributed capital	44,000
Dividends	-14,080
Adjustments to equity	-7,520
Financing cash flows	**132,400**
Net change in cash	**$91,600**

Reconcile the Change in Cash with the Cash Flow Statement.

Starting cash	$51,000
Ending cash	142,600
Net change in cash on balance sheet	$91,600
Net change on cash flow statement	$91,600
Do they match?	Yes

How to Analyze Working Capital

Working capital should be sufficient to allow a firm to conduct its business without un-necessary attention to liquidity problems. The following analysis examines the adequacy of working capital for a group of entrepreneurs that started McDonald Company.

Activities at Start-Up of the McDonald Company.

Sold common stock	$75,000
Purchased a factory	55,000
Took out a mortgage	45,000
Bought goods to sell	24,000
Paid cash for the goods	14,400

Summary Activities for Year 1.

Revenues	$125,000
Cash expenses	$55,200
Noncash expenses	$6,000
G&A expenses	$21,600
Interest on debt	$6,240
Tax rate	20%
Paid dividends	$17,261

Adjustments at End of Year 1.

Increase in receivables	$78,000
Increase in inventory	96,900
Increase in fixed assets	20,000
Increase in payables	110,400
Increase in contributed capital	20,000
Increase in long-term debt	33,000
No accounting adjustments were made to retained earnings.	

From these data, we can prepare the comparative balance sheet, working capital pool, income statement, cash flow statement, and cash reconciliation to allow us to analyze the management of working capital.

McDonald Company Balance Sheet.

	January 1	December 31
Cash	$50,600	$30,607
Accounts receivable	0	78,000

	January 1	December 31
Inventories	24,000	120,900
Fixed assets	55,000	75,000
Total Assets	**$129,600**	**$304,507**
Payables	$9,600	$120,000
Long-term debt	45,000	78,000
Contributed capital	75,000	95,000
Retained earnings	0	11,507
Total Liabilities and Equity	**$129,600**	**$304,507**

McDonald Company Working Capital Pool.

	January 1	December 31
Cash	$50,600	$30,607
Accounts receivable	0	78,000
Inventories	24,000	120,900
Total sources	**$74,600**	**$229,507**
Payables	$9,600	$120,000
Total uses	$9,600	$120,000
Net working capital	**$65,000**	**$109,507**

McDonald Company Income Statement.

Revenues	$125,000
Cash expenses	-55,200
Noncash expenses	-6,000
Cost of sales	-$61,200
Gross margin	$63,800
Administrative expenses	-21,600
Operating income	$42,200
Interest expense	-6,240
Pretax income	$35,960
Taxes 20%	-7,192
Net income	$28,768
Dividends	$17,261

McDonald Company Adjustments to Retained Earnings.

Net income	$28,768
Dividends	-17,261
Expected change in retained earnings	$11,507

Actual change in retained earnings	$11,507
Adjustments to retained earnings	0

McDonald Company Statement of Cash Flows.

Cash flows from operations	
Net income	$28,768
Current asset adjustment	-174,900
Current debt adjustment	110,400
Operating cash flows	**-$35,732**
Cash flows from investing	
Investing in fixed assets	$20,000
Investing cash flows	**20,000**
Cash flows from financing	
Long-term debt	$33,000
Contributed capital	20,000
Dividends	-17,261
Adjustments to retained earnings	0
Financing cash flows	**35,739**
Net change in cash	**-$19,993**

McDonald Company Cash Reconciliation.

Starting cash	$50,600
Ending cash	30,607
Net change in cash	-$19,993

Chapter
4
Operating Budgets

NATURE OF BUDGETING: IMPORTANCE OF THE OPERATING BUDGET

Peter Drucker, an important business strategist, claimed that the only strategic goal of an organization is to create a customer. He believed that such a goal statement oriented the organization to the market. It focused everyone on a common business purpose. This is the role of the operating budget.

Is a single goal too narrow for those who develop budgets? Maybe not. Does the firm ask itself, "What is our business?" and, "Who are our customers?" Or does it take last year's numbers and increase them based on the rate of inflation or changing conditions in current markets? What is the financial risk? Simply stated, you may be in the wrong business, or you may not have the right customers.

Then the budgeting process can take a leap ahead. The questions change: "What will our business be?" and, "Who will our customers be?" If the firm takes this approach to budgeting, it has a future orientation. It is not accepting the status quo. It does not assume that what worked in the past will work in changing conditions in the future.

We can go further to dramatically increase the value of the budgeting process. We can ask, "What should our business be?" and, "Who should our customers be?" Now we are adding financial risk management to our thinking. We focus on our capabilities as matched to emerging market trends. Enterprise risk management brings exposures and opportunities into our span of vision. The operating budget gives numbers to a changing world. This is the framework for the tools in this chapter. A *budget* is a formal plan expressed in a unit of currency. *Budgeting*, also called *financial planning*, uses financial statements to plan for future business. A *pro forma* income statement is a forecast of future revenues, expenses, and profits.

Implied in the process is an assumption that an organization has set goals and is seeking to reach them. Thus, the actual budget is preceded by a planning process in which events are predicted and alternative scenarios are evaluated. In most organizations, the budget process is coordinated by a department of one or more persons designated as corporate planning, long-range planning, or budgeting. These individuals receive inputs from operating areas and assemble them into a coherent budget. The purpose of the effort is to ensure that all units are working to achieve the same goals.

Goals of Budgeting

By tying the budgeting process to the organization's long-range plan, the organization seeks to use the budget as a component of its financial risk management efforts. Goals include:

- *Mitigating problems and seeking opportunities.* Budgeting involves managers at all levels of the organization. Department heads interact with division managers on staffing, operating expenses, sales forecasts, and major projects. These interactions encourage key personnel to identify possible problems and seek potential opportunities. As an example, in a university, the budget might be prepared through the interaction of department chairpersons, deans, and the chief financial officer.
- *Improve coordination of actions.* Because budget centers interact with one another and compete for resources, managers must take care to coordinate their courses of action. If this is done early, an organization increases the likelihood of achieving its goals because of better communication and the reduction of conflicts. The setting of goals gives different operating areas a common focus and encourages all units to work together for their mutual benefit.
- *Assistance in control.* A budget that is matched against the firm's goals can be used to monitor progress. Since each unit may have goals and the means to reach them, higher-level managers can watch for deviations from the plan and step in to provide assistance or tighten controls.
- *Providing standards of performance.* A comparison of the budget with actual performance during the budget year and afterwards can be used to evaluate each unit's success or failure. Did a unit achieve its stated goals? If it did not, what happened? Answers to such questions help the organization adjust to risks and opportunities that might arise in the next budgeting cycle.

FORECASTING REVENUES

The specific steps in budget preparation vary from one organization to the next. A business that sells products or services has one approach. A government agency will have another approach. In the framework of financial risk management, the first step should be to forecast revenues. It is the level of revenues that determines the cash needed to support operations and produce profits and positive cash flow for the organization. This forecasting may start in two different places:

- *Centralized forecast.* A revenue forecast may be undertaken by a planning department, controller, chief financial officer, or some other individual or group that is responsible for bringing together all information on the sale of products or the provision of services. Inputs will be provided by the marketing department, customer service, technical support, research and development, and other areas of the organization. The forecast itself is then put together for the entire company.

- *Budget center forecast.* Alternatively, a revenue forecast may be made in budget centers. A *profit center* is a budget center with responsibilities for forecasting both revenues and expenses. With this approach, the organization consolidates the forecasts of all the profit centers and uses their estimates to prepare a consolidated revenue forecast.

Evaluation of Goals in an Operating Budget

An operating budget might contain any of the following goals. Each one is judged on its value to the budget.

Goal: The company wants to expand into South America.

Value: Fair. The goal identifies a specific objective, but it is vague on the meaning. Which countries? With which products? How much volume?

Goal: The department wants to cut overhead by 10 percent.

Value: Excellent. The goal is specific and quantitative.

Goal: The marketing department wants to increase consumer awareness of the Conchita brand.

Value: Fair. The goal focuses on an important issue, but it is vague.

Goal: The factory wants to cut defects in finished goods to less than 1 percent of products shipped.

Value: Good. However, what is the definition of "defect"? Why not catch defects before shipping and achieve 100 percent quality items?

Goal: The human resources department wants to complete all payrolls every month.

Value: Poor. This kind of goal is what is supposed to be done. It does not contain any information on improving conditions.

Goal: The project manager wants to complete the new building on time and under budget.

Value: Fair. This is a worthwhile goal, but it is broadly stated. Also, intermediate benchmarks may be needed to ensure that the schedule and budget are being met.

Goal: The accounting department wants to complete the monthly closing of the accounting system by the third week of the next month.

Value: Good. However, the goal would be better if it included a statement of how accurate the closing would be.

Goal: The sales department wants to cut returns of goods sold from 6 percent to less than 3 percent of sales in the next six months.

Value: Excellent. This goal is measurable and specific.

Goal: The department wants every person to complete two hours of sexual harassment training during the next year.

Value: Excellent. This is specific in terms of both the goal and the time period.

Goal: The maintenance department wants all machinery in the factory to be serviced during the year.

Value: Poor. This is a laudable goal, but what does it mean? Preventive maintenance? Repaired when it breaks? How quickly after it breaks? How many breakdowns are acceptable?

Risk of Cost Centers

Many organizations start the budgeting process in cost centers rather than centrally or in profit centers. This adds risk to the budgeting process. A cost center is a unit that spends money but does not generate revenues to pay for its disbursements. Typical cost centers are the accounting department, human resources, and data processing. As a cost center does not fund itself, it may not have knowledge of the revenue forecasts. Problems can arise when cost centers are influential in the budgeting process but ignore the reality of creating revenues and cash flows to cover their disbursements. The organization can spend too much money on functions that have no possibility of producing cash inflows and wind up reducing budget lines for units that can earn a considerable profit on the budget allocation.

Market Demand

The most important budget questions revolve around the demand for the goods or services provided by an organization. Management evaluates such demand for each product, service, or line of business. The budget manager interprets economic and demographic trends and their impact on different budget centers. Decisions to discontinue, expand, or create products or services are made based on the assumptions and available information related to demand. In a manufacturing firm, competitive conditions determine the products that are sold. A good economy helps to encourage business activity. A bad economy or high interest rates are harmful. Service providers and nonprofit institutions also are helped or hurt by market factors.

Financial risk management asks, "What will happen if market demand does not develop in line with budget estimates?" The answer is twofold. If demand outstrips the forecast, the firm should have contingency plans to spend more money to seize the opportunities that arise. If market demand is disappointing compared to the forecast, the firm should also have a plan for reducing expenditures that are not generating revenues.

Pricing of Products and Services

The price charged will affect the number of units sold or the volume of services provided. Is the price of each item reasonable in light of competitive factors? Is it adequate to cover the risk of producing the good or providing the service? If not, why not? When asking these questions, the organization should challenge previous assumptions. Occasionally, the market and pricing data will indicate the need to withdraw from a market. In other cases, the firm will decide to expand its operations. The organization should make these decisions before allocating monies to expense areas.

As with market demand, the firm should also have contingency plans for dealing with changing circumstances that would justify raising or lowering prices.

Capability to Meet Demand

Does the organization have the structure and resources to meet the varying demands? In this step, the firm reviews the table of organization. It examines the funds allocated to routine operating expenses and noncompetitive expenditures. The approximate size of the competitive pool is determined. Each budget center works with the assumptions and guidelines provided by management and prepares initial budgets that are in line with the suggested targets. The organization must have adequate skilled direct line personnel and support staff. It also allocates money to provide administrative support that maintains the structure of the operation.

LIFE-CYCLE STAGES IN BUDGETING

In the process of forecasting revenues, the organization faces a number of risks as various units interact to create a combined budget. One way to view these exposures is to examine the challenges that arise from profit centers in various stages of the organizational life cycle. The stages are:

- *Start-up.* This refers to the birth of a unit. The organization has made a conscious decision to develop a new product or service and has formed a unit and created a budget to pursue the task
- *Growth.* A unit in this stage has been working for a period of time, has created a product or service, has identified a market, and is generating revenues from its operations. Generally, the revenues are not sufficient to cover the expenses, the cash inflows lag the cash outflows, or the unit is not earning a sufficiently high return on the company's investment in it. Thus, the budgeting process is seeking a rapid expansion of products and markets to reach an acceptable level of return for the risk of the operation.
- *Peak.* A unit in this stage has mature products and markets, with strong profits and usually slow growth. Such units are the bread and butter of many successful enterprises. Budgets are designed to maintain a strong competitive position and allow the unit to continue to grow, earn profits, and create cash inflows.
- *Declining.* A unit in this stage was once a peak unit that made significant contributions to the firm. Now it is not doing so well and is either losing money or earning an inadequate return. The company is trying to figure out what to do with the unit. The budgeting options are renewal or closure.

Units in each of these stages have different goals and priorities in the budgeting process. The organization has to deal with the exposures that are created by each unit's perspective on the budget.

Life-Cycle Budgeting Goals

Each stage of the life cycle creates different budgeting goals for profit centers. Specifically:

- *Start-up.* A unit in this stage needs to create a marketable product or service. It takes money to achieve this goal, and progress is often uncertain, as technological and other delays can disrupt the schedule of development. Funding allocated to such a unit often needs to be revised after the budget is approved.

- *Growth.* A unit in this stage has a goal of developing a market for a relatively new product or service. The expenditures are usually less variable than those for a start-up unit. The revenues, on the other hand, can be highly unpredictable, as the market may grow more or less quickly than the forecast.
- *Peak.* A unit in this stage is rolling along and seeks to continue to bring in profits and cash. It also looks for new markets and opportunities to sell its existing products or services. Most employees are confident that they can achieve their budget goals and hope to benefit personally from salary, bonuses, and perks as a result of a successful operation.
- *Declining.* The goal of a unit in this stage is quite simple: It seeks survival. It is trying to hang on as it looks for new products and markets so that it can avoid downsizing or closure. In some cases, the budget reflects real opportunities to modify products, services, or strategies. In other cases, budgeting is largely a matter of figuring out what costs to reduce.

Sources of Financing to Achieve Goals

In the budget process, the organization finances its ongoing activities with cash provided by operations. Where does it obtain the cash needed for each of the profit centers? This question has a fairly simple answer: All the money comes from peak units. They are making more money than they need for the slow expansion of their activities. They are the source of cash for the other units.

This reality poses considerable risk for the budgeting process. Peak units do not need a large new allocation of cash, so they can usually get through the budgeting process without rancor. For the other units, however, budgeting is more problematic. For declining units, times are tough anyway. An inadequate expense budget just makes thing worse. For growth units, time is not on their side. They must reach a viable market demand level as soon as possible, particularly if they are experiencing rising competition. For start-up units, product development should finish as soon as possible. Changing technology or customer preferences can endanger the entire effort. These units have a big stake in the development of the budget.

Life-Cycle Political Risk

We know who needs funding. Do we also recognize the politics of budgeting? Let us use a simple measuring tool. How many vice presidents will we find in each unit? Let us assume that a peak unit has 14 vice presidents. This means that the start-up and growth units might have a few, and the declining units, may have the most. Figure 4-1 shows a possible scenario.

Financial risk management recognizes the impact of the number of vice presidents. In many cases, the units with the most senior executives have the most clout in discussions on allocating funds. As a result, we commonly see the creation of budgets in which organizations spend more to keep declining units alive than to start, grow, or maintain the success of other units. It is an everyday peril in the world of budgeting.

Unit	Number of VPs
Start-up	2
Growth	3
Peak	14
Declining	26

Figure 4-1. Vice Presidents Involved in Budgeting.

The Charge for Top Management

The success or failure of budgeting revenues is laid directly at the door of the organization's top management. Senior executives must resist the pressure to allocate funds to activities that do not achieve organizational goals. Management must review the budget and the budget process and address inconsistencies or invalid assumptions or beliefs. Political risk can create dangers that exceed the organization's ability to succeed.

High-Level Review

In addition to reviewing the politics of the budget, senior management and the board of directors should ask pointed questions:

- *Is the forecasted market demand realistic?* Every unit has made some assumptions concerning the level of goods that it can sell or services that will be purchased. If these assumptions are unrealistic, the rest of the budget is in danger. Management should require full support for market share assumptions as it examines and even challenges them in detail. A company forecasts changes in conditions based on management's view of the strength of each unit and the market demand for its products or services.

- *Is the pricing correct?* The price charged for goods or services is a critical variable in the conduct of business. If the price is too high, the number of units sold will decline, and revenue goals will not be achieved. If the price is too low, the firm will not earn a proper return for the level of risk it incurs. The pricing of all product lines and services should be critiqued prior to approval of the budget. Many organizations use different pricing for each of their units. This reflects a belief that products have different values in various segments of the market.

- *Is the revenue forecast realistic?* We are forecasting revenues. We are concerned about the bottom line. Businesses are seeking sufficient revenues to cover their expenses, pay off their liabilities, and earn a return for their shareholders. Nonprofit organizations usually seek at least a balanced budget. If the bottom line is not adequate given the risks facing the organization, the budget must be reviewed and perhaps be redone. This does not mean that the firm prefers short-term profits to long-term financial health and stability. It does mean that the short-term results must fit in with the long-range plans of the organization.

RISKS IN REVENUE FORECASTING

Organizations often portray revenue forecasting as a relatively static process. The company had sales last year. Let us increase the forecast by the rate of inflation, and that will be our next revenue budget. This is a poor process indeed. Let us develop the logic.

Why do organizations spend money? The answer leads us directly to the revenue forecast. Firms and nonprofit organizations spend money to make money. The only way they can do this is to achieve revenues. If we assume revenues to be static, we have little guidance in how to complete the rest of the budget.

A better approach is to start with the opportunities to sell products or services. What are the hot markets? What are the unmet needs? Where can we make acceptable profits? Once these are identified, we can budget expenses to reach those markets. The revenue budget thus becomes dynamic. We are not selling last year's stuff to last year's customers. We are setting ourselves up to take advantage of new opportunities.

Stages of the Market

Revenue budgets should always be prepared with a goal of selling something. The first question is the nature of the market itself. Three conditions are possible, each with its own opportunities and exposures:

- *Production stage—demand exceeds production.* For a new product or market, demand might exceed supply. In this case, a primary emphasis is on the manufacturing and distribution of the product. The revenue budget simply has to reflect a reasonable selling price in terms of value to purchasers. Then, a company should be able to sell all it can produce.
- *Selling stage—productive capacity exceeds demand.* Some products or services are sold in situations where no shortages exist. The revenue budget must reflect efforts to "sell" the product. The budget center cannot assume that sales will occur just because a product is produced. The budget manager must evaluate revenues in light of advertising and other promotional efforts that will be used to convince customers to buy the company's products rather than the products sold by a competitor.
- *Marketing stage—highly competitive markets.* Many countries of the world have reached levels of high sophistication in demanding specialized products and services. In this situation, the revenue forecast examines whether the organization's products or services have competitive advantages over the competition. The budget manager should determine whether research has been undertaken on the product and on the needs of customers. Is the budget center offering distinctive products that will attract purchasers?

Level of Economic Activity

Revenue forecasts are the most uncertain part of budget preparation. This is true because sales are affected directly and often dramatically by the level of activity in national economies. We can control production costs. We can manufacture a high-quality product or provide a first-class service. However, we do not control the national or the global economy. Times may be good, and people may have money to spend. Or unemployment and tight money may hurt sales. In this context, it may be helpful to identify the concept of a *business cycle*. This may be defined as a circular pattern of economic activity that is commonly experienced in many nations. The stages are:

- *Prosperity.* A period of economic growth during which people and companies expand their spending and marketing and seek to capitalize on the good times.
- *Recession.* A period of economic decline. People cut spending, and businesses reduce production. Marketing efforts are directed toward preserving markets and profits.
- *Recovery.* A period during which the recession is ending and the groundwork is being laid for prosperity. Marketing efforts are expanded as firms seek to improve their sales efforts.

Changing Price Levels

A second reason for uncertainty in the revenue budget is caused by the central bank's seeking to match the money supply with the goods and services available to purchase in an economy. This is often outside the view of the budget manager. This is a big mistake. Two things can occur when the money supply and the supply of goods are not in balance:

- *Inflation.* This is a rise in the prices of goods and services, often caused by excessive money in the economy. If prices are rising, the organization's revenue estimates may be lower than the amount of money actually collected. At first, this sounds good. However, a problem arises if costs are rising faster than selling prices. A second problem arises when we evaluate actual performance against a budget. We may achieve a revenue figure, but not make the profit we expected.
- *Deflation.* This is a decline in prices, often caused by an excessive supply of goods and services. If prices are falling, it can be quite difficult to achieve the revenue forecast.

Other Risks in the Revenue Budget

As a company develops a revenue budget, it can consider any factors that increase uncertainty. It should also incorporate factors that offer a competitive advantage. Some considerations are:

- *Market saturation.* In some cases, the local market is mature. New products are not demanded, and additional units cannot be sold.
- *Export growth.* Foreign markets may offer the potential to increase sales on a profitable basis.
- *Comparative advantage.* This refers to a unique resource that gives a nation an advantage in the production of a good or service. Some countries have natural resources. Others have low-cost labor. And still others have technological skills. Comparative advantage encourages a nation to produce some goods and services and import others. The company can look for situations in which its comparative advantage opens new sources of revenues.

- *Competitors.* Many markets are highly competitive. Others are not. Is market entry relatively easy or relatively difficult? This affects revenues during the early years of a product launch. Does a competitor dominate the potential market? If so, pricing can get nasty.
- *Competitive advantage in production.* The company itself may have a production advantage that will drive revenues up. Does it know how to design and produce excellent products at reasonable costs? If so, demand for new products or in new markets might be high.
- *Competitive advantage in strong marketing.* The company may have excellent advertising, brand recognition, and selling channels in its primary markets. Can it extend these strengths to new markets? If so, the revenue forecast can be boosted.
- *Competitive advantage in research and development.* The company may know more about products and customer trends than its competitors do. This increases the likelihood of successful sales in new markets.

Budgeting Risk from Government Regulations

Companies often make the mistake of ignoring government regulations when preparing a revenue budget. Laws affect sales in a variety of ways. Governments regulate competition, protect consumers, forbid certain competitive practices, protect domestic companies from foreign competition, and impose reporting requirements on businesses. Revenue strategies should deal with existing and pending legislation, including:

- *Taxes.* Government tax policies affect the sales of goods and services. Luxury items may be taxed at higher rates than other goods. Tax breaks may encourage the sale of some products at the expense of others. A tax break for products sold in a low-income area encourages retail outlets in that area. A tax on imported wines will raise prices and switch buying patterns to domestic wine.
- *Environmental regulations.* Governments are paying increasing attention to problems of pollution, noise, and other quality-of-life issues. This results in laws that shape the design of products and the ability of companies to sell them. A law requiring recycling of newspapers creates one industry. A law banning glass bottles eliminates another.
- *Safety regulations.* Governments prescribe rules to protect workers and consumers from dangerous conditions. Such regulations create markets for new products and eliminate other markets. A requirement for safety glass in automobiles opens a market. A ban on all-terrain vehicles kills a market.
- *Subsidies.* Most countries subsidize industries that are deemed to be essential to the local economy or the political scene. Revenues are affected by subsidies to mass transportation, farmers, airlines, telecommunications companies, and heavy industry.
- *Monetary policy.* This refers to regulating a nation's money supply, price levels, and interest rates. If the money supply is not adequate or interest rates are excessive, goods and services will not be purchased. In periods in which money is not

available or is costly, successfully achieving revenue targets may require a company to provide assistance to a customer who wants to make a purchase.

- *Fiscal policy*. This refers to a government's efforts to manage its budget, tax collection, and spending. If the government is having problems balancing its budget, it may raise taxes and hurt sales.

Budgets of Nonprofit Organizations

A nonprofit organization or government agency forecasts funding using a format that is appropriate for its environment. All of the previous factors may play a role. At the same time, adjustments must be made. Some examples include:

- *Hospitals*. Funds may come from patients, government agencies, employers, or private donors. Cash may be earned from operating a cafeteria or collecting parking fees.
- *Universities*. A college or university collects tuition and fees from students, provides food service and housing to students, operates a bookstore, receives donations from alumni and benefactors, and has a variety of other revenue sources.
- *Department of Motor Vehicles*. This government agency may be financed by tax dollars from the government, or it may collect and retain fees for licensing individuals to drive automobiles or registration of vehicles.
- *Labor unions*. These organizations may collect dues from individuals or receive commissions from the sale of health insurance or other services provided to their members.
- *Trade associations*. Members of groups such as travel agents or lawyers may belong to an association that provides information on the profession. Such an association may have revenues from dues, publication of a journal, annual meetings, or providing services to members.

EXPENSE ALLOCATIONS

Once the revenue forecast is done, the budget center manager can bring expenses into the picture. The difference between revenues and expenses becomes a profit goal for an organization.

An expense occurs when a company uses an asset to produce revenues. It is a cost of doing business during an accounting period. A cost is money used to purchase an asset or pay a bill. The cost may be an immediate expense if revenue is produced. An example is money paid to a worker who sells products. A cost is not an immediate expense if revenue is not produced. An example is when a company purchases a product to sell at a later time.

A cost center or budget center has the task of forecasting the money it will need in order to conduct its operations. It also must live within the guidelines set by higher levels of management.

Foundations for Expense Estimates

The budget manager has the task of forecasting next year's expenditures. The forecast can be built upon a number of sources of information:

- *Historical data.* The most widely used foundation for operating budgets is the actual expenditures for last year or the current year. If 100 workers produced 50,000 units of a product last year, the same might be expected next year. If new technology is introduced, the level of productivity may rise or the number of workers may fall. Still, the historical data are a starting or reference point for the forecast. *Financial risk:* The future will not be similar to the past.
- *Comparative data.* A company may be starting up a new line of business. It has expenditure data from another area of the company. The budget manager may seek historical results from the other area and use them to estimate expenditures in the new business. *Financial risk:* The company may compare the new line of business to the wrong area.
- *Relationships among variables.* The budget manager may notice relationships among variables that affect future expenditures. A change in one factor may cause a future change in another. The planned level of production affects the cost of utilities and the amount of overtime. Predictions of shortages of raw materials affect the price of such materials. *Financial risk:* The budget manager may choose the wrong variables or miss changing circumstances related to the right variables.
- *Period-to-period trends.* The budget manager may look through historical data for relationships that are changing. Increased computerization of manufacturing processes may be reducing the cost of labor in finished goods. Improved telecommunications services may be reducing travel costs. *Financial risk:* The firm may not observe the reversal of trends or the development of factors that cause new trends that affect products or markets.

Cost of Merchandise

The first expense involves the cost of the goods or services sold. The simplest calculation occurs when a company buys a product and resells it. This creates an expense that can be called *cost of merchandise*.

Cost of Goods Sold

A more complex expense occurs when a firm converts raw materials into a finished product. *Cost of goods sold* represents an accounting allocation of the costs of raw materials, labor, overhead, and other expenses that can be matched against the goods sold by the firm. It contains a mixture of fixed and variable costs.

Cost of goods sold reflects manufacturing expenses to change raw materials into finished products. Initially, the costs become inventory. Then, when the goods are sold, they become an expense. Items commonly included in cost of goods sold are:

- *Materials expense.* The cost of the steel, wood, electric circuits, transistors, plastic components, or any other materials that become an integral part of the finished product and can be conveniently traced to the product.
- *Direct labor expense.* The salaries, benefits, or contractual charges for assembly line workers, carpenters, machine operators, and others who process the raw materials and convert them into finished products.
- *Manufacturing overhead.* All the other costs of production, including heat, electricity, maintenance, property taxes, insurance, and other expenses of the factory.

Cost of Services

Service companies do not have materials, labor, and manufacturing overhead costs, but they have similar expenses for facilities, equipment, and people.

General and Administrative Expenses

These expenses support nonproduction activities, such as marketing, corporate staff salaries, and miscellaneous expenses.

Interest Expense

The fixed charges paid by the firm on the money that it borrows are reported as interest expense. Unlike cost of goods sold, depreciation, and general and administrative expenses, interest is not an operating expense; rather, it is related to the financial structure of the firm. This is a large expense for firms with considerable amounts of debt; it is relatively small for firms with mostly equity financing.

An Expense Budget

Let us assume that a business is opening. During the first year, it expects a variety of operating expenses. The expense budget is shown in Figure 4-2.

Although firms may have similar profit margins, controlling costs can increase profits. Areas where this is possible are:

- *Producing goods or delivering services.* Producing goods involves materials, labor, and overhead costs. Delivering services involves labor costs and other disbursements. Good management strives to control costs.

Materials expenses	$250,000
Direct labor expenses	350,000
Overhead	100,000
Selling expenses	700,000
Administrative expenses	50,000
Administrative salaries	150,000
Insurance expense	30,000
Annual budget	**$1,630,000**

Figure 4-2. Expense Budget.

- *Marketing expenses.* It costs money to create a marketing force and advertise products and services. A firm seeks to spend these funds properly.
- *Handling and delivery.* The storage, shipment, and safeguarding of goods can be expensive. Maintaining high quality when delivering services can involve special expenses. Costs should be examined to see if distribution channels are efficient.
- *Administrative expenses.* Indirect costs should be reviewed frequently to avoid unnecessary overhead.

ACCOUNTING BUDGETS

Budgeting in a profit center involves matching revenues and expenses. It is not enough to figure out what we need to spend to be in operation. The business also verifies that the budgeted expenses are producing the desired results in terms of revenues to cover them and provide a return to investors. We will illustrate a profit center budget using accounting data for the Keaton Medical Devices Company, a manufacturer of medical products.

Keaton Approved Budget

Figure 4-3 shows a budget for next year for the Keaton Medical Devices Company. The firm produces equipment in two divisions: Surgical Devices and Nonsurgical Products. The budget is based upon existing operations, is supported by years of past experience, and has been approved for next year.

The Opportunity

In preparing for the future, companies come upon new opportunities. These are often addressed by creating a new budget. Keaton has discovered a market niche for a new emergency room product line. The company has investigated the market and believes that the new products would bring in additional revenues and involve additional costs as shown in Figure 4-4.

The company prepared the revised budget shown in Figure 4-5. It appears that the new venture is promising, with the prospect of doubling operating income.

Surgical Devices revenues	$12,450
Nonsurgical Products revenues	7,800
Total revenues	**$20,250**
Staff salaries	$8,910
Staff benefits	2,138
Variable costs, Surgical Devices	2,241
Variable costs, Nonsurgical Products	1,482
Fixed costs	4,658
Total expenses	**$19,429**
Operating income	**$821**

Figure 4-3. Accounting Budget for Keaton Medical Devices (000s).

Additional revenues	$2,400
Additional staffing costs	360
Additional variable costs	720
Additional fixed costs	432

Figure 4-4. Additional Revenues and Expenses (000s).

CASH BUDGETING

The cash budget is a second form of forecasting future results. It builds upon the revenue and expense accounts, but it makes an adjustment for the lags that occur in collecting or paying cash. Some of the cash adjustments are:

- *Starting cash.* Does the firm have enough cash to finance its assets on the first day of the month?
- *Cash collections.* How much cash will be collected from the current month's and prior months' revenues?
- *Cash disbursements.* How much cash is needed to pay for supplies and other expenses?
- *Safety level.* At the end of each period, will the firm achieve a target safety level of cash?

Starting Cash

The cash budget recognizes that a company needs to finance assets to conduct its business. A cash budget identifies the assets needed and the sources of financing. As an example, a firm has a unit that will need to buy machinery and supplies at the start

	Original Budget	New Line of Business	Revised Budget
Surgical Devices revenues	$12,450		$12,450
Nonsurgical Products revenues	7,800		7,800
Emergency Room Supplies revenues	_____	$2,400	2,400
Total revenues	**$20,250**	**$2,400**	**$22,650**
Staff salaries	$8,910		$8,910
Staff benefits	2,138		2,138
Additional staffing costs		$360	360
Variable costs, Surgical Devices	2,241		2,241
Variable costs, Nonsurgical Products	1,482		1,482
Additional variable costs		720	720
Fixed costs	4,658	4,658	
Additional fixed costs	_____	432	432
Total expenses	**$19,429**	**$1,512**	**$20,941**
Operating income	**$821**	**$888**	**$1,709**

Figure 4-5. Keaton Revised Budget (000s).

of a budget period. The unit wants to maintain a target level of cash in the bank as a contingency. The firm can borrow to finance part of the expenditures. Figure 4-6 shows the data and the budgeted amount of starting cash.

Cash Collections

A company needs to budget the cash that will be received from cash and credit revenues. Commonly, the accounts receivables manager uses historical data to forecast the collections pattern. A firm is budgeting credit revenues for January, February, and March. Cash revenues are also budgeted for each month. The receivables manager knows that a different percentage of revenues is collected each month over a three-month period. A small percentage represents bad debts. Assuming that the operation starts in January, Figure 4-7 shows the cash collections pattern.

Cash Disbursements

A company budgets its cash payments for supplies and other expenses. Once again, historical data are a guideline. The company budgets the purchase of supplies each month. The accounts payable manager knows the terms of trade and the payment pattern that the company follows. He also knows the cash disbursements other than those for supplies. Figure 4-8 shows the budget for cash disbursements for the firm over a three-month period, assuming that the firm starts up in May.

Safety Level

A safety level is the minimum amount of cash that a firm is required to have on hand at all times. The goal of maintaining a safety level is to avoid the risks or costs of errors in cash budgeting. The risks of running out of cash are:

- *Default.* The failure to pay interest or make principal payments on a firm's fixed obligations is a default. It may result in liquidation or legal action by the firm's creditors.
- *Overdue bills.* The failure to pay short-term obligations, such as payables, is less serious than default on long-term debt, but it may result in a lowering of the firm's credit rating in the business community. This may be accompanied by higher interest rates when the firm applies for future loans, or it may cause creditors to refuse to ship supplies on credit.
- *Lost savings on purchases.* Inadequate cash may cause the firm to lose opportunities to make special purchases or to take generous trade discounts on purchases of goods.

Cost of machinery	$300,000
Cost of supplies	50,000
Cash balance to be maintained in bank.	25,000
Less debt financing	-125,000
Cash needed to start	$250,000

Figure 4-6. Budgeting the Starting Cash.

	January	February	March
Cash sales	$5,000	$5,000	$5,000
Credit sales	$10,000	$15,000	$20,000
Collections in:			
Same month	20%	20%	20%
Next month	40%	40%	40%
Second month	35%	35%	35%
Never	5%	5%	5%
Cash collections	$7,000	$12,000	$18,500

Figure 4-7. Cash Collections.

Positions in the Cash Budget

When the safety level is matched with the cash budget, four positions are possible:

- *Surplus.* This occurs at the end of any period in which the budget forecasts holding more cash than the safety level.
- *Optimum.* This occurs when the cash budget shows approximately the same amount of cash as the safety level.
- *Shortage.* This occurs when the forecasted cash level is positive, but is less than the safety level.
- *Deficit.* This occurs when the cash budget shows a negative cash position.

Example of a Cash Budget

A simplified cash budget is presented in Figure 4-9. The firm is forecasting a starting balance for January. Collections and disbursements during each month produce ending balances that are compared to a safety level of $4,000. Three situations are visible:

- *Surplus.* This occurs in May only, when the forecasted cash balance is $5,300, a net position $1,300 above the safety level.
- *Shortage.* This occurs in January (-$500), March (-$2,700), and April (-$1,200). The cash balances are positive at $3,500, $1,300, and $2,800, but the cash levels are below the safety level of $4,000.

	May	June	July
Cash disbursements	$5,000	$5,000	$50,000
Purchase of supplies	$25,000	$30,000	$40,000
Cash paid for supplies in:			
Same month	0%	0%	0%
Next month	60%	60%	60%
Second month	40%	40%	40%
Cash disbursements	$5,000	$20,000	$78,000

Figure 4-8. Cash Disbursements.

- *Shortage and deficit.* This occurs in February. The deficit is $1,400, and the shortage is $5,400.

Knowing that it expects to have shortages and even a deficit, the firm can take steps to avoid running low on cash or out of cash. Then, it can revise the budget to make spending plans that keep cash above the safety level.

DETAILS OF BUDGETING

We have now seen accounting and cash flow budgets on a summary basis. We need to recognize that they are built from details. In most cases, budgets have subcategories where details are used and then are rolled up to higher units and eventually to the entire organization. In this section, we will examine such a process.

Darnell Volume of Business Activity

The Darnell Walk-in Clinic is preparing an operating budget for the next year. The starting point is the company's expectations with respect to the amount of business that will be available. This is expressed in terms of the number of physicians it will need for each seasonal quarter of the year and the number of staff members needed to support the operations. The firm also makes an assumption concerning the number of patients that will be seen by each physician during a typical day and the number of days that the clinic will operate, a number that fluctuates in each quarter. The company also estimates the average fee for seeing a physician. The fee varies by procedure, but the company has historical data on the mix of services and is comfortable forecasting an average fee.

Figure 4-10 shows the data for Darnell's expectations of business activity for each quarter next year.

Darnell Variable Costs

Darnell has variable costs that essentially match the number of patients served. As shown in Figure 4-11, these consist of medical supplies, other supplies, and laboratory costs.

Darnell Fixed Costs

A walk-in clinic has a number of fixed costs, as shown in Figure 4-12. These include the salaries and benefits paid to full-time staff, including part-year staffers who work during peak periods. They also include the total of operating costs not associated with personnel.

Darnell Revenue Budget

Once all this information is brought together, Darnell forecasts revenues. Figure 4-13 shows the revenues budget.

Darnell Variable Cost Budget

Darnell uses the volume data to prepare a forecast of variable costs. Figure 4-14 shows the variable cost budget.

	January	February	March	April	May
Cash on hand, start	$4,000	$3,500	-$1,400	$1,300	$2,800
Collections of cash	0	3,000	4,000	3,500	4,000
Cash revenues	1,000	1,100	1,200	1,000	1,000
Cash payments	-1,500	-9,000	-2,500	-3,000	-2,500
Ending cash	$3,500	-$1,400	$1,300	$2,800	$5,300
Safety level	$4,000	$4,000	$4,000	$4,000	$4,000
Net position	-$500	-$5,400	-$2,700	-$1,200	$1,300

Figure 4-9. Cash Budget.

	Quarter 1	Quarter 2	Quarter 3	Quarter 4
Physician services:				
Number of physicians	5	7	9	6
Number of staff members	3	4	5	3
Daily patients per physician	16	16	16	16
Average days in period	75	80	90	70
Average fee for physician service	$75	$75	$75	$75
Medical procedures:				
Total patients	6,000	8,960	12,960	6,720
Percent needing procedures	20%	20%	20%	20%
Total procedures	1,200	1,792	2,592	1,344
Average fee for procedure	$65	$65	$65	$65

Figure 4-10. Volume of Activity Data.

	Quarter 1	Quarter 2	Quarter 3	Quarter 4
Medical supplies per patient	$10	$10	$10	$10
Other supplies per patient	$5	$5	$5	$5
Laboratory costs per procedure	$30	$25	$25	$30

Figure 4-11. Variable Cost Data.

	Quarter 1	Quarter 2	Quarter 3	Quarter 4
Average physician salary	$60,000	$60,000	$60,000	$60,000
Average staff salary	$15,000	$15,000	$15,000	$15,000
Staff benefits, percent of salary	25%	25%	25%	25%
Nonpersonnel operating costs	$72,000	$72,000	$72,000	$72,000

Figure 4-12. Fixed Cost Data.

	Quarter 1	Quarter 2	Quarter 3	Quarter 4
Physician services:				
Total patients	6,000	8,960	12,960	6,720
Average fee for physician service	$75	$75	$75	$75
Physician revenues	$450,000	$672,000	$972,000	$504,000
Medical procedures:				
Total procedures	1,200	1,792	2,592	1,344
Average fee for procedure	$65	$65	$65	$65
Procedure revenues	$78,000	$116,480	$168,480	$87,360
Total revenues	$528,000	$788,480	$1,140,480	$591,360

Figure 4-13. Revenue Budget (000s).

	Quarter 1	Quarter 2	Quarter 3	Quarter 4
Number of patients	6,000	8,960	12,960	6,720
Medical supplies per patient	$10	$10	$10	$10
Other supplies per patient	$5	$5	$5	$5
Number of procedures	1,200	1,792	2,592	1,344
Laboratory costs per procedure	$30	$25	$25	$30
Variable costs for patients	$90,000	$134,400	$194,400	$100,800
Variable costs for procedures	$36,000	$44,800	$64,800	$40,320
Total variable costs	$126,000	$179,200	$259,200	$141,120

Figure 4-14. Variable Cost Budget.

Darnell Fixed Cost Budget

Figure 4-15 shows the budget for fixed costs, which, as we already noted, are fixed in a seasonal pattern.

Darnell Summary Budget

The budget comes together in a format similar to that of an income statement. The summary budget is shown in Figure 4-16.

CONCLUSION

Budgeting is a risky process, as we would expect it to be, considering that it deals with financial projections in an uncertain future. Still, organizations can take steps to reduce the risk of a disastrous outcome. The process itself must be protected from the political risk that accompanies the participation of units in various stages of the organizational life cycle. Budget managers must have an understanding of their products and markets. Revenue forecasts must recognize conditions both within and external to the organization. Expenses must pursue revenues, cash, and profits. The budgeting process must lead

	Quarter 1	Quarter 2	Quarter 3	Quarter 4
Number of physicians	5	7	9	6
Physician quarterly salary	$60,000	$60,000	$60,000	$60,000
Number of staff members	3	4	5	3
Staff quarterly salary	$15,000	$15,000	$15,000	$15,000
Physician salaries	$300,000	$420,000	$540,000	$360,000
Staff salaries	$45,000	$60,000	$75,000	$45,000
Staff benefits 25%	$86,250	$120,000	$153,750	$101,250
Nonpersonnel operating costs	$72,000	$72,000	$72,000	$72,000
Fixed costs	**$503,250**	**$672,000**	**$840,750**	**$578,250**

Figure 4-15. Fixed Cost Budget.

	Quarter 1	Quarter 2	Quarter 3	Quarter 4
Physician revenues	$450,000	$672,000	$972,000	$504,000
Procedure revenues	78,000	116,480	168,480	87,360
Total revenues	$528,000	$788,480	$1,140,480	$591,360
Variable costs for patients	$90,000	$134,400	$194,400	$100,800
Variable costs for procedures	36,000	44,800	64,800	40,320
Physician salaries	300,000	420,000	540,000	360,000
Staff salaries	45,000	60,000	75,000	45,000
Staff benefits	86,250	120,000	153,750	101,250
Total expenses	$557,250	$779,200	$1,027,950	$647,370
Operating income	**$-29,250**	**$9,280**	**$112,530**	**$-56,010**

Figure 4-16. Summary Budget.

clearly from data, assumptions, and beliefs to a bottom line. Finally, the firm must be prepared to make adjustments in response to changing conditions.

CHAPTER 4 APPENDIXES

How to Prepare a One-Year Operating Budget

Two doctors plan to open an adult treatment facility that accepts referrals from the military to treat active-duty and retired soldiers, sailors, marines, and air force personnel. They have prepared a budget for the first year using the following steps.

Step 1. Volume of Business (Number of Referrals and Average Charge for Providing Treatment).

	Quarter 1	Quarter 2	Quarter 3	Quarter 4
Substance abuse referrals				
Number	60	80	90	60

	Quarter 1	Quarter 2	Quarter 3	Quarter 4
Average fee for treatment	$6,000	$6,000	$6,000	$6,000
Psychological trauma referrals				
Number	60	70	70	60
Average fee for treatment	$8,000	$8,000	$8,000	$8,000

Step 2. Revenue Forecast.

	Quarter 1	Quarter 2	Quarter 3	Quarter 4
Substance abuse referrals				
Number	60	80	90	60
Average fee for treatment	$6,000	$6,000	$6,000	$6,000
Substance abuse revenues	**$360,000**	**$480,000**	**$540,000**	**$360,000**
Psychological trauma referrals				
Number	60	70	70	60
Average fee for treatment	$8,000	$8,000	$8,000	$8,000
Trauma revenues	**$480,000**	**$560,000**	**$560,000**	**$480,000**

Step 3. Variable Cost of Treatments.

	Quarter 1	Quarter 2	Quarter 3	Quarter 4
Substance abuse referrals				
Electronic medical record	$40	$60	$60	$40
Blood and other testing	150	150	150	150
Cost per treatment	$190	$210	$210	$190
Number of referrals	60	80	90	60
Substance variable costs	**$11,400**	**$16,800**	**$18,900**	**$11,400**
Psychological trauma referrals				
Electronic medical record	$50	$60	$60	$50
Blood and other testing	120	120	120	120
Cost per treatment	$170	$180	$180	$170
Number of referrals	60	70	70	60
Trauma variable costs	**$10,200**	**$12,600**	**$12,600**	**$10,200**

Step 4. Quarterly Fixed Costs of Operating the Facility.

	Quarter 1	Quarter 2	Quarter 3	Quarter 4
Medical salaries	0	$100,000	$100,000	0
Non-medical salaries	$140,000	$150,000	$150,000	$140,000
Benefits, % of salaries (25%)	35,000	62,500	62,500	35,000
Medical expenses	30,000	40,000	40,000	30,000

	Quarter 1	Quarter 2	Quarter 3	Quarter 4
Rent of facility	$72,000	$72,000	$72,000	$72,000
Administrative expenses	20,000	25,000	25,000	20,000
Utilities	30,000	35,000	35,000	30,000
Insurance	220,000	220,000	220,000	220,000
Miscellaneous Costs	22,000	25,000	25,000	22,000
Annual fixed costs	**$569,000**	**$729,500**	**$729,500**	**$569,000**

Step 5. Prepare the Budget.

	Quarter 1	Quarter 2	Quarter 3	Quarter 4
Substances abuse revenues	$360,000	$480,000	$540,000	$360,000
Trauma revenues	480,000	560,000	560,000	480,000
Substance treatment costs	-11,400	-16,800	-18,900	-11,400
Trauma treatment costs	-10,200	-12,600	-12,600	-10,200
Fixed costs	-569,000	-729,500	-729,500	-569,000
Share for doctors	**$249,400**	**$281,100**	**$339,000**	**$249,400**

How to Estimate Start-Up Costs and Desired Profit

A company has sent out a request for proposal (RFP) to provide computing and tele-communications services to align its customers with investment systems. An investor has formed a group of technicians who are certified by a computer institute to provide such services. Before submitting a proposal, the investor wants to know the profit that must be built into the proposal so that he can earn a desired profit on his capital. He performed the following analysis.

Step 1. Identify the Start-up Costs and Desired Profit.

Start-up costs (legal, accounting, planning)	$120,000
Desired profit	20%

Step 2. Forecast Level of Business Activity. Last year the company paid the following for services:

Likely revenues	$3,000,000

Step 3. Calculate the Required Assets.

Machinery and equipment at cash cost	$800,000
Buildings and land at cash cost	$300,000
Assets needed, percent of first-year revenues:	
Cash	6%

Receivables	15%
Inventory	15%

Step 4. Identify the Sources of Financing. As a percentage of start-up costs and assets:

Payables	12%
Line of credit	6%
Short-term bank note	8%
Medium-term bank loan	14%
Owner's capital	60%

Step 5. Calculate Starting Cash Needed.

Start-up costs	$120,000
Cash	180,000
Receivables	240,000
Inventory	420,000
Fixed assets	1,100,000
Total cash needed	$2,060,000

Step 6. Calculate Sources of Financing.

Payables	$247,200
Line of credit	123,600
Short-term bank note	164,800
Medium-term bank loan	288,400
Owner's capital	1,236,000
Total sources of financing	$2,060,000

Step 7. Profit to Be Included in Proposal.

Total cash to be provided	$2,060,000
Desired profit	20%
Profit needed	$412,000

How to Develop a Self-Funding Budget

The Approved Budget. A subsidiary forecasts the following budget for next year:

Revenues forecast	$3,100,000
Direct labor	-670,000
Materials expense	-350,000
Overhead expense	-460,000
Cost of goods sold	-$1,480,000

Gross margin	$1,620,000
Indirect labor	-325,000
Administrative expense	-595,000
Rent expense	-160,000
Depreciation expense	-210,000
Operating expenses	-$1,290,000
Interest expense	-145,000
Pretax income	$185,000
Income tax 20%	-37,000
Forecasted income/loss	**$148,000**

The income is not sufficient to allow the declaration of dividends at the desired level. The desired level of dividends is $500,000.

The Opportunity. The company could offer a new product line that would have the following impact:

Additional revenues	$2,400,000
Additional cost of goods sold	$850,000
Additional operating expenses	$910,000

Where Will the Firm Get the Money to Finance the New Line of Business? *Answer:* The money is not in the budget. It is in the bank.

Assume that we have to borrow the full amount	-$1,760,000
Assume that the number of days we need the money is	90
Assume that the number of days in the year is	365
Assume that the borrowing cost us	11%
Interest costs would be	$47,737

The Revised Budget.

	Old Line of Business	New Line of Business	Total
Revenues forecast	$3,100,000	$2,400,000	$5,500,000
Direct labor	-$670,000		
Materials expense	-350,000		
Overhead expense	-460,000		
Cost of goods sold	-$1,480,000	-$850,000	-$2,330,000
Indirect labor	-$325,000		
Administrative expense	-595,000		
Rent expense	-160,000		

	Old Line of Business	New Line of Business	Total
Depreciation expense	-210,000		
Operating expenses	-$1,290,000	-$910,000	-$2,200,000
Operating income	$330,000	$640,000	$970,000
Interest expense	-$145,000	-$47,737	-$192,737
Pretax income	$185,000	$592,263	$777,263
Income tax 20%	-$37,000	-$118,453	-$155,453
After-tax income/loss	**$148,000**	**$473,810**	**$621,810**

Analysis. The subsidiary is now expecting sufficient profits to pay the dividend to the parent company.

Lesson Learned: We do not need to find the money in the budget. We need to get approval to get the money from the bank.

How to Build the Details of a Budget

The process for preparing a budget varies from organization to organization. Each company has its own guidelines, budget forms, and policies. Whatever the structure, the only way to learn how to budget is to prepare a budget. A new budget manager tackles the guidelines, figures out the forms, and develops a budget that seems reasonable and workable.

Although the forms are different, the process is usually the same. It follows the steps of producing goods or services, marketing and supporting them, then distributing the products or delivering the services. Typical elements are:

- *Organization and staffing.* This covers the people who will make, market, and deliver the product or service.
- *The product or service.* What does it cost? What will be the selling price? What will be the level of activity? What will it cost to deliver the units produced or the services promised? These and similar questions are asked in the budgeting process.
- *Organization and staffing.* This covers the people who will make, sell, and deliver the product or service.
- *Operating expenses.* It takes money to run a business and carry on day-to-day activities. Everything from copy machines to telephones must be budgeted for.
- *Marketing costs.* The firm must plan to cover the marketing and promotional support expenses for the product or service.
- *Miscellaneous costs.* Any other expenses that will be incurred should be estimated and budgeted for. An example is fringe benefits that must be paid in addition to salaries.

Budgets are usually built upward from units as an accumulation of likely revenues and expenses needed to achieve them. The following analysis demonstrates this process.

The Situation. Two partners plan to buy medical equipment in Germany and sell it in the United States. One of the partners has many years of experience selling medical devices to hospitals and skilled nursing facilities. The partners forecast the following:

	Quarter 1	Quarter 2	Quarter 3	Quarter 4
Units likely to be sold	300	400	500	200
Average price per unit	$14,000	$14,000	$14,000	$14,000
Collections on sales		$4,200,000	$5,600,000	$7,000,000

The other partner will manage the purchase and distribution of the equipment. After negotiations with the German supplier and a freight forwarder, the following costs are estimated:

	Quarter 1	Quarter 2	Quarter 3	Quarter 4
Cost to purchase one unit	$7,700	$7,700	$7,700	$7,700
Ocean transport for one unit	$1,680	$1,680	$1,680	$1,680

The People Who Handle the Product. The company will set up a warehouse in Baltimore, Maryland. The warehouse will receive shipments by ocean and store the equipment until it is purchased. Then the units will be shipped. Six full-time and part-time workers will be employed at the following costs:

	Quarter 1	Quarter 2	Quarter 3	Quarter 4
Warehouse manager	$13,750	$13,750	$13,750	$13,750
Assistant manager	9,500	9,500	9,500	9,500
Stock person	7,750	7,750	7,750	7,750
Truck driver	3,000	3,000	3,000	3,000
Inventory control person	1,500	1,500	1,500	1,500
Accounting assistant	1,200	1,200	1,200	1,200

Operating Budget. Operating expenses for the business have been estimated based on prior experience of the partners as follows.

	Quarter 1	Quarter 2	Quarter 3	Quarter 4
Warehouse costs	$2,100	$2,100	$2,100	$2,100
Delivery costs	825	743	668	668
Lease of warehouse equipment	600	600	600	600
General repairs	1,350	1,350	1,215	1,094
Purchased services	600	600	600	600
Professional services	375	338	304	304
Postage	225	225	203	182
Data processing costs	825	825	825	825
Lease of the warehouse	3,600	3,600	3,600	3,600
Replacement of equipment	450	405	365	365
Miscellaneous	900	900	810	729

Selling Costs. It will cost money to pay the two individuals who will make calls on hospitals and other medical facilities. The marketing expenses are estimated as follows:

	Quarter 1	Quarter 2	Quarter 3	Quarter 4
Marketing manager	$11,250	$11,250	$11,250	$11,250
Assistant marketing manager	8,750	8,750	8,750	8,750
Sales support	29,750	25,500	21,250	8,500

In addition, the company will pay commissions and bonuses as a percentage of revenues as follows:

	Quarter 1	Quarter 2	Quarter 3	Quarter 4
Percent commission	3.0%	3.0%	3.0%	3.0%

The company knows that it has to support the selling effort with advertising and sales promotion expenses.

	Quarter 1	Quarter 2	Quarter 3	Quarter 4
Travel to conferences	$6,300	$5,400	$4,500	$1,800
Brochures and promotional materials	2,800	2,400	2,000	800

Miscellaneous Expenses. The partners will pay retirement and health benefits to their employees. Under the tax code and insurance regulations, the fringe benefits are estimated as a percentage of base salaries.

	Quarter 1	Quarter 2	Quarter 3	Quarter 4
Percentage of fringe benefits	25%	25%	22%	20%

Brief Format. The company has prepared a rough budget based on the assumptions just given.

Unit sales	1,400
Average price per unit	$14,000
Revenues	$19,600,000
Units purchased	1,400
Cost per unit	$7,700
Ocean transport per unit	$1,680
Cost of goods purchased	$13,132,000
Operating personnel	$146,800
Fringe benefits 25%	36,700
Other warehouse operating expenses	93,800
Administrative expenses	$277,300
Sales personnel	$80,000
Fringe benefits 25%	20,000
Commissions and bonuses 3%	588,000

Advertising and promotion	26,000
Selling expenses	$714,000
First-year profit	**$5,476,700**

The partners also prepared a more detailed budget.

Revenues Budget.

	Quarter 1	Quarter 2	Quarter 3	Quarter 4
New England:				
Units likely to be sold	30	40	50	20
Average price per unit	$14,500	$14,500	$13,500	$13,500
New York:				
Units likely to be sold	75	100	125	50
Average price per unit	$16,000	$16,000	$16,000	$16,000
Mid-Atlantic:				
Units likely to be sold	60	80	100	40
Average price per unit	$15,500	$15,500	$15,000	$14,500
Ohio-Pennsylvania:				
Units likely to be sold	45	60	75	30
Average price per unit	$14,000	$14,000	$13,500	$13,500
South:				
Units likely to be sold	90	120	150	60
Average price per unit	$12,500	$12,500	$12,000	$12,000
Total units	**300**	**400**	**500**	**200**
Average price per unit	$14,400	$14,400	$13,975	$13,875
Revenues	**$4,320,000**	**$5,760,000**	**$6,987,500**	**$2,775,000**

Purchases Budget.

	Quarter 1	Quarter 2	Quarter 3	Quarter 4
Total units	300	400	500	200
Cost to purchase one unit	$7,700	$7,700	$7,700	$7,700
Ocean transport for one unit	$1,680	$1,680	$1,680	$1,680
Cost of goods sold	**$2,814,000**	**$3,752,000**	**$4,690,000**	**$1,876,000**

Personnel Costs.

	Quarter 1	Quarter 2	Quarter 3	Quarter 4
Warehouse manager	$13,750	$13,750	$13,750	$13,750
Assistant manager	9,500	9,500	9,500	9,500
Stock person	7,750	7,750	7,750	7,750

	Quarter 1	Quarter 2	Quarter 3	Quarter 4
Truck driver	3,000	3,000	3,000	3,000
Inventory control person	1,500	1,500	1,500	1,500
Accounting assistant	1,200	1,200	1,200	1,200
Marketing manager	11,250	11,250	11,250	11,250
Assistant marketing manager	8,750	8,750	8,750	8,750
Salary totals	$56,700	$56,700	$56,700	$56,700
Percent fringe benefits	25.0%	25.0%	25.0%	25.0%
Salary plus fringes	**$70,875**	**$70,875**	**$70,875**	**$70,875**

Operating Expenses.

	Quarter 1	Quarter 2	Quarter 3	Quarter 4
Warehouse costs	$2,100	$2,100	$2,100	$2,100
Delivery costs	825	743	668	668
Lease of warehouse equipment	600	600	600	600
General repairs	1,350	1,350	1,215	1,094
Purchased services	600	600	600	600
Professional services	375	338	304	304
Postage	225	225	203	182
Data processing costs	825	825	825	825
Lease of the warehouse	3,600	3,600	3,600	3,600
Replacement of equipment	450	405	365	365
Miscellaneous	900	900	810	729
Operating expenses	**$11,850**	**$11,685**	**$11,289**	**$11,066**

Sales Support Costs.

	Quarter 1	Quarter 2	Quarter 3	Quarter 4
Sales support	$29,750	$25,500	$21,250	$8,500
Travel to conferences	6,300	5,400	4,500	1,800
Brochures and promotional materials	2,800	2,400	2,000	800
Sales support expenses	**$38,850**	**$33,300**	**$27,750**	**$11,100**

Budget Summary.

	Quarter 1	Quarter 2	Quarter 3	Quarter 4	Total
Revenues	$4,320,000	$5,760,000	$6,987,500	$2,775,000	$19,842,500
Cost of goods sold	-2,814,000	-3,752,000	-4,690,000	-1,876,000	-$13,132,000
Salary plus fringes	-70,875	-70,875	-70,875	-70,875	-$283,500
Operating expenses	-11,850	-11,685	-11,289	-11,066	-$45,890

	Quarter 1	Quarter 2	Quarter 3	Quarter 4	Total
Sales support	-38,850	-33,300	-27,750	-11,100	-111,000
Commissions					-595,275
Profit	$1,384,425	$1,892,140	$2,187,586	$805,959	$5,674,835

Comparison of Two Budgets.

	Brief Budget	Detailed Budget
Revenues	$19,600,000	$19,842,500
Cost of goods sold	-13,132,000	-13,132,000
Salary plus fringes		-283,500
Operating expenses	-277,300	-45,890
Commissions		-595,275*
Sales support	-714,000	-111,000
Profit	$5,476,700	$5,674,835

*In the detailed format, Commissions are in the $714,000 Sales Support calculation.

Analysis. Do we see any problems with the budget?

Yes. The cash collections lag the revenues. Thus the budget manager needs to have a plan to pay for expenses before the revenues are collected.

	Quarter 1	Quarter 2	Quarter 3	Quarter 4
Collections	$0	$4,200,000	$5,600,000	$7,000,000
Cost of goods sold	-2,814,000	-3,752,000	-4,690,000	-1,876,000
Salary plus fringes	-70,875	-70,875	-70,875	-70,875
Operating expenses	-11,850	-11,685	-11,289	-11,066
Sales support	-38,850	-33,300	-27,750	-11,100
Gap	-$2,935,575	$332,140	$800,086	$5,030,959

Lesson learned: The budget manager needs to have a plan to pay for expenses before the revenues are collected.

Part 3 | Analyzing Operating Risks

Financial risk managers know that firms do not declare bankruptcy because they fail to make accounting profits. The name of the game is liquidity. Do not run out of cash. The term *burn rate* refers to the negative cash flow when a company starts operations with shareholder capital and maybe also debt financing. It is a measure of how much time can pass before the firm must either generate a positive cash flow, raise additional funds, or cease operations. It is an appropriate term, as it is painful to "burn." It highlights the role of cash.

Having pointed out the importance of cash, we immediately emphasize that profits pave the road to liquidity. If a firm is not profitable, sooner or later it will not be liquid. Thus, the tools for measuring financial risk involve a mixture of measures of the firm's ability to pursue profits while maintaining liquidity. In this part we cover three topics:

- *Profit planning.* First, a firm pursues a breakeven point where it erases the burn rate and starts to generate profits, which should be accompanied by positive cash flows. As it grows, so do its profits and cash flow. The concept of marginal analysis helps the risk manager understand the dimensions of risk.
- *Leverage.* This term refers generally to increasing the impact of one action by taking another action. In financial management, leverage is the use of debt to enhance profits and cash flow. Stated in financial risk terms, it is the use of credit to allow a firm to speculate that it can earn more that its costs to finance its assets. This is a big deal in managing liquidity and profitability risk.
- *Financial analysis.* With the profit planning and leverage concepts as a foundation, how do we quickly assess financial risk in terms of liquidity and profitability?

The answer is ratio analysis. Ratios give symptoms of problems and success. Thousands of them exist. We need to select the ratios that help us see emerging risks and positive trends.

At the conclusion of these three chapters, the reader should have a grasp of new tools for understanding how to use the balance sheet and income statement to measure liquidity and profitability.

Chapter
5

Profit Planning

PLANNING

A major role of the financial manager is setting corporate goals and the policies to achieve them. The major departments, including marketing, production, personnel, and finance, participate in the activity of determining the firm's direction and courses of action. This involves the management of resources and decision making, both in the near and in the long term.

Planning is the specific process of setting goals and developing ways to reach them. Stated another way, planning represents the firm's efforts to predict events and be prepared to deal with them. In many firms, the task of planning is coordinated by a department of one or more persons designated as the corporate planning department, the long-range planning department, or the budgeting department. Whatever the title, these individuals are responsible for receiving inputs from sales, production, finance, and other operating areas of the company. By coordinating the planning process, management ensures that the different departments are working toward the same goals and taking actions that are consistent with the overall objectives of the firm.

In this chapter, we will examine the basic principles of profit planning. We will look at breakeven analysis and profit-volume analysis, two tools for managing assets in the near term. We will also cover marginal analysis as a technique for forecasting operating results with the aid of the income statement. We will conclude with a method for estimating the value of the firm's common stock, using the technique of future earnings per share. All of these techniques are designed to assist the firm in managing its assets over the next accounting period, normally a single year.

Planning Process

As a general rule, the firm's formal planning process involves the efforts of many operating and financial managers. Once plans are agreed upon by the operating units, they are usually presented to the management committee or chief operating officer of the firm. At this level, they are challenged and either approved with possible modifications or returned to the operating units for further analysis. The final plans, whether short or long term, become the blueprint for the firm's operations.

Planning basically involves two major areas for analysis:

• *External factors.* The starting point in the planning process is the environment in which the firm operates. The planner evaluates the outlook for the economy as a whole. Will the firm be operating during a period of economic growth and expansion, or will the next one to three years be a period of recession and stagnation? As part of the total environment, the firm considers the expected level of activity in its industry and possible changes in the market for its products. Is the industry anticipating growth or decline? Does the firm have a stable market for its products? Is the firm's competition gaining or losing strength? Thus, the analysis of external factors considers both the overall economy and the individual industry as a framework for the next operating periods.

• *Internal factors.* Some factors are internal in the sense that they are under the control of the firm. For example, such items as cash levels, inventories, and the nature of the fixed assets are operating elements that can be varied by the firm. This is not true for the external factors, such as a national recession or an industry decline.

Controllable Internal Factors

The most developed portion of the firm's short- and long-term plans deals with internal factors and stresses:

• *Market demand for the firm's product line or services.* The firm can decide, after a careful evaluation of the external factors, what mix of products or services it will offer in the marketplace. If the firm produces its existing product line, what sales are likely? If it changes or modifies its products, will sales increase or decrease? These kinds of questions are analyzed in this part of the plan.

• *Future costs.* A firm may have a number of opportunities to reduce the costs of its products in future periods. The purchase of new and more modern equipment may increase fixed costs while reducing variable costs. Should the equipment be purchased? Better scheduling or planning may help minimize production or administrative expenses. High-cost areas in the firm may be examined to see how economies could be achieved.

• *Sources of funds.* As the firm plans expenditures, it analyzes the funds available to finance its activities. If sufficient funds are not predicted, steps are taken to locate the money needed at reasonable costs.

These factors are internal only in the sense that the firm has the ability to influence them to a greater or lesser degree. The firm cannot have very much impact on the overall level of economic activity for the entire nation, but it can affect the demand for its product by more aggressive advertising or changes in product pricing or design. It cannot control inflation, but it can take actions to reduce its costs. It cannot make money available in the economy, but it can find institutions and individuals who will make funds available to meet its needs.

Benefits of Planning

As a result of the planning process, the firm realizes a number of benefits:

- *Anticipation of problems and opportunities.* Planning involves people at different levels in the organization and forces them to think ahead. This encourages managers at varying levels to anticipate possible problems and to attempt to identify potential opportunities.
- *Coordination of actions.* Because they are involved in planning discussions with others in management positions, managers begin to coordinate courses of action. Frequently, early coordination facilitates the achievement of company goals by increasing communication and reducing potential conflicts. The very process of setting goals and subgoals gives the different operating areas a common focus and encourages everyone to pursue compatible courses of action.
- *Assistance in control.* Plans may be used as tools to help managers control their areas of operation. A detailed plan gives departments and divisions specific goals to pursue and means to achieve these goals. As the firm conducts its operations, managers can watch for variations from the plan that indicate a need for tighter supervision and control.
- *Standards of performance.* A comparison of the plan with actual performance during the planning period can be used to provide a standard of achievement. Did the company reach the goals outlined in the plan? If not, why not? Did certain areas perform exceptionally well? Answers to such questions help the firm evaluate its own performance during a recent operating period.

BREAKEVEN ANALYSIS

A fundamental profit-planning tool involves the determination of the likely profits at different levels of production. To develop the necessary calculations, the financial manager builds on the basic tool of breakeven analysis and expands it through profit-volume analysis.

Marginal Contribution

Breakeven formulas recognize the fundamental relationship between sales and profits. The key concept is *marginal contribution*, defined as the excess of sales over variable costs. Stated differently, it is the direct profit from operations. This excess may be used to cover fixed costs that are not related to the volume of sales or operations. It is also available to cover any financing charges, such as interest on a mortgage, to pay federal income taxes, and to provide a profit to shareholders.

Breakeven Point

The *breakeven point* is the level of operations at which a firm neither makes a profit nor loses money. At this level, the firm operates at a zero profit level and therefore is able to cover its operating costs from the profits of the business. Breakeven analysis makes use of fixed costs, variable costs, and revenues and may be expressed graphically or mathematically.

Graphic Approach to Breakeven Analysis

The graphic approach to breakeven analysis plots dollars on the vertical axis and units on the horizontal axis, as shown in Figure 5-1. The costs that are included in the analysis are:

- *Fixed costs.* These remain the same at all levels of production. An example would be the rent paid on a building. Graphically, the fixed costs are a horizontal line.
- *Variable costs.* These change directly with the number of units produced. At zero units of production, the firm incurs no variable costs. As production rises, the variable costs rise proportionately. Two aspects of variable costs are important and should be noted:
  - *Variable costs plotted as total costs.* If the variable costs are plotted from the zero point on the graph, the line reflects only the variable costs of production. It is more common, however, to plot them from the left-hand side of the fixed costs line. When this is done, the line represents total operating costs.
  - *Variable costs plotted as constant costs.* It is traditional to plot unit variable costs using a straight line. This implies that unit variable costs are constant costs; that is, they are the same at all levels of production. If the first unit costs $3, the second also costs $3, and so on until the last.

Revenues, or sales, are needed to complete the picture of the breakeven analysis. The total revenues are plotted diagonally, beginning at zero dollars, and the slope of the line rises more quickly than that of the total costs line. This is true because the firm

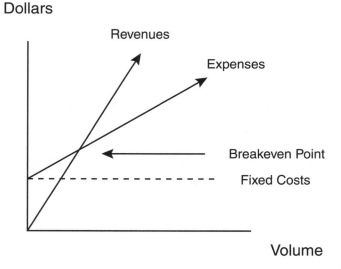

Figure 5-1. Breakeven Analysis.

(we hope!) will receive more revenues per unit of production than the variable cost of producing each unit.

This completes the profit picture for the firm. The breakeven point occurs at the crossing of the revenues and total costs lines. Above this production level, the firm will be profitable. Below it, the firm will incur a loss. Note that the profits are measured in the triangle above the breakeven point and losses in that below the breakeven point, in each case in the area defined by the revenues and total costs lines.

Nonlinear Breakeven Analysis

Even as we plot revenues and variable costs as a straight line, we recognize that the two lines curve with changes in production levels. At a low volume of production, revenues rise quickly and expenses are largely fixed. At another point, the firm has to lower its prices to achieve more sales, and revenues grow more slowly. At some point, expenses rise rapidly as the firm reaches its capacity to produce goods or services.

Although nonlinear analysis is theoretically superior, linear analysis is more commonly used in industrial settings. This is appropriate in most cases, since firms are usually dealing with decisions that involve relatively constant unit variable costs. In these situations, the firm is planning for operations only in the range in which production is efficient, that is, in a range where setup costs are overcome, but below levels where bottlenecks occur. Since production in this efficient range involves fairly constant costs, the calculations are quite accurate, and realistic decisions are reached.

Figure 5-2 illustrates nonlinear breakeven relationships. Note that there are two breakeven points, and a point can be seen for the maximum profit from operations. This differs from linear breakeven analysis, where a single breakeven point can be located and profits grow indefinitely once the breakeven point is reached. With nonlinear breakeven analysis, the firm strives for an optimum output in a range of efficient production.

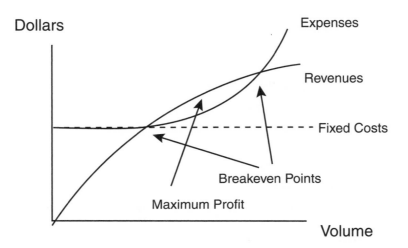

Figure 5-2. Nonlinear Breakeven Relationships.

Mathematical Approach to Linear Breakeven Analysis

Within a forecasted range of production and sales, a firm can treat the breakeven calculation as a linear relationship. Within this range, the breakeven point may be calculated by the formula:

$ Sales = Fixed Cost/Marginal Contribution %

where $ Sales = dollar sales volume at the breakeven point

Marginal Contribution % = marginal contribution as a percentage of the selling price

We have already seen marginal contribution as revenues minus variable costs. When expressed as a percent, the formula is (Selling Price – Variable Costs)/Selling Price, where all numbers occur on the basis of a single unit. Figure 5-3 shows a breakeven calculation using marginal contribution.

> *Example.* A restaurant chain is considering a 24-hour operation for some of its outlets. With the following data, what is the breakeven point for adding the overnight schedule?

Data

Average charge to customers	$25.00
Average cost of food served	$8.00
Fixed costs for the operation	$750,000

Answer

Selling price minus variable costs	$17.00
Divided by average charge	$25.00
Equals marginal contribution [(SP - VC)/SP]	68.0%
Divided by fixed costs	$750,000
Equals breakeven in dollars	**$1,102,941**

Figure 5-3. Calculation of Breakeven Point.

PROFIT-VOLUME ANALYSIS

A modification of the breakeven formula results in a tool that relates profits to sales at different operating levels. By writing the breakeven formulas so that fixed costs are replaced by both fixed costs and profits, the manager can solve for the sales volume needed to produce a desired profit level. The general form of the formula is:

$ Sales = (Fixed Cost + Profit)/Marginal Contribution %

where $ Sales equals the dollars of sales needed to achieve a desired profit

Calculating Maximum Fixed Costs

The profit-volume formulas may be applied to different measures of profit. One example is shown in Figure 5-4, where the technique is used to calculate the maximum

Example. A chain of auto repair shops is considering adding a new line of business to customize automobiles for customers. Given the following data, what is the maximum fixed costs that will allow the business to break even at the likely number of customers per year?

Data

Likely customers per year	35,000
Average fee charged for service	$120
Fee paid to specialist who does the work	$75

Answer

Annual customers	35,000
Times single fee	$120
Equals revenues	$4,200,000
Minus variable costs	-$2,625,000
Equals maximum fixed costs at breakeven	**$1,575,000**

Figure 5-4. Calculating Maximum Fixed Costs.

fixed costs that a firm can cover when it has a forecasted level of sales and a likely selling price.

Calculating Volume of Sales to Reach Target Profit

Figure 5-5 shows another example of profit-volume analysis. Here the firm is calculating the volume of business needed to achieve a target operating income when it is considering the purchase of equipment.

MARGINAL ANALYSIS

We have already been introduced to marginal analysis, which was defined as breaking down an income statement into fixed and variable costs. The formulas for profit-volume analysis use the concept of marginal analysis because they define costs and profits using fixed and variable costs. In this section, we will work directly with the income statement to show how marginal analysis helps the manager forecast the effect of differing selling prices, costs, and sales levels on the firm's net income.

Marginal Analysis to Compare Profit Decisions

The technique of marginal analysis can be applied to different scenarios, which are then compared to see which ones create the most profit. Figure 5-6 shows an example of an electronic testing facility that is expanding its operations. It has a choice of two locations to set up an additional operation. The locations are quite different in terms of demographics and population. Figure 5-6 shows the data on each location and the higher profit from location 2. The answer is calculated using marginal analysis.

Example. A physicians' internal medicine practice is considering the purchase of expensive MRI equipment. With data as follows, how many scans must be made each year to provide the target operating income?

Data

Fixed costs of MRI scanner	$175,000
Average fee for single scan	$600
Variable radiologist cost	$125
Other variable costs	$25
Target operating income	$250,000

Answer

Fee minus variable costs	$450
Divided by fee	$600
Equals marginal contribution	75.0%
Divided into fixed costs plus profit	$425,000
Equals dollars in revenues needed	$566,667
Divided by fee	$600
Equals individual scans needed	**944**

Figure 5-5. Units Needed to Achieve Target Profit.

Data

	Location 1	Location 2
Likely fee for service	$325	$525
Variable cost of service	$120	$140
Likely number of tests	600	400
Fixed costs	$20,000	$35,000

Answer

Revenues	$195,000	$210,000
Variable costs	-72,000	-56,000
Fixed costs	-20,000	-35,000
Operating income	$103,000	$119,000
Which is higher?	**Location 2**	

Figure 5-6. Comparing Profit Alternatives.

Trading Off Variable and Fixed Costs

Marginal analysis can also help firms make decisions on upgrading technology. Figure 5-7 shows data for an insurance carrier that operates a claims processing unit for other insurance companies. It is considering automation that would lower the variable costs of processing claims while raising fixed costs. Which strategy provides the largest earnings before interest and taxes? The question is answered using marginal analysis.

FUTURE EARNINGS PER SHARE

In profit planning, it is important that the firm consider the effect of different courses of action on the value of the stock. If the firm takes actions that cause a decline in the market price of the common stock, management may be criticized by angry shareholders. A valuable tool for analyzing the future market price of the stock is the calculation of future earnings per share.

Why Future Earnings per Share Are Critical

In profit planning, two measures of corporate profits are especially important:

- *Return on investment (ROI).* This is an operating indicator of profits and a key measure of the success of the firm's management. If this ratio is high, the firm is generating sufficient sales on its asset base and is making sufficient profit margins on its sales. The use of ROI allows a financial manager to make comparisons of the operating profits of different firms or of the same firm in different time periods.
- *Earnings per share (EPS).* This is a market indicator of profits and the most important profit measure for stockholders and other individuals outside the firm. If the earnings continue to increase on a per-share basis, the firm is judged to be increasingly

Data

	Strategy 1	Strategy 2
Fee received for outsider claim	$135	$135
Variable cost to process claim	$65	$85
Fixed costs	$600,000	$300,000
Annual claims volume	30,000	30,000

Answer

Revenues	$4,050,000	$4,050,000
Variable costs	-1,950,000	-2,550,000
Fixed costs	-600,000	-300,000
Total costs	-2,550,000	-2,850,000
EBIT	$1,500,000	$1,200,000
Which is higher?	**Strategy 1**	

Figure 5-7. Analyzing Variable and Fixed Costs.

successful. On the other hand, a drop in earnings per share is viewed as a symptom of problems.

Given the important role of earnings per share in the eyes of shareholders and the investing public, the firm must be particularly conscious of actions that will affect the reported earnings. For this reason, profit planning focuses on how different alternatives will affect the future earnings per share reported by the firm.

Comparing Future Events at the Margin

The technique of forecasting future earnings per share measures the effect of each decision at the margin. That is, the technique recognizes that the firm will have some future earnings per share without any decisions being required. When the firm considers new investments, the revenues and expenses associated with the investments will change the projected earnings. To determine the effect of each project, the firm does the following:

- *Forecasts EPS without a new project.* The analyst estimates the sales and expenses for the next period without a new investment.
- *Forecasts the proposal's effect on EPS.* The analyst forecasts EPS on a combined basis. If the EPS is higher with the proposal than without it, the analyst knows that the proposal helps increase EPS. If the EPS is lower with the proposal, the analyst knows that the proposal weakens future profitability.

Comparing future events at the margin means that each proposed investment is evaluated separately to see how it will affect the firm's sales and profits. If, for example, two projects were combined, the undesirable effects of one project might be obscured by the desirable effects of the other. This is avoided by individually combining each new proposal with the existing operations.

Normal Price-Earnings Multiple

A *price-earnings ratio* (P/E) is calculated by:

Market Price/EPS

If a firm's stock has a market price of $90 and earnings per share of $6, the price-earnings multiple is 15, or 15:1 (90/6).

A *normal price-earnings multiple* is the ratio that is expected when a firm is realizing a satisfactory return on its capital, and the stock market is not disturbed by unusual psychological or economic factors. It may be determined by analyzing historical data, similar firms, and industry norms, or by common sense.

If, for example, a firm's stock sells at a 12 multiple this year, we may expect it to continue to sell at this multiple. If the firm maintains this norm and its EPS rises from $2 to $3, the market price of the stock may rise from $24 to $36. To analyze likely future market prices, we forecast future earnings per share and multiply EPS by the normal P/E.

Question. A firm is considering accepting Project A. Without the project, its EPS next year will be $2.15. With the project, EPS will be $2.35. Its normal P/E is 10. What will be its market value next year with and without the project?

Answer.

$23.50 with the project ($2.35 × 10)

$21.50 without the project ($2.15 × 10)

Forecasting Future Earnings per Share

A company forecasts $5.5 million in operating income next year. It has $10 million in debt at a cost of 9.5 percent. It has 200,000 shares of common stock outstanding. The company is evaluating a new project that will create an operating income of $1.1 million. The project will cost $5 million, which can be financed with debt at 11 percent or common stock sold to net $100 a share. The firm's effective tax rate will be 20 percent. The normal price-earnings multiple for this firm is 7. If it finances the project with debt, the normal P/E will drop to 6. If it finances the project with common stock, the normal P/E will rise to 8. What are the future earnings per share with and without the project?

Figure 5-8 shows the calculation of future earnings per share and future market price. The key elements of the example are:

- *Future EPS without project.* The middle column shows the income statement without the project. The firm forecasts next year's income, earnings per share, and market price at an assumed normal price-earnings ratio.
- *Project with debt financing.* A new project costing $5 million can be financed with debt at 11 percent. The net income is shown in the first column.
- *Project with stock financing.* The project can also be financed by selling common stock at a net selling price of $100 per share. This means that 50,000 new shares would have to be issued.
- *Combined with debt financing.* The future earnings per share with the project financed by debt are shown in the fourth column. Because of the debt, added risk confronts shareholders. Thus, the normal price-earnings ratio has dropped.
- *Combined with stock financing.* The final column shows the future earnings per share with stock financing for the project. The normal price-earnings multiple rises to reflect the lower risk from additional equity financing.

Other Factors Related to Future EPS

It should be noted that a company does not make its decision solely on the basis of the future EPS. Other factors also affect the future market price, including:

- *Risk from high levels of debt.* Borrowing is less costly because it avoids the dilution of earnings associated with stock financing. But debt involves more risk than equity financing. If interest payments are not made, the firm may face unpleasant consequences, including bankruptcy. This danger is increased if the firm incurs variable-rate debt in a period of low interest rates and then must pay more interest when rates rise. The market value of the stock will drop if the firm makes excessive use of borrowed funds and incurs a high level of risk as a result.

	Forecast for Next Year				
	Project with Debt	Project with Stock	Without Project	Combined	
				with Debt	with Stock
Original debt			$10,000		
Original interest rate			9.5%		
Original interest			$950		
New debt	$5,000				
New interest rate	11.0%				
New annual interest	$550				
Project cost		$5,000			
Net price		$100			
Shares Needed		50			
Operating Income	$1,100	$1,100	$5,500	$6,600	$6,600
Interest	-550	0	-950	-1,500	-950
Earnings before taxes	$550	$1,100	$4,550	$5,100	$5,650
Taxes 20%	-110	-220	-910	-1,020	-1,130
Net income	$440	$880	$3,640	$4,080	$4,520
Shares	0	50	200	200	250
Earnings per share			$18.20	$20.40	$18.08
Times likely P/E			7	6	8
Future market price			$127.40	$122.40	$144.64

Figure 5-8. Solved Future EPS Example.

- *Growth.* The future EPS technique makes a projection only one year into the future. Long-term growth will be a different factor from next year's earnings, and the expected growth characteristics of a proposal as well as the likely short-term profits will affect the firm's future market value.
- *Difficulties in implementing proposals.* In some cases, a firm will not want to accept a profitable project that may cause complications for its other operations. The proposal may be highly complex and may require extensive time from key operating personnel, time that will have to be taken from other areas. The project may cause the firm to receive adverse publicity or to experience other difficulties that make it undesirable. These difficulties can affect the market price of the firm's stock and will influence the firm's acceptance of a project.
- *Risk from uncertain ventures or unstable returns.* Any proposal contains the risk that the firm will be unable to achieve the projected returns. This risk may arise from changes in the general level of economic activity, the entry of strong competitors into a firm's primary market, or other factors. The degree of business risk and the expected stability of returns are factors that affect the decision to accept or reject a proposal.

CONCLUSION

The techniques of profit planning offer tools that can quickly allow financial risk managers to test the sensitivities of assumptions, estimates, and forecasts. They help managers see the risks when pursuing the breakeven point for new operations and can also allow various scenarios to be examined for their effect on profits.

CHAPTER 5 APPENDIXES

How to Assess Basic Profit Planning Risks

Calculating the Breakeven Point. A firm has the following data. What is the breakeven point?

Data

Forecasted sales	35,000
Selling price per unit	$4.00
Variable costs per unit	$2.50

Answer

Marginal contribution percent	37.5%
Divided into fixed costs	$2,250
Equals breakeven, dollars	$6,000

Breakeven at Projected Sales Level. How much fixed costs can the following firm have and break even at its projected unit sales?

Data

Projected unit sales	35,000
Selling price	$6.00
Variable costs	$125,000

Answer

Projected unit sales	35,000
Times price	$6.00
Equals dollar sales	$210,000
Minus variable costs	$125,000
Equals fixed costs at breakeven	$85,000

Projecting Sales Needed for Target Operating Income. A firm has the following data. What is the dollar amount of sales needed to achieve the target operating income?

Data

Target operating income	$14,000
Fixed costs	$5,500
Selling price	$30
Variable costs	$20

Answer

Total to be covered	$19,500
Marginal contribution, percent	33.3%
Dollar sales needed	$58,500

Target Earnings Before Taxes. A firm has the following data. What is the dollar sales needed to achieve the target earnings before taxes?

Data

Selling price	$8.00
Variable costs	$3.00
Debt	$200,000
Interest rate	12%
Fixed costs	$75,000
Target pretax income	$150,000

Answer

Fixed costs	$75,000
Interest	$24,000
Target pretax income	$150,000
Total to be covered	$249,000
Divided by marginal contribution %	62.5%
Equals sales needed	$398,400

Forecasting Maximum Debt. At the forecasted sales number, how much more debt could be financed before the firm reached zero earnings before taxes?

Data

Forecasted sales in units	6,000
Selling price per unit	$10
Variable cost per unit	$6
Fixed costs	$20,000
Debt	$12,000
Interest rate	9%
Interest rate for additional debt	10%

Answer

Revenues	$60,000
Variable costs	$36,000
Fixed costs	$20,000
Operating income	$4,000
Interest	$1,080
Earnings before taxes	$2,920
Divided by interest rate	10%
Additional debt that can be financed	$29,200

Choosing a Selling Price. A firm forecasts sales at two different selling prices. Given the following data, which selling price yields the highest forecasted earnings before taxes?

Data

	Price 1	Price 2
Selling price per unit	$12	$15
Variable cost per unit	$7	$7
Units that can be sold at price	600	400
Fixed costs	$1,000	$1,000
Interest	$200	$200

Answer

Revenues	$7,200	$6,000
Variable costs	$4,200	$2,800
Fixed costs	$1,000	$1,000
Interest	$200	$200
Earnings before taxes	$1,800	$2,000
Which is higher?	**Price 2**	

Choosing a Mix of Variable and Fixed Costs. A firm is considering automation that would affect variable costs and fixed costs. The data follow. Which strategy provides the larger earnings before taxes?

Data

	Strategy 1	Strategy 2
Selling price per unit	$15	$15
Variable cost per unit	$5	$7
Units that can be sold	1,400	1,400
Fixed costs	$2,000	$1,500
Interest	$200	$200

Answer

Revenues	$21,000	$21,000
Variable costs	$7,000	$9,800
Fixed costs	$2,000	$1,500
Interest	$200	$200
Earnings before taxes	$11,800	$9,500
Which is higher?	**Strategy 1**	

Forecasting the Future Market Price of Stock. A firm has the following data, including current EPS, a forecasted rise in EPS, and a normal P/E multiple. What are the expected current and future market prices?

Data

	Current	**Future**
Earnings per share	$4.00	
Forecasted rise in EPS	15%	
Normal P/E multiple	8.00	8.00

Answer

Future EPS		$4.60
Normal P/E multiple	8.00	8.00
Market price	$32.00	$36.80

How to Set the Selling Price for a Product or Service

Situation. One company would manufacture a product. A second company would distribute it. The two companies have estimated the following:

First-year sales, units	20,000
Average final selling price per unit	$200

The estimated expenses for each partner in the venture will be:

Cost per Unit for	**Manufacturer**	**Distributor**
Production	$10	
Packaging	$2	
Distribution		$8
Marketing		$45
Postsale servicing	$15	

The Issue. What should be the intermediate price that the distributor pays to the manufacturer?

The Financial Impacts of Different Prices.

	Manufacturer	Distributor	Totals
Units sold			20,000
Price per unit			$200
Revenues			$4,000,000
Production costs	$200,000		
Packaging costs	$40,000		
Distribution costs		$160,000	
Marketing costs		$900,000	
Postsale service costs	$300,000		
Total costs	$540,000	$1,060,000	$1,600,000
Profit			$2,400,000

Each Party's Profits at Four Possible Prices to Distributor.

	$80	$100	$120	$140
Manufacturer				
Revenues	$1,600,000	$2,000,000	$2,400,000	$2,800,000
Variable expenses	-540,000	-540,000	-540,000	-540,000
Profit	$1,060,000	$1,460,000	$1,860,000	$2,260,000
Distributor				
Revenues	$4,000,000	$4,000,000	$4,000,000	$4,000,000
Cost of product	-1,600,000	-2,000,000	-2,400,000	-2,800,000
Variable Expenses	-1,060,000	-1,060,000	-1,060,000	-1,060,000
Profit	$1,340,000	$940,000	$540,000	$140,000

Which Price Should Be Set? There is no single correct answer. The price should make sense for both parties. It appears that a number in the $80 to $100 price range gives both parties a reasonable profit.

How to Evaluate the Profits from Channels of Distribution

A company can manufacture dolls in Mexico and ship them to a warehouse in Massachusetts. Variable costs would be:

Average cost per doll	$12.00
Packing the doll for shipment	$0.25
Truck transport	$0.75

At the warehouse, inventory costs would be:

Processing into warehouse	$0.40
Physical storage and safeguarding	$1.20
Processing out of warehouse	$0.40

The company can distribute through either a specialty store or a direct mail channel. The sales, pricing, and unit expenses would be:

	Specialty Channel	Direct Mail
Annual unit sales	140,000	90,000
Selling price per unit	$30.00	$50.00
Average discount	($3.00)	($5.00)
Unit shipping costs from warehouse	$1.30	$5.00
Customer servicing costs per unit	$1.25	$3.00
Insurance per unit	$2.00	$2.00

Advertising and promotion annual fixed costs would be:

	Specialty Channel	Direct Mail
Graphics design	$15,000	$60,000
Printing	20,000	300,000
Distribution of materials	25,000	100,000

First-Year Budget for Each Channel.

		Specialty Channel	Direct Mail
Average selling price		$30.00	$50.00
Average discount		($3.00)	($5.00)
Net price		$27.00	$45.00
Unit sales		140,000	90,000
Net sales		$3,780,000	$4,050,000
Cost of dolls	$12.00 each	-$1,680,000	-$1,080,000
Marginal contribution		$2,100,000	$2,970,000

Graphics design		-$15,000	-$60,000
Printing		-$20,000	-$300,000
Distribution of materials		-$25,000	-$100,000
Advertising and promotion		-$60,000	-$460,000

To the warehouse	$1.00	-$140,000	-$90,000
Storage costs	$2.00	-$280,000	-$180,000
Unit shipping, specialty channel	$1.30	-$182,000	$0
Unit shipping, direct mail channel	$5.00	$0	-$450,000

		Specialty Channel	Direct Mail
Insurance per unit	$2.00	-$280,000	-$180,000
Servicing, specialty channel	$1.25	-$175,000	$0
Servicing, direct mail channel	$3.00	$0	-$270,000
Shipment of dolls		-$1,057,000	-$1,170,000
Total distribution cost		-$1,117,000	-$1,630,000
Profit after distribution		**$983,000**	**$1,340,000**

How to Compare Profits from Branded Products Versus Unbranded Products

Firms X and Y sell similar products under their own brand names. The current sales are:

	Unit Sales	Selling Price per Unit	Variable Costs per Unit	Profit per Unit	Total Profit
Brand X	9,000	$150	$145	$5	$45,000
Brand Y	5,000	$150	$145	$5	$25,000

Firm X would like to increase the price of its product. If it does so, it forecasts a loss of sales to Firm Y. The forecast is:

	Unit Sales	Selling Price per Unit	Variable Costs per Unit	Profit per Unit	Total Profit
Brand X	7,000	$160	$145	$15	$105,000
Brand Y	7,000	$150	$145	$5	$35,000

Firm X also has an offer to sell the product to a distributor as a private brand product. The new product would be priced lower than current pricing for either Brand X or Brand Y and would cut into the sales of both companies. The forecast is:

	Unit Sales	Selling Price per Unit	Variable Costs per Unit	Profit per Unit	Total Profit
Brand X	6,000	$160	$145	$15	$90,000
New	4,000	$140	$145	-$5	-$20,000
Brand Y	4,000	$150	$145	$5	$20,000

Should Firm X sell the unbranded product to the distributor?

Answer

Future profit for X, one brand	$105,000
Future profit for X, two brands	$70,000
Difference in profit	-$35,000
Should the brand be introduced?	No

How to Conduct a Profit-Volume Analysis

Everstrong Electrical is a manufacturer of lamps. The following applies to next year:

Sales of lamps in units	2,300
Average selling price of each lamp	$28
Variable cost of each lamp	$22

The company could change the price and also the likely sales, as follows:

Lowered price	$26
Likely sales in units at this price	2,900

A further reduction would increase sales even more.

Lowered price	$24
Likely sales in units at this price	3,300

Everstrong also can adjust its relationship of fixed and variable costs. It can buy new equipment. The results would be:

Cost of the equipment	$3,000
Debt financing at an interest rate of	12%
Current fixed costs	$1,100
Increase in fixed costs with the equipment	$600
New level of variable costs with the equipment	$18

Without the new equipment, Everstrong would have the following next year:

Debt	$37,500
Interest cost on the debt	11%
Corporate tax rate	18%

Required. Which selling price would yield the highest net income next year? Would the new machinery increase or decrease net income next year?

Solution.

	No Changes	Same Price, New	Lower Price, Old	Lower Price, New	Lowest Price, Old
			Equipment		
Unit sales	2,300	2,300	2,900	2,900	3,300
Selling price	$28	$28	$26	$26	$24
Revenues	$64,400	$64,400	$75,400	$75,400	$79,200
Unit variable cost	$22	$18	$22	$18	$22
Variable costs	$50,600	$41,400	$63,800	$52,200	$72,600
Original fixed costs	$1,100				
Original debt	$37,500				

	No Changes	Same Price, New	Lower Price, Old	Lower Price, New	Lowest Price, Old
			Equipment		
Interest rate	11%				
Old interest	$4,125				
New debt		$3,000		$3,000	
Interest rate		12%		12%	
New interest		$360		$360	

Income Statements.

	No Changes	Same Price, New	Lower Price, Old	Lower Price, New	Lowest Price, Old
			Equipment		
Revenues	$64,400	$64,400	$75,400	$75,400	$79,200
Variable costs	-50,600	-41,400	-63,800	-52,200	-72,600
Marginal contribution	$13,800	$23,000	$11,600	$23,200	$6,600
Original fixed costs	-1,100	-1,100	-1,100	-1,100	-1,100
New fixed costs	0	-600	0	-600	0
Operating income	$12,700	$21,300	$10,500	$21,500	$5,500
Original interest	-4,125	-4,125	-4,125	-4,125	-4,125
New interest	0	-360	0	-360	0
Earnings before taxes	$8,575	$16,815	$6,375	$17,015	$1,375
Taxes 18%	-1,544	-3,027	-1,148	-3,063	-248
Net income after taxes	$7,032	$13,788	$5,228	$13,952	$1,128

Recommendation: The lower price with new machinery gives a higher net income than simply continuing without the machinery. Given the risk of new investments, the firm probably should decline the purchase of new equipment.

How to Forecast Future Earnings per Share

Finley Products is a producer of chemicals. Last year's income statement was:

Revenues	$154,546
Cost of goods sold	82,304
Gross margin	$72,242
Administrative costs	17,695
Operating income	$54,547
Interest	9,500
Earnings before taxes	$45,047

Taxes 20%	9,009
Net income	$36,038
Shares outstanding	8,000
Earnings per share	$4.50

The company expects its revenues and operating income to grow next year at a rate of 10 percent.

Finley can accept a new project with data as follows:

Project revenues	$60,000
Project operating income	$18,000
Investment required in the project	$90,000

The company has two financing choices for the project.

| Debt at an interest rate of | 13% |
| Common stock sold to net per share | $28 |

The tax rate for the company is 20 percent. The normal price-earnings multiple is 7.

Should the new project be accepted? If so, how should it be financed? To answer this question, we can perform the following analysis.

Solution. First, we calculate the new operating income from the project.

Data	Next Year			
	Last Year	No Project	Debt Project	Equity Project
New financing			$90,000	$90,000
Interest rate			13%	
New interest			$11,700	
Proceeds per share				$28
New revenues			$60 000	$60,000
New operating income			$18,000	$18,000

Then, we calculate the future market price under the different assumptions.

Data	Next Year			
	Last Year	No Project	Debt Project	Equity Project
Growth rate		10%		
Total revenues	$154,546	$170,001	$230,001	$230,001
Operating income	$54,547	$60,002	$78,002	$78,002
Original interest	9,500	9,500	9,500	9,500
New interest			11,700	
Pre-tax income	$45,047	$50,502	$56,802	$68,502
Taxes 20%	9,009	10,100	11,360	13,700
Net income	$36,038	$40,401	$45,441	$54,801
Original shares	8,000	8,000	8,000	8,000

Data	Last Year	Next Year		
		No Project	Debt Project	Equity Project
New shares				3,214
Total shares	8,000	8,000	8,000	11,214
EPS	$4.50	$5.05	$5.68	$4.89
Normal P/E ratio	7	7	7	7
Future market price	**$31.53**	**$35.35**	**$39.76**	**$34.21**

Finally, we need to choose an option that matches our appetite for risk. From the analysis we can see that the new project does not justify equity financing. The increase in stock value that is forecasted when the project is financed with debt is offset by the added risk of debt financing. The company must decide whether the added likely profits and increase in stock price are acceptable in light of the added debt exposure.

Chapter

6

Leverage

Financial risk managers pay considerable attention to ways in which firms accept higher levels of risk in order to achieve higher likely returns. Leverage is one of those tools. A general dictionary definition of *leverage* would refer to an increased means of accomplishing some purpose. In some cases, as with lifting heavy objects, leverage allows us to accomplish things that are not otherwise possible at a given level of effort. This concept is valid in running a company. The financial manager can identify many different types of leverage. In most cases, the effects are reversible, so that the leverage may be favorable or unfavorable. This is the risk accepted by the firm.

In this chapter, we will use leverage to link measures of profit with other areas of the firm's operating or financial situation. Each type of leverage will be analyzed to determine what it measures and what it shows with respect to the firm's operations or financing. As we will see, each type of leverage may be used as a tool of profit planning to provide insights into specific areas of the firm's anticipated profits. Each type of leverage also needs to be monitored in the event that circumstances change and the leverage backfires.

RETURN ON INVESTMENT LEVERAGE

A firm is able to obtain leverage in its operations. Essentially, this is a matter of increasing profits without the same percentage increase in sales or assets. Leverage that affects return on investment is covered in this section.

Concepts of Profits

From a profit planning perspective, there are two major categories of profits.

- *Profits in relation to sales.* It is important from a profit standpoint that the firm be able to generate adequate profit on each unit of sales. If sales lack a sufficient margin of profit, it is difficult for the firm to cover its fixed costs and interest and provide a profit for shareholders.

- *Profits in relation to assets.* It is similarly important that profit be compared to the capital invested by owners and creditors. If the firm cannot produce a satisfactory profit on its asset base, it will not be attractive as an investment.

Profit Margin

The *profit margin* is the percent of profit earned on the company's revenues. It is calculated using two figures normally taken from the income statement:

Profit Margin = Operating Income/Revenues

The significance of this ratio is that it helps measure the relationship between sales and operating profits. If the profit margin is inadequate, the firm cannot achieve satisfactory returns for its investors. The profit margin is an indicator of the firm's ability to withstand adverse conditions, which may arise from several sources:

- *Falling prices.* If the general price level in the marketplace experiences a decline, does the firm have a sufficient margin to lower its price and still show a profit on individual sales?
- *Rising costs.* If the firm is caught in a period of rising costs when it cannot raise its prices, will it continue to be profitable?
- *Declining sales.* Can the firm withstand unexpected drops in sales and still show a profit?

Similarly, the profit margin may be used as an indicator of possible success under favorable conditions, such as:

- *Rising prices.* If the firm is able to raise its prices, how quickly will profits rise?
- *Lowered costs.* If supplies and materials decline in price, what profits can be expected?
- *Increasing sales.* If the firm is able to gain large increases in sales without price or cost effects, what would be the profit forecast?

Asset Turnover

The *asset turnover* is a measure of the volume of revenues obtained from the firm's invested assets. It is calculated by:

Asset Turnover = Revenues/Total Assets

The ability to produce a large volume of sales on a small asset base is an important part of the firm's profit picture. Idle or improperly used assets increase the firm's need for costly financing and the expenses for maintenance and upkeep. By achieving a high asset turnover, a firm reduces costs and increases the eventual profit to its owners.

In the calculation of asset turnover, assets may be defined in three ways:

- *Total assets.* The most common definition uses total assets reported on the balance sheet. This is basically the book value of current and fixed assets. It is the most readily available calculation, since it can be taken directly from accounting records or a firm's annual report.

- *Operating assets.* A more accurate measure of the assets used to generate a given volume of revenues is the actual operating assets. The analyst might eliminate excess current assets, capital tied up in expansion activities, or other assets that are not used in the firm's operations. The difficulty in using operating assets is identifying them. If the firm is constructing a $25 million factory, this may be noted in the annual report. Since it is not operating yet, it can be subtracted from the total assets. But there may be other unused assets that are not known.
- *Total assets plus estimated value of leased assets.* When a firm leases plant or equipment, it is earning a return on an asset that is not shown on the balance sheet. When comparing different firms, the approximate value of each firm's leased assets should be included.

Return on Investment (ROI)

Individually, the profit margin and the asset turnover have certain weaknesses. The profit margin ignores the money invested by the firm to earn the profit. On the other hand, the asset turnover does not consider the profits made through the use of the assets. To overcome these individual weaknesses, the two ratios may be combined to form the *return on investment (ROI)*, which may be calculated in two ways:

- *Operating income (EBIT) divided by assets.* The firm's return on investment is a ratio of its operating income to the assets used to produce the income.
- *Asset turnover times profit margin.* The size of a firm's return on investment is a function of the margin of profit on sales and the amount of sales generated on the asset base.

The formulas are:

$$\text{Return on Investment} = \text{Profit Margin} \times \text{Asset Turnover}$$

or

$$\text{ROI} = \text{EBIT/Revenues} \times \text{Revenues/Assets} = \text{EBIT/Assets}$$

As illustrated in the formula, when the multiplication is performed, the sales in the denominator of the profit margin and the sales in the numerator of the asset turnover cancel out, leaving operating income/assets.

Return on investment is the key indicator of profitability for a firm. It matches operating profits with the assets available to earn a return. Firms that are using their assets efficiently have a relatively high return. Less efficient firms have a lower ROI.

Asset Leverage

The term *asset leverage* is the tool that links the firm's return on investment with its degree of efficiency in employing assets. It is important for two reasons:

- *Similar profit margins are common.* When comparing firms that produce similar products, we might expect them to have approximately the same profit margins. This recognizes that their costs will be about the same and that they will be forced by market factors to establish equal selling prices for the goods. In this situation, it is difficult to increase ROI by increasing profit margin; thus, the employment of assets becomes very important.

- *Asset turnover reflects efficiency.* The ability to generate a large volume of sales on a small asset base is a measure of a firm's operating efficiency. Firms with excessive or idle assets tend to be poorly managed and are sluggish in their operating characteristics. Aggressive, profit-minded firms strive for a rapid turnover in order to gain the benefits of asset leverage.

Question

What are the major factors that determine norms for profit margin, asset turnover, and return on investment?

Answer

To determine what is normal, which also means what is reasonable in normal times, we can compare ratios to different benchmarks. These include those for the industry that the firm is in, economic and market cycles that affect supply and demand, level and intensity of competition, and even the pricing and other strategies pursued by the firm.

Asset turnover is the tool that we use to monitor the employment of assets on a comparative basis. If a firm has a relatively high asset turnover compared to other firms, we say that it has a high degree of asset leverage. If its turnover is low, it has a low degree of asset leverage. Note that a firm cannot have absolutely high or low asset leverage; it has a relatively high or low leverage.

Profit Margin Leverage

Although firms in the same business may have similar profit margins, careful cost control can increase profit margin, with a levering effect on ROI. Some major areas where cost control is possible are:

- *Production.* Producing goods involves a variety of costs, including manufacturing facilities and equipment, maintenance, labor, and losses caused by equipment that is not operating properly. Good management can usually control these costs.
- *Selling expenses.* In addition to salaries and salespeople's expenses, advertising and sales-support activities cost money. The firm tries to identify essential items and minimize others as a part of cost control.
- *Distribution.* The movement of goods from the factory to warehouses and on to the customer involves many handling and inspecting steps. These should be examined to see if all of them are necessary and if more streamlined distribution channels would reduce costs.
- *Administrative expenses.* The firm's miscellaneous and general expenses should be reviewed frequently to ensure that all are needed in the conduct of the daily business.

Example. A firm has a profit margin of 6 percent and an asset turnover of 3. If it improves its profit margin by 1 percent, what will be the effect on return on investment?

Answer. It will grow by 3 percent.
Originally:

$$6\% \times 3 = 18\%$$

Afterwards:

$$7\% \times 3 = 21\%$$

Example. Company A and Company B both have profit margins of 5 percent. Company A has an asset turnover of 3; Company B has a turnover of 4. If market conditions change so that profit margins rise to 7 percent, which firm will benefit the most?

Answer. Company B, because it has higher asset leverage. A's ROI moves from 15 to 21 percent; B's ROI moves from 20 to 28 percent.

Levering ROI Through Tighter Management

Figure 6-1 shows a more detailed example of how the control of costs can help a firm to lever its ROI. Small reductions in the size of operating assets combined with small decreases in operating costs can have significant effects. Careful planning can help the firm achieve the lower costs, which result in better use of assets and higher reported profits.

To put numbers to the diagram in Figure 6-1, suppose we have a company with the starting information shown in Figure 6-2. This company makes relatively small adjustments that produce the following changes in accounts:

- *Current assets.* Increased efficiency allows an overall decline approaching 10 percent.
- *Fixed assets.* The decline is near 3 percent.
- *Revenues.* The rise is 2 percent.
- *Cost of services.* The drop is 4.5 percent.

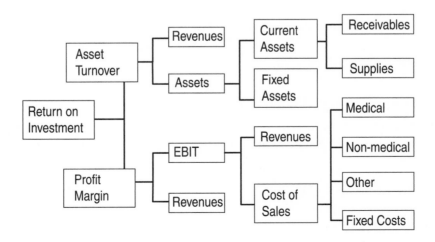

Figure 6-1. Levering Return on Investment Through Asset and Profit Margin Leverage.

Category	Original	Adjusted	Percent Change
We start with assets, sales, and expenses.			
Cash	$12,000	$11,000	-8.3%
Receivables	22,000	20,000	-9.1%
Inventories	27,000	25,000	-7.4%
Fixed assets	70,000	68,000	-2.9%
Sales	200,000	204,000	2.0%
Production costs	125,000	119,000	-4.8%
Selling costs	14,000	13,000	-7.1%
Distribution costs	13,000	12,000	-7.7%
Fixed costs	25,000	25,000	0.0%
Administrative expenses	10,000	9,000	-10.0%
We group the balance sheet accounts.			
Current assets	$61,000	$56,000	-8.2%
Fixed assets	70,000	68,000	-2.9%
Total assets	$131,000	$124,000	-5.3%
We group the income statement accounts.			
Sales	$200,000	$204,000	2.0%
Cost of sales	-177,000	-169,000	-4.5%
Administrative expenses	-10,000	-9,000	-10.0%
EBIT	$13,000	$26,000	100.0%
We measure the degree of leverage			
Asset turnover	1.53	1.65	7.8%
Profit margin	6.5%	12.7%	96.1%
Return on investment	9.9%	21.0%	111.3%

Figure 6-2. Leverage Return on Investment with Minor Changes.

The first visible results are a small rise in asset turnover but a doubling of profit margin. The impact on return on investment shows the leverage effect of small changes, as ROI rises by more than 100 percent.

OPERATING LEVERAGE

Operating leverage exists when changes in revenues produce greater changes in operating income. Several important points should be noted about operating leverage:

- *Related to fixed costs.* The degree of operating leverage is related to the fixed costs of the firm. If the firm has relatively large fixed costs, much of its marginal contribution (revenues minus variable costs) must be applied to cover fixed costs. Once the breakeven point is reached (revenues = fixed + variable costs), all the marginal contribution becomes operating income.

• *Greatest leverage near breakeven point.* After the firm reaches its breakeven point, small percentage increases in sales cause larger percentage increases in operating income. In the same manner, a small drop in sales can erase the entire operating income if the firm is near its breakeven point.

Example. A firm has a marginal contribution of $5 per unit and sells one unit of an item above the breakeven point. Operating income is $5. If the firm sells a second unit, what happens to operating income?

Answer. It doubles to $10, a 100 percent rise in operating income with a far smaller percentage rise in revenues.

Calculating the Degree of Operating Leverage

The degree of operating leverage at any single sales volume can be calculated from the ratio of marginal contribution to operating income. If the marginal contribution is $900,000 and the operating income is $450,000, the operating leverage is 900/450, or 2/1. Thus, any percentage increase in sales results in twice that percentage increase in operating income. Two formulas can be used to calculate operating leverage:

Marginal Contribution/Operating Income

(Revenues – Variable Costs)/(Revenues – Variable Costs – Fixed Costs)

Example. A firm has sales of 100,000 units at $5, variable costs of $3, and fixed costs of $100,000. What is operating leverage?

Answer. Operating leverage is 2/1, calculated as (500 - 300)/(500 - 300 - 100).

Check. If the firm's sales rise to 200,000 units (a 100 percent increase), what will happen to operating income?

Answer. It should rise by 200 percent, and it does. Operating income would grow from $100,000 to $300,000, as follows:

	Original	Afterwards	Another Rise
Revenues	$500,000	$1,000,000	$2,000,000
Variable costs	300,000	600,000	1,200,000
Marginal contribution	$200,000	$400,000	$800,000
Fixed costs	100,000	100,000	100,000
Operating income	$100,000	$300,000	$700,000

Note that the rise in sales in the example produces a new degree of operating leverage at 200,000 units. The new level is 1.33 (400,000/300,000). Another rise in sales will be accompanied by only 1.33 times as large an increase in operating income. Operating leverage decreases with each increase in sales above the breakeven point, because fixed costs become relatively smaller compared to revenues and variable costs. In the example, another 100 percent rise in revenues raises operating income by 133 percent.

Significance of Operating Leverage

What does operating leverage tell the financial manager? It tells the impact of changes in sales on operating income. If a firm has a high degree of operating leverage, small changes in sales will have large effects on operating income. If the change is a small rise in sales, profits will rise dramatically. But if the change is a small decline in forecast sales, operating income may be wiped out and a loss may be reported.

As a general rule, firms do not like to operate under conditions of a high degree of operating leverage. This is a high-risk situation in which a small drop in sales can be excessively damaging to the firm's efforts to achieve profitability. The firm prefers to operate sufficiently above breakeven to avoid the danger of a fluctuation in sales and profits.

Operating leverage works when sales are decreasing as well as when they are increasing.

FINANCIAL LEVERAGE

Financial leverage refers to a situation in which both of the following exist:

- *The firm has limited-cost securities.* The firm must be financing a portion of its assets by using debt with a limited cost to the firm. It can be fixed- or variable-rate securities, but the return to the holder must be limited.
- *ROI is not equal to the cost of the limited-cost securities.* The firm's ROI must not be equal to the percentage of interest being paid on the limited-cost securities.

Three Possible Situations with Debt

The sole criterion for determining whether a firm has financial leverage with its debt involves a comparison of the firm's ROI with the average interest rate. Three situations are possible.

- *ROI is greater than the interest rate.* If the ROI exceeds the interest rate, the firm is making money as a result of borrowing. It may be making 15 percent on its assets but paying only 10 percent to its creditors. The extra five percentage points will be divided between the government (in the form of income taxes) and the shareholders. In this situation, it makes sense to borrow. When the ROI exceeds the interest rate, we say that the firm has *favorable financial leverage*. Another common term used to describe this situation is to say that the firm is *trading on the equity*.
- *ROI equals the interest rate.* In this situation, the firm is earning on the money exactly what it pays for the use of the money. It neither makes sense nor is totally objectionable to borrow in this situation, unless other factors are involved.
- *ROI is less than the interest rate.* When this happens, the firm is borrowing and then losing money on the use of the funds. It does not make sense to borrow, conduct operations, and then make less than the cost of the borrowed money. This situation is called *unfavorable financial leverage*.

Importance of Financial Leverage

Many financial managers would argue that financial leverage is the most important of the leverage concepts. It finds particular application in capital-structure management. A firm's *capital structure* is the relationship between the debt and equity securities that the firm uses to finance its assets. A firm with no debt is said to have an all-equity capital structure. Since most firms have capital structures that include both debt and equity elements, the financial manager is highly concerned with the effects of borrowing. If a firm is making money on its borrowing (has favorable financial leverage), the shareholders are realizing higher earnings per share than they would in the absence of debt.

Financial Leverage and Capital-Structure Management

To demonstrate the effect of financial leverage in a firm's capital structure, consider four firms, each with $500,000 of assets. All four firms earn a 12 percent return on investment. Each firm has sold common stock for $10 a share. Firm A sold $500,000 of stock, while Firms B, C, and D each sold $300,000 of stock. Firms B, C, and D borrowed the remaining $200,000 at different interest rates. Firm B borrowed at 8 percent and, with the 12 percent return on investment, has favorable financial leverage. Firm C borrowed at 12 percent and has neither favorable nor unfavorable financial leverage. Firm D borrowed at 16 percent and has unfavorable financial leverage. Financial data for each firm are given in Figure 6-3.

Analyzing each situation in turn, we can see the effects of financial leverage. Even though the stock sold for $10 and each firm has a 12 percent ROI, the after-tax earnings and EPS vary. Firm A, with no debt, earns $0.90 per share (a 9 percent return on equity). This is also the situation for Firm C, the firm that borrows at the same interest rate as its

	Firm A	Firm B	Firm C	Firm D
	No Debt	Favorable Leverage	No Leverage	Unfavorable Leverage
Data				
ROI	12%	12%	12%	12%
Interest rate	0%	8%	12%	16%
Equity	$500,000	$300,000	$300,000	$300,000
Debt	$0	$200,000	$200,000	$200,000
Total assets	$500,000	$500,000	$500,000	$500,000
Shares outstanding	50,000	30,000	30,000	30,000
Tax rate	25%	25%	25%	25%
Calculations				
EBIT	$60,000	$60,000	$60,000	$60,000
Interest	0	-16,000	-24,000	-32,000
Earnings before taxes	$60,000	$44,000	$36,000	$28,000
Taxes	-15,000	-11,000	-9,000	-7,000
Net income	$45,000	$33,000	$27,000	$21,000
Divided by shares	50,000	30,000	30,000	30,000
Earnings per share	**$0.90**	**$1.10**	**$0.90**	**$0.70**

Figure 6-3. Effects of Favorable Financial Leverage.

ROI. But Firm B, the firm that borrows at less than its ROI, levers its profits to $1.10 by paying only 8 percent to its creditors, who provide 40 percent of the assets ($200,000 of $500,000).

Firm D has the reverse effect from Firm B. Firm D is paying 16 percent interest, which is more than its ROI. This firm must use a portion of the profits that would otherwise be designated for the shareholders in order to pay its creditors.

This example shows that it is logical for a firm to borrow up to reasonable amounts if it can earn a higher return on the money borrowed than it pays for the money. Similarly, a firm should not borrow if it cannot earn more than the cost of the money.

Leverage Impact with Changing Return on Investment

A second way to analyze financial leverage is to consider the effects of different profit levels with each situation. A firm is not guaranteed a 12 percent ROI, and management may consider the effects of achieving a lower or higher return. In the preceding situation with Firms A, B, C, and D, we may evaluate how different ROIs will affect EPS for each firm. Figure 6-4 shows the EPS for each firm with a lower return on investment, and Figure 6-5 shows the EPS for each firm with a higher return on investment.

Figures 6-4 and 6-5 illustrate the general pattern of effects for leveraged firms. When the ROI is high, the firms with favorable financial leverage report the highest earnings. Similarly, when the ROI drops, the firms with the largest interest payments report the

	Firm A	Firm B	Firm C	Firm D
	No Debt	Favorable Leverage	No Leverage	Unfavorable Leverage
Data				
ROI	8%	8%	8%	8%
Interest rate	0%	8%	12%	16%
Equity	$500,000	$300,000	$300,000	$300,000
Debt	$0	$200,000	$200,000	$200,000
Total assets	$500,000	$500,000	$500,000	$500,000
Shares outstanding	50,000	30,000	30,000	30,000
Tax rate	25%	25%	25%	25%
Calculations				
EBIT	$40,000	$40,000	$40,000	$40,000
Interest	0	-16,000	-24,000	-32,000
Earnings before taxes	$40,000	$24,000	$16,000	$8,000
Taxes	-10,000	-6,000	-4,000	-2,000
Net income	$30,000	$18,000	$12,000	$6,000
Divided by shares	50,000	30,000	30,000	30,000
Earnings per share	**$0.60**	**$0.60**	**$0.40**	**$0.20**

Figure 6-4. Leverage with Drop to 8 Percent Return on Investment.

	Firm A	Firm B	Firm C	Firm D
	No Debt	Favorable Leverage	No Leverage	Unfavorable Leverage
Data				
ROI	18%	18%	18%	18%
Interest rate	0%	8%	12%	16%
Equity	$500,000	$300,000	$300,000	$300,000
Debt	$0	$200,000	$200,000	$200,000
Total assets	$500,000	$500,000	$500,000	$500,000
Shares outstanding	50,000	30,000	30,000	30,000
Tax rate	25%	25%	25%	25%
Calculations				
EBIT	$90,000	$90,000	$90,000	$90,000
Interest	0	-16,000	-24,000	-32,000
Earnings before taxes	$90,000	$74,000	$66,000	$58,000
Taxes	-22,500	-18,500	-16,500	-14,500
Net income	$67,500	$55,500	$49,500	$43,500
Divided by shares	50,000	30,000	30,000	30,000
Earnings per share	**$1.35**	**$1.85**	**$1.65**	**$1.45**

Figure 6-5. Leverage with Rise to 18 Percent Return on Investment.

largest losses or smallest earnings. The firm with no debt has lower earnings in high-profit periods and higher earnings in low-profit periods than firms with debt.

WEAKNESSES OF PROFIT PLANNING

Financial risk management points out the fact that various profit-planning and leverage concepts pose weaknesses that should be noted by the financial manager:

- *Short-term outlook.* Usually we are projecting income statements only a year or two into the future. In fact, a more powerful tool is to plan for all cash flows over a five- to seven-year planning horizon.
- *Accounting profits, not cash.* Profit planning does not measure cash. Business decisions should be made on a cash basis.
- *Assets at book, not market, value.* Market value is the correct basis for making business decisions. Profit planning uses book values.

CONCLUSION

Leverage is a powerful tool that cannot be ignored by modern corporations. Enterprise risk management tells us that the firm needs to establish its appetite for risk. Then, it can use leverage in its profit planning to reach the desired profit goals at a risk level that is acceptable to it.

CHAPTER 6 APPENDIXES

How to Assess Risks from Leverage

Firm A has the following data:

Sales	$9,250
Variable costs	$5,500
Marginal contribution	$3,750
Fixed costs	$1,100
Operating income	$2,650
Average debt cost	12.0%
Debt	$6,000
Equity	$7,200
Assets	$13,200

The industry norm for asset turnover is 2.3.
Three ratios are:

EBIT	$2,650
Revenues	$9,250
Profit margin	**28.6%**

Revenues	$9,250
Assets	$13,200
Asset turnover	**0.7**

EBIT	$2,650
Assets	$13,200
Return on investment	**20.1%**

Calculate Financial Leverage.

Return on investment	20.1%
Is ROI higher than interest rate?	Yes
If yes, leverage is favorable.	

Is Asset Leverage High? Identify the industry norm for asset turnover: 2.3. Measure whether Firm A exceeds this norm.

	Sales	Assets	Turnover	Norm
Assets	$9,250	$13,200	0.7	2.3
High asset leverage?				No

Calculate the Degree of Operating Leverage for Firm A.

Marginal Contribution	EBIT	Operating Leverage
$3,750	$2,650	1.42

Test to See What Happens to EBIT If Sales Drop. Assume sales drop to $6,000.

Original sales	$9,250
New sales	$6,000
Percent change in sales	-35.1%
Times operating leverage	1.42
Percent change in operating income	-49.7%
Times original operating income	$2,650
Drop in EBIT	-$1,318
New EBIT	$1,332

Calculate Drop in Sales Needed to Erase EBIT.

Percent decline in operating income	100%
Divided by operating leverage	1.42
Percent decline in sales to erase EBIT	70.7%

How to Analyze Financial and Operating Leverage

Garfield produces swimming pools and products for the pool patio. Its current balance sheet and income statement are:

Balance Sheet

Cash	$3,250
Accounts receivable	8,500
Inventory	5,000
Fixed assets	76,500
Total Assets	**$93,250**
Current liabilities	$6,000
Long-term debt 10%	37,000
Common stock	15,000
Retained earnings	35,250
Total Liabilities and Equity	**$93,250**

Income Statement, Current Year

Sales	$90,000
Variable costs	60,300
Marginal contribution	$29,700

Fixed costs	<u>10,430</u>
Operating income	$19,270
Interest	<u>3,700</u>
Pretax earnings	$15,570
Taxes 25%	<u>3,893</u>
Net income	**$11,678**

The firm is forecasting the following for next year:

Sales	$120,000
Variable costs as a percent of sales	67%
Rise in fixed costs	15%

The firm can invest in a project to make chaise lounges. The data are:

Investment in machinery	$35,000
Debt (100%)	$35,000
Additional sales	$30,000
Variable costs as a percent of sales	70%
Additional fixed costs	$3,000

The firm could also invest in a project to make patio umbrellas. The data are:

Investment in machinery	$50,000
Debt (100%)	$50,000
Annual sales	$42,000
Variable costs as a percent of sales	60%
Fixed costs	$5,000

Other financial information is:

Financing for the project would involve a 10-year loan at an interest rate of	13%
The tax rate is	25%
The number of shares of stock outstanding is	5,000

Leverage Analysis. We can check the impact of each project on earnings per share.

Income Statement	Alone	With Lounges	With Umbrellas
Original sales	$120,000	$120,000	$120,000
New sales	_____	<u>30,000</u>	<u>42,000</u>
Total sales	$120,000	$150,000	$162,000
Original variable costs	80,400	80,400	80,400
New variable costs	_____	<u>21,000</u>	<u>25,200</u>
Marginal contribution	$39,600	$48,600	$56,400

Income Statement	Alone	With Lounges	With Umbrellas
Original fixed costs	11,995	11,995	11,995
New fixed costs	0	3,000	5,000
Operating income	$27,606	$33,606	$39,406
Original interest	3,700	3,700	3,700
New interest	_____	4,550	6,500
Pretax income	$23,906	$25,356	$29,206
Taxes 25%	5,976	6,339	7,301
Net income	$17,929	$19,017	$21,904

Shares outstanding	5,000	5,000	5,000
Earnings per share	**$3.59**	**$3.80**	**$4.38**

We can check the impact of each project on measures of leverage.

Sales	$120,000	$150,000	$162,000
Assets	$93,250	$128,250	$143,250
Asset turnover	**1.29**	**1.17**	**1.13**

Marginal contribution	$39,600	$48,600	$56,400
Operating income	$27,606	$33,606	$39,406
Operating leverage	**1.43**	**1.45**	**1.43**

Operating income	$27,606	$33,606	$39,406
Assets	$93,250	$128,250	$143,250
Return on investment	30%	26%	28%
Debt	$43,000	$78,000	$93,000
Interest	$3,700	$8,250	$10,200
Interest cost	8.6%	10.6	11.0%
Favorable financial leverage?	**Yes**	**Yes**	**Yes**

Conclusion. Adding either chaise lounges or patio umbrellas significantly increases earnings per share even as it drops return on investment. This occurs because the firm would be using debt to finance all the new assets in a situation of favorable financial leverage. The question for decision makers becomes one of appetite for risk. Is the rise in EPS the right compensation for the rise in risk?

How to Use Leverage to Assess a Firm's Appetite for Risk

H&G Industries is considering the acquisition of two companies. One is owned by Joe Haynes. The other is managed by Charles Grady. From the following data and questions, we can assess our view of the appetite for risk in each unit.

Which balance sheet is stronger?

Balance Sheet (000s)

	Haynes	Grady
Current assets	$6,000	$7,000
Fixed assets	22,000	28,000
Total Assets	$28,000	$35,000
Liabilities	$10,000	$22,000
Equity	18,000	13,000
Total Liabilities and Equity	$28,000	$35,000

Which income statement is stronger?

Income Statement (000s)

	Haynes	Grady
Sales	$24,500	$32,000
Variable costs	18,000	11,000
Marginal Contribution	6,500	21,000
Fixed costs	1,000	10,000
Operating income	$5,500	$11,000
Interest rate	11%	14%
Interest	1,100	3,080
Pretax income	$4,400	$7,920
Taxes	1,100	1,980
Net income	$3,300	$5,940

Does the difference in earnings per share show a strength or weakness of either unit? Why or why not?

	Haynes	Grady
Shares	1,000	3,000
Earnings per share	$3.30	$1.98

Which unit makes better use of operating leverage?

	Haynes	Grady
Marginal contribution	$6,500	$21,000
Operating income	$5,500	$11,000
Operating leverage	1.18	1.91

Which unit can sustain a larger drop in revenues and still break even?

	Haynes	Grady
Drop in operating income	100%	100%
Divided by operating leverage	1.18	1.91
Drop to erase operating income	85%	52%

Which unit makes better use of financial leverage?

	Haynes	Grady
Operating income	$5,500	$11,000
Assets	$28,000	$35,000
Return on investment	20%	31%
Cost of debt	11%	14%
Favorable financial leverage?	Yes	Yes

Which unit makes the larger contribution to earnings?

	Haynes	Grady
Net income	$3,300	$5,940
Percent of net income from each unit	36%	64%

Overall, which unit is better managed?

The answer to this question will vary with a person's appetite for risk. A majority of individuals seem to prefer Grady. Both units are well managed and would be a nice fit as an acquisition. Haynes has lower profits and lower risk. Grady has higher profits and higher risk. On balance, Grady seems to offer the most to H&G Industries, a factor that should affect the offer to purchase the stock of both companies.

Chapter
7
Financial Analysis

RATIO ANALYSIS

Financial analysis is the process of determining the significant operating and financial characteristics of a firm from accounting data and financial statements. The goal is to determine the efficiency and performance of management, as reflected in the financial records and reports. The analyst measures the firm's liquidity, profitability, and other indicators to see whether its business is being conducted in a rational and orderly way. If a firm does not achieve the financial norms for its industry or if relationships among data do not seem reasonable, the analyst notes the deviations. The burden of explaining the apparent problems may then be placed upon management.

In this chapter, we will develop ratio analysis as the primary tool for examining the firm's financial position and performance. We will recognize two viewpoints in receiving and evaluating financial data:

- *External analysis.* This is performed by outsiders to the firm, such as creditors, stockholders, or investment analysts. It makes use of existing financial statements and involves limited access to confidential information on a firm.
- *Internal analysis.* This is performed by the corporate finance and accounting departments and is more detailed than external analysis. It uses current information that is not available to outsiders. Internal analysts are able to produce a more accurate and timely analysis of the firm's strengths and weaknesses.

Separating Causes and Symptoms of Problems

Financial analysis offers insights into the operating and financial problems confronting the firm. We must be careful, however, to distinguish between the cause of a problem and a symptom of it. A *cause* is an event that produces a result or effect; in our case, the result is a problem. A *symptom* is a visible indicator that a problem exists. The firm may observe symptoms of problems, such as a low level of profits, but it must deal with the causes of those problems, such as high costs. If it does not deal with the cause of a problem, the firm will probably not be able to correct that problem.

As we will see, financial ratios are used to locate symptoms of problems. Once the symptoms have been located, the analyst determines the cause of any problem. Then a solution must be found. Examples of symptoms, causes, and solutions of problems are given in Figure 7-1.

Financial Ratios

A *ratio* may be defined as a fixed relationship in degree or number between two quantities. In finance, ratios are used to point out relationships that are not obvious from the raw data. Some uses of ratios are the following:

- *To compare different companies in the same industry.* Ratios can highlight the factors associated with successful and unsuccessful firms. They can reveal strong and weak firms, overvalued and undervalued firms.

Symptom:
Abnormal liquidity ratio
    Check for:
    Inadequate cash
    Excessive receivables or inventory
        Solutions:
        Raise additional funds
        Restrict terms of trade
        Institute a more aggressive collection policy
        Improve inventory management
        Obtain additional long-term financing

Symptom:
Abnormal profitability ratio
    Check for:
    High production costs
    Idle assets
    Inadequate sales
    Inadequate selling price
    High administrative expenses
    Excessive interest payments
        Solutions:
        Raise selling price
        Reduce administrative expenses
        Seek lower cost debt financing
        Seek equity financing
        Institute cost-cutting measures
        Sell excess or obsolete assets
        Increase size and quality of sales force
        Improve advertising

Figure 7-1. Symptoms, Problems, and Solutions

- *To compare different industries.* Every industry has its own unique set of operating and financial characteristics. These can be identified with the aid of ratios.
- *To compare performance in different time periods.* Over a period of years, a firm or an industry develops certain norms that may indicate future success or failure. If these relationships change over time, the ratios may provide clues to trends and future problems.

From all the financial accounts on the balance sheet, income statement, and flow-of-funds statement, it is possible to formulate countless ratios. To be successful in financial analysis, the analyst must select only those ratios that provide significant information.

Users of Ratios

Different analysts desire different kinds of ratios, depending largely on the training of the analyst and the goals of the evaluation. Some users of ratios are the following:

- *Short-term creditors.* These persons hold obligations that will soon mature, and they are concerned with the firm's ability to pay its bills promptly. In the short run, the amount of liquid assets that the firm has determines its ability to pay its current liabilities. These persons are interested in liquidity.
- *Long-term creditors.* These persons hold bonds or mortgages against the firm and are interested in current payments of interest and eventual repayment of principal. The firm must both be sufficiently liquid in the short term and have adequate profits for the long term. These persons examine both liquidity and profitability.
- *Stockholders.* In addition to liquidity and profitability, owners are concerned about the policies of the firm that affect the market price of its common stock. Without liquidity, the firm will not be able to pay cash dividends. Without profits, the firm will not be able to declare dividends. With poor policies, the common stock will trade at low prices in the market.

Comparative Ratios

The most effective use of ratios is to compare them to industry averages or norms for similar firms. A *comparative ratio* is defined as a fixed relationship between numbers that is derived from industry averages or other data that can provide a benchmark for evaluating an individual firm. As an example, if an industry average shows a ratio of 6:1 and an individual firm has a ratio of 8:1, we can say that, on a comparative basis, the firm exceeds the industry average.

Comparative ratios are provided by a number of organizations. Dun & Bradstreet is probably the most widely known organization providing such ratios. It provides data on different ratios showing business activity for some 125 business categories under the general headings of manufacturing and construction industries, wholesalers, and retailers. A second source of ratios is Robert Morris Associates, which is a national organization of bank lending officers. This association compiles and publishes averages based upon financial statements received by commercial banks in connection with business loans made by the banks. Other sources of comparative ratios are individual commercial banks, industry trade associations, and the Federal Trade Commission.

Kinds of Ratios

Financial ratios may be classified in a number of ways. One classification scheme uses three major categories:

- *Liquidity ratios.* These examine the adequacy of the firm's funds, the solvency of the firm, and the firm's ability to pay its obligations when due.
- *Profitability ratios.* These measure the efficiency of the firm's activities and its ability to generate profits.
- *Ownership ratios.* These are generally linked directly or indirectly to profits and liquidity. They assist the stockholder in evaluating the firm's activities and policies that affect the market price of the common stock.

LIQUIDITY RATIOS

A firm's ability to pay its debts can be measured partly through the use of liquidity ratios. Short-term liquidity involves the relationship between current assets and current liabilities. If a firm has sufficient net working capital (the excess of current assets over current liabilities), it is deemed to have sufficient liquidity. Two ratios are commonly used to measure liquidity directly: the current ratio and the quick ratio, or acid test ratio.

Current Ratio and Quick Ratio, or Acid Test Ratio

The *current ratio* is calculated by:

Current Assets/Current Liabilities

A low ratio is an indicator that a firm may not be able to pay its future bills on time, particularly if conditions change, causing a slowdown in cash collections. A high ratio may indicate excessive current assets and management's failure to utilize the firm's resources properly. To determine whether this ratio is high, low, or just right, the analyst should consider such factors as the firm's past history, its goals, and the current ratios of similar companies. As a general rule, a 2:1 ratio is considered acceptable for most firms.

The *quick ratio*, or acid test ratio, is a more stringent measure of liquidity than the current ratio because inventories, which are the least liquid of current assets, are excluded from the ratio. The quick ratio may be calculated by:

(Current Assets - Inventories)/Current Liabilities

Inventories require a two-step process in order to be converted into cash. They must be sold, at which time they are converted into receivables (with the markup), and then the receivables must be collected. The acid test ratio is so named because it shows the ability of a firm to pay its obligations without relying on the sale of its inventories.

As a guideline, a 1:1 quick ratio has traditionally been deemed adequate for most firms. A higher ratio may have several meanings. It could indicate that the firm has excessive cash or receivables, both of which are signs of lax management. A low ratio is usually an indication of possible difficulties in the prompt payment of future bills.

Accounts Receivable Turnover

The *accounts receivable turnover* is used to measure the liquidity of a firm's accounts receivable. It is calculated as:

Revenues/Accounts Receivable

The receivables turnover is a comparison of the volume of sales and the amount of uncollected bills from customers. If the firm is having difficulty collecting its money, it will have a large receivables balance and a low ratio. If it has a strict credit policy and aggressive collection procedures, it will have a low receivables balance and a high ratio.

Several techniques are available to help analyze the significance of the receivables turnover and average collection period:

- *Make comparisons with other firms in the industry.* Since conditions concerning the terms of trade and selling practices are usually similar throughout an industry, this comparison can indicate whether the firm is lax or strict in its collection and sales policies.
- *Compare ratios with the terms of trade.* The terms of trade are an important factor in analyzing receivables. Suppose Firms A and B both have turnovers of 8 times a year. Firm A has terms 2/10 net 30 (a 2 percent discount for payment within 10 days, with full payment due in 30 days). A turnover of 8 means that a number of receivables are still uncollected on the final due date of 30 days. Firm B has terms of 2/10 net 60. For this firm, a turnover of 8 means that collections are probably well within the 60-day period. Without further information, we could conclude that Firm B is doing a better job of collecting its receivables.
- *Use only net credit sales.* Sales figures may include both cash and credit sales. Since only credit sales become receivables, a more accurate turnover uses only credit sales.
- *Use average receivables figures.* The average of the beginning and ending receivables balance for a year may give a more accurate picture of turnover than a single ending figure. A monthly view (adding the ending monthly balances and dividing by 12) might be even more accurate.
- *Avoid cyclical figures.* The analyst must always beware of applying ratio analysis to industries with cyclical sales. The busy season will distort the ratios in one direction; the quiet season, in the other. Even the average of the busy and quiet periods may not be useful. It would be better to develop two sets of ratios: the turnover during (1) the busy period and (2) the quiet period.

Inventory Turnover

The liquidity of a firm's inventory may be calculated by:

Cost of Goods Sold/Inventory

The cost of goods sold is for the period being studied, normally one year. Two factors are important in calculating this ratio:

- *Physical turnover of inventory is measured.* The sales figure includes a markup for profit. Thus, a $50 sale may turn over only $30 of inventory. The cost of goods sold would be $30, and the ratio would measure the actual movement of inventory.
- *Average inventory may be used.* The inventory may be calculated using an average figure in a manner similar to averaging accounts receivable.

The significance of inventory turnover is that it helps measure the adequacy of goods available to sell compared to the actual sales. In this context, the carrying of inventory involves two risks:

- *Running out of goods to sell.* In some industries, customers place orders and are willing to wait for delivery. In most industries, however, running out of stock means a loss of sales. When a customer immediately needs an item that the firm does not stock, the customer will purchase it elsewhere, with a consequent loss of profit for the firm.
- *Excessive carrying charges resulting from excessive inventory.* Carrying inventory involves costs for storing goods, protecting them from theft or breakage, and handling them. Unneeded inventory means unnecessary costs.

Because the manager must compromise between running out of goods to sell and investing in excessive inventory, either a high or a low ratio may be an indication of poor management, as follows.

- *High turnover may indicate future shortages.* A high inventory turnover results when the firm maintains low stocks of goods or raw materials. A low level of finished goods may indicate a future loss of sales because of an inability to deliver goods promptly. A low level of raw materials could lead to shutdowns of the production line, resulting in higher costs.
- *Low turnover may indicate overstocking of inventory.* A low inventory turnover results from excessive inventory. The firm may be incurring high costs from overstocking finished goods or raw materials. At the same time, the firm may be carrying obsolete goods in its inventory.

Different firms turn over their inventories at markedly different rates. A firm that has many items at varying stages of production might be expected to have a relatively low turnover. If the inventory contains only a few fast-moving items, a high turnover would be expected. High and low turnovers are relative terms. The current turnover must be compared to that in previous periods or to some industry norms before it is designated as high, low, or normal. The nature of the business should also be considered in analyzing the size of the turnover.

Alternative Calculation of Inventory Turnover

An alternative calculation of inventory turnover is:

$$\text{Sales/Inventory}$$

This differs from the first formula in that the markup for profit when a sale is made is included. Because revenues are generally higher than costs, the alternative calculation gives a higher turnover. Which calculation is more useful? The calculations measure different things, but both are useful. With cost of goods sold, we are measuring physical turnover. We can identify a sluggish inventory (low turnover) or inadequate inventory (high turnover). With sales, we are measuring the dollars generated in the normal course of business. The ratio measures liquidity if the firm continues to sell at its normal markup.

Example. A firm sells 1,000 units of a product at $10 per unit during a one-year period. The cost of each unit is $6. The firm's inventory is 100 units. What is the inventory turnover in units and in dollars?

Answer. The turnover in units is 10:1:

$$\text{Cost of Goods Sold/Inventory} = 6,000/600$$

The turnover in dollars is 16.67:1:

$$\text{Sales/Inventory} = 10,000/600$$

In using comparative ratios, the analyst must be aware of which calculation is being used, so that a valid comparison is made. Dun & Bradstreet, for example, regularly publishes inventory turnover for sales. In order to have figures that can be correctly compared with Dun & Bradstreet figures, the analyst must use the sales-to-inventory method of calculation.

Analyzing Liquidity

The cash, receivables, and inventory ratios should be used together to gain an overall grasp of the liquidity of the firm. With respect to Banner Incorporated, whose financial information is given in Figure 7-2, the ratios are:

Banner Liquidity Ratios	Start of Year	End of Year
Current ratio	4.4	2.4
Quick ratio	2.4	1.3
Accounts receivable turnover	11.0	8.3
Inventory turnover (cost of goods sold)	3.6	3.0
Inventory turnover (sales)	8.0	6.6

Banner has a current ratio of 2.4:1, which exceeds the 2:1 guideline. Its acid test ratio is 1.3:1, which exceeds the 1:1 guideline. Similarly, the receivables and inventory turnover are high, but the trend is declining. Since all ratios are higher than the norms, the company appears to be sufficiently liquid. Although the figures may still be adequate, the analyst may wish to investigate the reasons for the downward trends. A problem seems to be the large increase in accounts payable from $32,000 to $67,000. Although increases in receivables and inventories accompany the increase in payables, the analyst should inquire as to the cause of the payables rise.

Balance Sheet				Income Statement	
	Start of Year	**End of Year**			**This Year**
Cash and equivalents	$33,000	$28,000		Net sales and other revenues	$495,000
Accounts receivable	45,000	60,000			
Inventories	62,000	75,000		Cost of goods sold	225,000
Current assets	**$140,000**	**$163,000**		Gross margin	$270,000
Plant and equipment	$185,000	$246,000		Administrative expenses	115,000
Accumulated depreciation	130,000	135,000			
Other fixed assets	60,000	60,000		Operating income	$155,000
Total Assets	**$385,000**	**$469,000**		Interest on debt	21,000
Payables	$32,000	$67,000		Earnings before taxes	$134,000
Long-term secured debt	75,000	70,000		Federal income taxes	53,600
Long-term unsecured debt	90,000	80,000		Net income after taxes	$80,400
Total debt	**$197,000**	**$217,000**		Shares outstanding	40,000
Contributed capital	$105,000	$105,000		Earnings per share	$2.01
Retained earnings	83,000	147,000		Market price per share	$18
Total Liabilities and Equity	**$385,000**	**$469,000**		Dividends per share	$1.00

Figure 7-2. Banner, Inc., Balance Sheet and Income Statement.

PROFITABILITY RATIOS

In the previous chapter, we discussed three ratios that measure profitability:

- *Profit margin.* This is calculated by dividing operating income by sales. If it is inadequate, the firm cannot achieve satisfactory returns for its investors.
- *Asset turnover.* This is calculated by dividing sales by total assets. It highlights the amount of assets the firm used to produce total sales.
- *Return on investment.* This is calculated by dividing operating income by assets. Also, it can be obtained by multiplying asset turnover by the profit margin. The return on investment is the key indicator of profitability because it matches operating profits with the assets available to earn a return.

Now we will add some additional profitability ratios.

Gross Profit Margin

A second ratio that links sales and profits is gross profit margin, calculated by dividing gross margin by sales. It shows profits relative to sales after the direct production costs are deducted.

Return on Equity

The return on equity (ROE) is an important profit indicator to shareholders of the firm. It is calculated by:

Net Income/Total Equity

This ratio shows whether operating income is being converted into after-tax income that can be claimed by shareholders. Stated differently, ROE measures the profits that accrue to the shareholders. It is useful in analyzing the ability of management to realize an adequate return on the capital invested by the owners of the firm.

Earning Power

Earning power is calculated by dividing net income by total assets. It is a measure of the after-tax return achieved by the company compared to the firm's resources. If a firm is using its assets efficiently, it has a high earning power when compared with similar firms. Earning power may be viewed as the firm's after-tax return on investment.

Analyzing Profitability

Many factors influence profitability. Each factor in turn affects the profitability ratios. The interrelationship of factors is shown in Figure 7-3. Note the cumulative effect of the individual factors. Every factor affects earning power, even though none leads to it directly. For example, high production costs, which affect gross profit margin, have an effect through the profit margin, return on investment, and return on equity, and finally earning power. One ratio explains another because the factors that affect it also affect other ratios.

For Banner, Inc., in Figure 7-2, the profitability ratios are:

Profit margin	31%
Asset turnover	1.1
Return on investment	33%
Gross profit margin	55%
Return on equity	32%
Earning power	17%

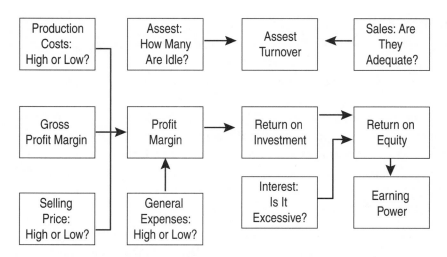

Figure 7-3. Factors Affecting Profit and Interrelation of Profitability Ratios.

For any company, these ratios would be high. A return on investment of 33 percent is a strong before-tax operating return. A 32 percent return on equity is an excellent return to shareholders. A 17 percent after-tax return on assets shows efficient use of the firm's resources.

OTHER RATIOS

A number of other ratios assist in analyzing the financial position of a company. They compare factors such as debt, dividends, earnings, and the market price of the stock. By understanding the profitability and liquidity ratios, we gain insights into the soundness of the firm's business activities. By investigating other ratios, we analyze factors that may affect the firm in the future.

In this section, we will analyze three categories of ratios:

- *Earnings ratios.* These provide information on how earnings affect the price of common stock. They are earnings per share, the price-earnings ratio, and the capitalization rate.
- *Capital structure ratios.* A firm's capital structure is the relation of debt to equity as sources of the firm's assets. The two ratios that reflect capital structure are the debt-equity ratio and the debt-asset ratio.
- *Dividend ratios.* These provide measures of the adequacy of dividend payments. The two ratios are dividend payout and dividend yield.

Earnings per Share (EPS)

Stockholders are concerned about the earnings that will eventually be available to pay them dividends or that are used to expand their interest in the firm because the firm retains the earnings. These earnings may be expressed on a per-share basis by dividing net income by the number of shares outstanding (net income/total shares). Shares that have been authorized but not issued, or that have been authorized, issued, and repurchased (treasury stock), are omitted from the calculation.

Price-Earnings Ratio

The price-earnings (P/E) ratio is calculated by dividing the market price of the stock by the earnings per share (market price/EPS). It is the most important measure of value used by investors in the marketplace. Many investors consider no other factors prior to making purchases.

The P/E ratio is a *going concern* method of valuing stock. As long as the firm is a viable business entity, its real (or going concern) value is reflected in its profits. The P/E ratio considers after-tax profits and market price, and links earnings per share to activity in the market. If a stock has a low P/E multiple, for example, 4:1, it may be viewed as an undervalued stock. If the ratio is 20:1, the stock may be considered overvalued.

The P/E ratio may be used in several ways:

- *To determine the expected market value of a stock.* Within any given industry, there is usually a wide variation in P/E multiples. One firm may trade at 6:1, while another trades at 10:1. If the firms are somewhat similar, the P/E ratio may help to identify the undervalued and overvalued stocks.

- *To determine the future market value of a stock.* If a stock is purchased for $27 and has $3 EPS, what will it be worth in five years when EPS is $7? If the P/E ratio stays at approximately 9:1, the stock will be worth $63 (7 × 9). If EPS goes only to $4, it will be worth $36 (4 × 9).

- *To determine the capitalization rate of a stock.* The P/E ratio may be used to measure the rate of return that investors demand before they purchase a stock. The reciprocal of the P/E ratio is EPS/market price and gives this return. If the stock has $3 EPS and sells for $27, the marketplace is demanding that the stock return 3/27, or 11 percent. This is the stock's *capitalization rate.* An 11 percent capitalization rate means that the firm earns 11 percent on the value of the common stock. If investors did not require this return, they would pay more for the stock and the rate of return or capitalization rate would drop.

Capital Structure Ratios

Two ratios are important in analyzing the relationship between the debt and equity components of the firm's capital structure:

- *Debt-equity ratio.* This is calculated by dividing the total debt by the total equity.
- *Debt-asset ratio.* This is calculated by dividing the total debt by the total assets.

These ratios show how much of the firm's assets is financed by debt and how much by equity and give important information about prospects for future financing. If a firm has an excessive amount of debt, it will have difficulty locating additional debt financing. The firm will be able to borrow only at high interest rates, if at all. On the other hand, if the ratio is low (virtually no debt), this may indicate a failure to use relatively lower-cost borrowed funds to raise the return earned on the common stock.

Analysts differ on whether short-term debt should be included in the capital structure ratios. One group reasons that accounts payable and similar short-term items allow a temporary use of assets (notably inventory) but are not really a form of borrowing to finance resources. In other words, current liabilities are not a permanent part of the capital employed by the firm. We will include current liabilities in the debt-equity and debt-asset ratios. The reasoning is that careful management of short-term debt provides inexpensive (frequently free) funds that the firm would otherwise have to borrow at higher rates. At the same time, short-term debt represents obligations of the firm. If capital structure ratios are to measure financial risk, they should reflect all debt owed by the firm.

There are three major uses of capital structure ratios:

- *Identify sources of funds.* The firm finances all its resources from either debt or equity sources. The amount of financing from each source is shown by these ratios.
- *Measure financing risk.* These ratios provide one measure of the risk from debt financing. If the firm has been increasing the percentage of debt in its capital structure over a period of time, this may indicate an increase in risk for its shareholders.

- *Forecast borrowing prospects.* If the firm is considering expansion and needs to raise additional money, capital structure ratios offer an indication of whether debt funds will be available. If the ratios are too high, the firm may not be able to borrow.

As a general guideline, the debt should not exceed 50 percent of the total sources of funds. It should be less than 50 percent for a firm in a risky business that produces wide swings in operating income. Thus, a debt-equity ratio of 1:1 or a debt-asset ratio of 0.5:1 should be the maximum for industrial firms.

Book Value per Share

The book value of a firm's common stock is calculated by dividing stockholders' equity by the number of shares outstanding. This ratio is somewhat related to the capital structure ratios, since it measures the accounting value of a portion of the firm's assets, the portion financed by the owners.

Book value is a reflection of the firm's accounting records rather than a measure of the real value of the firm's assets. If two otherwise identical firms used different depreciation schedules, the book value of their assets would be different. Historically, book value has resulted from the use of conservative accounting techniques and has been lower than the market value of the stock. For this reason, it is of limited use as an estimate of asset values. Three valid uses of book value may be identified:

- *Liquidation value.* When a firm is experiencing liquidity or profitability problems, it may consider selling its assets, paying off its debts, and distributing the remaining money, if any, to its shareholders. In cases of possible liquidation, the book value gives an indication of the amount that can be distributed to shareholders. If the firm can sell its assets for, say, 80 percent of the recorded asset value, and it pays its debt at 100 percent of value, the remainder is available for common shareholders.
- *Market price near book value.* In many cases, an interesting phenomenon occurs when market price nears book value. Investors note that the firm's assets support a certain price (book value) and do not allow the market price to drop below that price. In effect, the book value becomes a support level for the price of the common stock. In some cases, it may become a rallying point, and investor demand will begin to push up the price of the stock.
- *Legal proceedings.* In certain legal or tax proceedings, book value may be the taxable base for taxes on securities.

Dividend Ratios

Investors and creditors are concerned about the level of cash dividends. If the firm is paying insufficient dividends, the stock will not be attractive to investors who want current income. If it pays excessive dividends, it may not be retaining adequate funds to finance future growth.

To pay consistent and adequate dividends, the firm must be liquid and profitable. Without liquidity, it will not have the cash to pay dividends. Without profits, it will not have sufficient retained earnings to make dividend declarations. Firms cannot declare dividends if the balance in their retained earnings account is not at least as large as the amount of the dividend. A more important factor is that without profits, the firm will not have the resources to pay the dividends.

Two dividend ratios are particularly important:

- *Dividend payout [dividends per share (DPS)/EPS].* This is a ratio of dividends per share to earnings per share. It tells the percentage of earnings paid to the shareholder in dividends. The percentage that is not paid out is retained.
- *Dividend yield (DPS/Market Price).* This is a ratio of dividends per share to the market price per share. It gives the current return to investors as a percentage of their investment. It is of interest to potential shareholders who are considering purchasing the firm's stock and who desire dividends as a source of income.

Guidelines for these two ratios vary widely. Firms often attempt to pay approximately 50 percent of their earnings as dividends. However, if the firm needs funds to support its operations, it might allow the dividends to decline in relation to earnings. If the firm lacks opportunities to use the funds generated by retained earnings, it might allow the dividends to increase in relation to earnings. In either case, consistency of dividend payment is important to investors, so that changes should be gradual.

The dividend yield to a stockholder ranges from 0 to 10 or 12 percent. There is no dividend yield if a firm does not declare dividends. High-growth firms may declare dividends, but the yield may be only 2 or 3 percent. For mature industrial firms, the yield may be 7 or 8 percent. When stock prices are depressed or for the stock of public utilities or similar firms, the yield may reach 10 to 12 percent.

Analyzing Other Ratios

Using the data for Banner, Inc., we get the following ratios:

Earnings per share	$2.01
Price-earnings ratio	9:1
Capitalization rate	11%
Debt-equity ratio	86%
Debt-asset ratio	46%
Book value per share	$6.30
Market price per share	$18.00
Dividends per share	$1.00
Dividend payout	50%
Dividend yield	5.6%

From these ratios, we might draw the following conclusions for Banner:

- *Banner offers a moderate return to shareholders.* The price-earnings ratio and capitalization rate show a medium return to investors.

- *It has a reasonable capital structure.* The debt-equity and debt-asset ratios are close to a norm of 50 percent of a firm's assets being financed by debt.
- *It offers some current income.* The dividend ratios indicate that the firm is paying reasonable dividends.

From a potential owner's point of view, we might conclude that Banner offers a reasonable return, is financially balanced, and has long-term prospects for increases in market price and payment of cash dividends. With a high profit and high retention of earnings, the firm may be expected to grow rapidly, with an eventual increase in the price of its stock. Since the other ratios reveal that the firm is liquid and profitable, our external analysis indicates that it offers a good buy for the long-term investor.

DETERMINING FINANCIAL NORMS

One of the most difficult aspects of financial analysis is determining the appropriate norms against which an individual firm may be judged. At least five guidelines may be used:

- *Industry norms.* A firm may be compared against the financial ratios of other firms in the same industry. This is only partially satisfactory in most cases because the performance of firms within an industry varies widely from the strongest to the weakest firm in the grouping. Frequently, an average for the industry is of little use because the spread is so wide.
- *Similar firms.* If we compare the firm with similar firms in other industries, we often gain a better insight into its financial condition.
- *Historical trends.* We can compare a firm with itself, or rather with its own performance over a period of time. It is a good sign if the firm is maintaining or increasing its profits and a bad sign if its liquidity is dropping.
- *Future expectations.* Economists and analysts make efforts to forecast conditions in the future. These expectations can be used as norms against which to compare firms today. For example, in three years we may expect a surge of investor confidence and hence an increase in the normal price-earnings ratios. The future ratio can become the norm.
- *Common sense.* This is a guideline that is frequently ignored. If all else fails, we can use subjective judgment and reason. For example, a 2 percent return on investment can never be a norm because it is too low for rational investors. At the same time, a 60 percent ROI is too high. Common sense tells us that 20 percent is more reasonable as a norm.

CONCLUSION

In conclusion, we might perform certain steps to conduct a proper financial analysis. First, use liquidity, profitability, and ownership ratios together to gain a single, overall view of a firm. Then, determine the norms, using a combination of comparative ratios and common sense. Finally, perform further investigation to explain deviations from the norms.

CHAPTER 7 APPENDIXES

How to Apply Financial Analysis

Question 1: A firm has the following. What is its accounts receivable turnover?

Sales	$750,000
Accounts receivable	$94,000
Days in year	365

Answer

Accounts receivables turnover	8.0

Question 2: A firm has the following. What is its inventory turnover using sales and cost of goods sold?

Sales	$225,000
Cost of goods sold	$150,000
Inventory	$55,000

Answer

Inventory turnover using sales	4.1
Inventory turnover using cost of goods sold	2.7

Question 3: A firm has the following. How much can it have in current liabilities and still achieve its target current ratio?

Cash	$7,000
Receivables	$45,000
Inventories	$62,000
Target current ratio	3

Answer

Current assets	$114,000
Divided by target current ratio	3
Current liabilities	$38,000

Question 4: A firm has the following. Management has set a target goal for inventory turnover. How much is the inventory over or under the target?

Inventory	$80,000
Cost of goods sold	$150,000
Target inventory turnover	2

Answer

Target inventory	$75,000
Amount over	$5,000

Question 5: A firm has the following. What is its ROI?

Profit margin	12%
Asset turnover	3

Answer

Return on investment	36%

Question 6: A firm has the following. What are its sales?

Earnings before interest and taxes	$18,000
Assets	$50,000
Asset turnover	3

Answer

Sales	$150,000

Question 7: A firm has the following. What are its gross profit margin and profit margin?

Sales	$375,000
Cost of goods sold	$210,000
General and administrative expenses	$65,000

Answer

Gross profit margin	44%
Profit margin	27%

Question 8: A firm has the following. What is its ROE?

Earnings before interest and taxes	$23,500
Interest	$12,000
Taxes	$7,600
Assets	$110,000
Liabilities	$30,000

Answer

Net income	$3,900
Equity	$80,000
Return on equity	4.9%

Question 9: A firm has the following. What is the P/E ratio?

Net income	$13,500
Shares outstanding	5,000
Market price	$32.50

Answer

Earnings per share	$2.70
Price-earnings ratio	12

Question 10: A firm has the following. What is its debt-equity ratio? What is its debt-asset ratio?

Current liabilities	$12,500
Mortgage	$20,000
Unsecured long-term debt	$22,500
Equity	$65,000

Answer

Total debt	$55,000
Total assets	$120,000
Debt-equity ratio	85%
Debt-asset ratio	46%

Question 11: A firm has the following. What is its dividend yield? What is its dividend payout?

Net income	$300
Cash dividends	$120
Shares outstanding	60
Market price	$25.00

Answer

Dividends per share	$2.00
Earnings per share	$5.00
Dividend yield	8.0%
Dividend payout	40.0%

How to Use Ratios to Assess the Financial Position of a Firm

The Century Recreation Company has the income statement and balance sheet shown in Exhibits 7-1 and 7-2. The norms for this industry are shown in Exhibit 7-3. Using ratio analysis, is this a strong or a weak firm? Once again, different appetites for risk might produce different answers.

Exhibit 7-1. Century Income Statement.

Revenues	$110,000
Cost of services	81,400
Gross margin	$28,600
General and administrative expenses	17,908
Operating income	$10,692
Less interest	6,069
Earnings before taxes	$4,623
Less federal income tax 25%	1,156
Net income	**$3,467**
Dividends	$2,600

Exhibit 7-2. Century Balance Sheet.

Cash and short-term holdings	$2,200
Accounts receivable	26,400
Inventories	30,800
Other current assets	4,620
Depreciable fixed assets	116,895
Land and real estate	29,550
Total Assets	**$210,465**
Payables	$14,652
Short-term secured debt	2,198
Other current liabilities	879
Secured long-term debt	37,444
Unsecured long-term debt	73,892
Contributed capital	26,000
Retained earnings	55,400
Total Liabilities and Equity	**$210,465**

Exhibit 7-3. Industry Norms.

Current ratio	3.5
Acid test ratio	1.7
Accounts receivable turnover	8.0
Inventory turnover (sales)	6.0
Inventory turnover (cost of goods sold)	3.4
Profit margin	20%
Asset turnover	110%
Return on investment	23%
Return on equity	16%
Earning power	11%

Analysis of Ratios.

Ratio	Formula	Calculation	Norm	Exception
Current ratio	CA/CL	3.6	3.5	No
Acid test ratio	(CA - Inv)/CL	1.6	1.7	Yes
Receivables turnover	Sales/AR	4.2	8.0	Yes
Inventory turnover	Sales/Inv.	3.6	6.0	Yes
Inventory turnover	Cost of goods sold/Inv.	2.6	3.4	Yes
Profit margin	EBIT/Sales	9.7%	20.0%	Yes
Asset turnover	Sales/Assets	52.3%	110.0%	Yes
ROI	EBIT/Assets	5.1%	23.0%	Yes
ROE	Net Income/Equity	4.3%	16.0%	Yes
Earning power	Net Income/Assets	1.6%	11.0%	Yes

Assessment from Ratio Analysis. With receivables being slow to turn over and the same situation for inventory, liquidity problems could arise in the future.

The low return on investment is the result of both a low profit margin and a low asset turnover compared to the norms. This explains the low return on investment, return on equity, and earning power

Ratio analysis reveals both liquidity and profitability symptoms of stress. Further analysis is needed to find the sources of the numbers and assess whether the firm is as weak as the ratios seem to indicate.

Part 4 | Relationship of Risk and Return

We have to go back in history only to the early twentieth century to find a period when people had an inadequate grasp of the nature of risk. Assessment tools simply did not exist. Investment decisions were loosely based on a belief that money would be returned to the investor at some point in the future. Accompanying the lack of analytical tools, the time value of money was not considered. The sun rose and the sun set. This situation continues today in many areas of the world. People hoard gold and earn no return. They exchange currency outside of financial institutions and fail to invest it to build economic systems.

In contrast, modern business knows that in some periods, capital can be invested to earn massive returns as individuals and firms speculate in frenzied markets. At other times, the opportunities are quite limited. The firm should conserve capital; avoid high-risk, low-return investments; and wait until conditions improve. An understanding of risk and return is built upon two foundations:

- *Time value of money.* The financing of business ventures encourages us to calculate the costs of funding. As a simple example, how can we assess leverage in profit planning if we cannot determine the cost of debt? In the first chapter in Part IV, we examine the mathematics of short-term and intermediate-term financing. We develop the amortization schedule, which, we will see, plays a key role in assessing the return from capital investments.

- *Linkage of risk and return.* Our understanding of risk and return improved in the 1960s and 1970s with the pioneering work of three professors: Joel Dean in the area of capital budgeting, Harry Markowitz with modern portfolio theory, and William

Sharpe with the capital asset pricing model. Their work, and the work of those who followed them, provides our understanding of how firms make investment decisions. In our discussion, we create a framework for matching expected returns with the appetite for risk.

The two chapters in Part IV focus on the role of risk in investment decisions. They provide the foundation for maximizing the power of the capital budgeting process in the subsequent chapters.

Chapter
8

Time Value of Money

A firm or nonprofit organization derives its financing from a number of sources. Funds are provided by suppliers, creditors, owners, and customers. Some funds have a direct cost, as is the case with a bank loan, where interest is charged. Some funds have an indirect cost, as with capital supplied by owners, who eventually expect a return on their investment. Some funds have no cost at all, such as when the organization delays payment to a supplier who does not charge interest or a late fee.

In this chapter, we calculate the rate of return on investments and the effective cost of borrowing. Techniques using the time value of money are covered for different financing or investment vehicles. The format of an electronic spreadsheet to perform the calculations is integrated throughout the chapter.

SHORT-TERM FINANCING

Most organizations take advantage of some form of short-term financing. The firm can borrow for periods of a day to a year to achieve a number of goals. Flexibility is achieved when a short-term loan allows the organization to match funds against a seasonal or other cyclical need. Also, short-term sources can provide low-cost financing or can expand the total amount of money available to conduct operations. In this section, we will examine the characteristics and cost of funds provided from different short-term sources.

Sources of Short-Term Funds

The following sources routinely provide funds for businesses and nonprofit organizations:

- *Accounts payable.* These are created when a firm purchases raw materials, supplies, or other items on credit without signing a formal note. A payable is a form of unsecured financing, since no specific assets are pledged as collateral for the liability. Payables are an interest-free source of funds, since no interest is charged as long as the accounts are not overdue.
- *Accruals.* These are liabilities that occur when services have been received but payment has not been made. Typical accruals are wages payable and taxes payable.

Employees may work for up to one month and taxes may be owed for two weeks or more before being paid. In each case, the firm has the use of the money until payment is made. Like payables, accruals are interest-free.

- *Unsecured loans.* Banks and other financial institutions lend money to assist organizations in meeting cyclical needs. Two kinds of loans are common: (1) the single-payment note and (2) the line of credit. The cost of each of these will be covered in turn.

Amount Due on a Single-Payment Note

A *single-payment note* exists when a loan is repayable with interest at a specified time and maturity, often within 30 to 90 days. A *note* is a legal instrument that is signed by the borrower as proof of the existence of the debt. If the loan is made by a bank, a compensating balance and fees may be involved. A *compensating balance* is a requirement that the borrower maintain a stipulated portion, generally between 5 and 15 percent, of the outstanding loan balance in a demand deposit account at the lending institution. This forces the borrower to be a customer of the institution; it also raises the effective cost of the loan. A *fee* is a charge for approving the loan. It is frequently paid when the loan is accepted and ranges from ½ to 1 percent of the loan balance.

Figure 8-1 shows an approach to calculating the amount due on a single-payment note. The formula is:

$$FV = PV*(1+Int)^N$$

where FV = future value, or the amount owed at maturity
PV = present value, or the amount of the loan
Int = the annual rate of interest
N = the number of periods

Note that the figure shows three different amounts due, depending upon the compounding assumption:

- *Annual compounding.* If the loan assumes annual compounding, the period is expressed as a portion of a year, and the annual interest rate is used. The time period is 0.25 (90/365) of a year, and the rate is 12 percent. This produces a future value (amount due) of $102,834.
- *Periodic compounding (days in year over days of loan).* If the loan assumes compounding during a period equal to the loan period, the period is expressed as 1 and a periodic rate is used. This is calculated by multiplying the annual rate by the period, or 0.12 times 90/365. This produces a future value of $102,959.
- *Daily compounding.* If the loan assumes daily compounding, the period is expressed in terms of days and a daily interest rate is used. The number of time periods is 90, and the rate is 0.0003 (0.12/365). This produces a future value of $103,003.

Effective Cost of a Single-Payment Note

The actual or effective cost of a loan may be calculated by the formula:

$$Annual\ Cost = ((FV/PV)^{(1/N)})-1)*Periods\ in\ Year$$

The basic formula gives the rate or effective cost for the period of the loan. This is then multiplied by the number of periods in a year to get the annual rate. With annual compounding, the basic formula is multiplied by one. With periodic compounding, it is multiplied by the number of days in a year divided by the number of days of the loan. For daily compounding, it is multiplied by 365. Figure 8-2 shows the effective cost under each assumption.

Effect of a Compensating Balance

If a loan requires a compensating balance, the effective cost of the loan is raised. To calculate the annual rate, the amount of the loan and the amount due are both reduced by the compensating balance requirement. This correctly reflects the fact that the borrower does not have access to a portion of the loan and hence is paying the full amount of interest to use less than the face amount of the loan. As an example, consider the effect on the loan in

		Col. B	Col. C	Col. D	Col. E	Col. F	Col. G
Row Loan Data:							
6	Amount			$100,000			
7	Days of loan			90			
8	Days in year			365			
9	Rate			12.0%			
10	**Annual compounding**						
11				**Periods**	**Rate**	**Loan**	**Due**
12	Data			0.25	12.0%	$100,000	
13	Solution						$102,834
14	**Compounding by Days in Year/Days of Loan**						
15				**Periods**	**Rate**	**Loan**	**Due**
16	Data			1	3.0%	$100,000	
17	Solution						$102,959
18	**Compounding Daily**						
19				**Periods**	**Rate**	**Loan**	**Due**
20	Data			90	0.03%	$100,000	
21	Solution						$103,003

Formula: $FV = PV*(1+Int)^N$

Cell	Formula
G13	=F12*(1+E12)^D12
G17	=F16*(1+E16)^D16
G21	=F20*(1+E20)^D20

Figure 8-1. Solving for Amount Due on Single-Payment Note.

Figure 8-2 of a 10 percent compensating balance requirement. The borrower can use only $90,000 but still must pay $1,000 interest. The numbers become:

Amount	$90,000
Days of the loan	60
Amount due at maturity	$91,000

With annual compounding, the rate becomes 7 percent.

Effect of Fees Paid in Advance

Many lending arrangements require the borrower to pay a fee at the time the loan is received. In this case, the fee reduces the amount available, but the full amount must be repaid at maturity. This raises the effective cost. To illustrate this with the data in Figure

	Col. B	Col. C	Col. D	Col. E	Col. F	Col. G
Row Loan Data:						
31	Amount		$100,000			
32	Days of loan		60			
33	Days in year		365			
34	Amount due		$101,000			
35	**Annual Compounding**					
36			Periods	Rate	Loan	Due
37	Data		0.16		$100,000	$101,000
38	Solution			6.2%		
39	**Compounding by Days in Year/Days of Loan**					
40			Periods	Rate	Loan	Due
41	Data		1.00		$100,000	$101,000
42	Solution			6.1%		
43	**Compounding Daily**					
44			Periods	Rate	Loan	Due
45	Data		60.00		$100,000	$101,000
46	Solution			6.1%		

Formula: Rate = ((FV/PV)^(1/N)-1*Compounding Factor

Cell	Formula
E38	=((G37/F37)^(1/D37)-1)
E42	=((G41/F41)^(1/D41)-1)*D33/D32
E46	=((G45/F45)^(1/D45)-1)*D33

Figure 8-2. Solving for the Effective Cost of a Single-Payment Note.

8-2, consider the effects of a 1 percent fee payable in advance but no compensating balance. The numbers become:

Amount	$99,000
Days of the loan	60
Amount due at maturity	$101,000

With annual compounding, the rate becomes 12.9 percent. The large jump from the original 6.2 percent reflects the impact of a 1 percent fee for a 60-day loan.

INTERMEDIATE-TERM FINANCING

Intermediate-term financing may be viewed as borrowings with maturities greater than one year but less than five to seven years. Two types are common:

- *Revolving credit agreement.* This is a line of credit from a bank or other financial institution where funds are available on demand over a specified future period of time, say, three years. The maximum amount of the line and the rate are spelled out in the original agreement.
- *Term loan.* This is a loan from a financial institution that is repayable in fixed installments over a period of time.

In this section, we will examine the repayment schedules for revolving credit agreements and term loans under fixed- and variable-rate interest assumptions.

Key Terms

Several key terms are important when discussing intermediate-term financing:

- *Fixed-rate loan.* This exists when the stated interest rate does not change during the period of the loan.
- *Variable- or floating-rate loan.* This occurs when the interest rate is tied to some money market indicator, and interest charges vary as the indicator rises or falls. The *prime rate* is a widely published bank lending rate that is used in the United States as a money market indicator. Each bank publishes its own prime rate and ties its loans to that rate. Outside the United States, the London Interbank Offered Rate (LIBOR) is commonly used as a money market indicator.
- *Amortization.* This refers to the process of reducing the principal on a loan through a series of periodic payments to the lender. If the entire loan is paid off through the periodic payments, we say that the loan is *fully amortized*.
- *Payout period.* This is the length of time that it takes to fully amortize the loan. If the loan period is less than the payout period, the loan will require a *balloon payment*, which is defined as a final payment that is significantly larger than the periodic payments. As an example, a firm may be offered a three-year loan with a seven-year payout. This means that the periodic payments will be calculated as though the loan were made for seven years. The actual loan will be for three years with a balloon payment.

- *Caps, floors, and covenants.* Several technical terms may be contained in the loan agreement. A *cap* is a maximum rate that may be charged on a variable-rate loan. As an example, a loan may have a rate of prime plus 2 with a cap of 18 percent. If, during the life of the loan, the prime rate exceeds 16 percent, interest will be calculated based on the cap of 18 percent. A *floor* is a minimum rate on a loan. If the prime plus 2 loan had a floor of 12 percent and prime dropped to 9 percent, the 12 percent floor would be used in calculating interest. A *covenant* is a stipulation in a loan agreement whereby the borrower makes some formal promise to the lender. For example, a working capital covenant might require the borrower to maintain a minimum balance in a checking account. Covenants are sought by lenders to increase the likelihood of payment and are spelled out in the loan agreement.

The Periodic Loan Payment

An *annuity* exists when a firm has a series of equal cash receipts or payments that occur at the end of successive periods of equal duration. Thus, a loan payment of $12,000 a month for 36 months is an annuity of $12,000. In the case of a loan, each periodic payment usually contains some interest as well as an amount to retire the original principal. When a loan is repaid with an annuity, it is a *steady payment loan*.

A time value of money formula can be used to examine the relationship between the amount borrowed and the payments needed to retire the loan. The formula is:

PMT = (PV*Int)/(1-(1/(1+Int)^N))

Figure 8-3 shows the calculation of a periodic loan payment. With a loan amount of $100,000 for 36 months and an annual interest rate of 14 percent, the periodic payment is calculated with a rate of 1.17 percent (0.14/12) as follows:

	Col. B	Col. C	Col. D	Col. E	Col. F	Col. G
Row Loan Data:						
56	Amount		$100,000			
57	Periods of loan		36			
58	Periods in year		12			
59	Annual rate		14.0%			
60			**Periods**	**Rate**	**Loan**	**Payment**
61	Data		36	1.17%	$100,000	
62	Solution					$3,418

Formula:

PMT	=(PV*Int)/(1-(1/(1+Int)^N))
G62	=(F61*E61)/(1-(1/(1+E61)^D61))

Figure 8-3. Calculating a Periodic Loan Payment.

$$(100,000*0.0117)/(1-(1/(1+0.0117)^{\wedge}36)) = 3,418$$

Built-In Payment Function in Spreadsheets

Electronic spreadsheets offer a built-in payment function that simplifies the calculation of the periodic loan payment. It might take the form @PMT(Principal, Interest, Periods), =PMT(Principal, Periods, Interest), or some other form. Let us assume that our spreadsheet uses the @PMT format. In Figure 8-3, the principal is found at D56, the interest is at D59, and the periods are at D57. At G62, our spreadsheet calculates the payment with the entry

$$@PMT(D56,D57,D59/D58)$$

THE AMORTIZATION SCHEDULE

An *amortization schedule* is a listing over time of all payments, interest amounts, principal reductions, and ending balances for a loan. If the ending balance in the final period is zero, the schedule represents a loan that is fully amortized over the period.

Figure 8-4 shows an amortization schedule in which $100,000 is borrowed and repaid over a four-year period with a variable annual interest rate.

	Col. B	Col. C	Col. D	Col. E	Col. F	Col. G
Row Loan Data:						
70	Amount		$100,000			
71	Periods of loan		6			
	Amortization Schedule					
73			Period 1	Period 2	Period 3	Period 4
74	Periods remaining		6	5	4	3
75	Rate		15.0%	13.0%	11.0%	12.0%
76	Payment		$26,424	$25,184	$24,145	$24,566
77	Interest portion		$15,000	$11,515	$8,240	$7,080
78	Principal portion		$11,424	$13,669	$15,905	$17,485
79	Ending balance		$88,576	$74,908	$59,003	$41,517

Formulas: The formulas for Column D, which are parallel to the formulas in columns E, F, and G, are:

PMT	=(PV*Int)/(1-(1/(1+Int)^N))
D76	=(D70*D75)/(1-(1/(1+D75)^D71))
D77	=D70*D75
D78	=D76-D77
D79	=D70-D78

Figure 8-4. Amortization Schedule, Variable-Rate Loan.

Important Characteristics of Amortization Schedules

Some important characteristics of the schedule in Figure 8-4 are:

- *Periods remaining.* The schedule is set up so that the payout period can differ from the periods of the loan. The loan period is shown as four years, but the loan is being amortized over six years. A balloon payment will be required, since the loan period ends with a positive ending balance.
- *Fixed- or variable-rate loans.* The schedule shows the number of periods remaining on row 74. This year-by-year breakdown allows the schedule to be used for variable-rate loans, where each payment is calculated based on a new interest rate and the periods remaining. That is, the payments on row 76 are calculated in each column using the ending balance from the prior period, the interest rate for the current period, and the number of periods remaining.
- *Annual compounding.* The schedule is set up for compounding periodically. Since annual interest is given, the compounding must be annual. For other periods, an adjustment must be made. As an example, for monthly payments and compounding, the annual interest would have to be divided by 12 and the periods would be multiplied by 12, so that the schedule would have 48 periods.
- *Not fully amortizing.* The schedule finishes with a positive ending balance in period 4. Thus, the loan in this schedule is not fully amortizing.

Balloon Payment

An amortization schedule offers a straightforward method of calculating a balloon payment, as was illustrated in Figure 8-4. Another approach to calculating the balloon payment uses a four-step process, as is illustrated in Figure 8-5. The steps are:

- *Calculate periodic payment.* Using the built-in payment function, calculate the payment that would fully amortize the loan. In our example of a $100,000 loan, let us fix the interest at 15 percent for the 6 years and calculate the payment. This is shown to be $26,424 in Figure 8-5, with the formula for position D98 also shown.
- *Calculate the future value of the loan with no payments.* Take the original loan and determine its increase in value if no payments were made. For our loan, the future value is $174,901 at G101. The formula from Figure 8-1 is:

$$FV = PV*(1+Int)^N$$

- *Calculate the future value of payments.* Take the periodic payment and determine the value of a stream of payments at the end of the loan period. The future value in four years for our loan is $131,943 at G102. The formula is:

$$FV = PMT*(((1+Int)^N-1)/Int)$$

- *Subtract the future value of payments from the future value of the loan amount.* The difference is the balloon payment of $42,957 at G103.

	Col. B	Col. C	Col. D	Col. E	Col. F	Col. G
Row Loan Data:						
90	Amount		$100,000			
91	Periods		4			
92	Rate		15.0%			
93	Payout period		6			
94	Initial fee		0			
95	Compensating balance		0			
96	**Calculating Balloon Payment**					
97			**Period 1**	**Period 2**	**Period 3**	**Period 4**
98	Payment		$26,424	$26,424	$26,424	$26,424
99	Initial fee		0			
100	Compensating balance		0			
101	FV, principal					$174,901
102	FV, payments					$131,943
103	**Balloon payment**					**$42,957**

Formulas:

D98	=(D90*D92)/(1-(1/(1+D92)^D93))
G101	=D90*(1+D92)^D91
G102	=D98*(((1+D92)^D91-1)/D92)
G103	=G101-G102

Figure 8-5. Calculating a Balloon Payment, Fixed-Rate Loan.

Effective Cost with Fees and Balances

When a loan agreement calls for fees or compensating balances, the effective cost analysis must recognize the impact of each item. A *fee* is a charge made by a lender to guarantee the availability of funds or to cover the costs of approving a loan. It is normally paid up front; that is, it is paid on the date the loan is made. It commonly ranges from 1/2 to 1 percent of the amount of the loan.

A *compensating balance* is a requirement to maintain a stipulated portion, normally 5 to 20 percent, of the loan balance in a non-interest-bearing account at the lending institution. The effect of this requirement is to reduce the available funds from the borrowing; hence, the effective cost of the loan is increased.

The compensating balance may be required on the exercised portion of the loan, which is defined as the principal amount outstanding. Some loan agreements require a compensating balance on the total approved amount of the loan, whether it is fully exercised or not.

Figure 8-6 shows the calculation of the effective cost for a loan with a ½ percent fee and a 10 percent compensating balance. The loan is similar to the one in Figure 8-5. In this example, the borrower actually receives $89,500. He makes four payments of $26,424 plus a balloon payment of $42,957 at the end of the fourth period. The effective cost is calculated at D126 using the built-in internal rate of return formula. The 15 percent loan has an effective cost of 17.3 percent once the fee and compensating balance requirement are included.

Effective Cost, Interest-Only Loans

Figure 8-7 shows a variation of the loan in Figure 8-6. Instead of paying principal and interest each period, however, only interest is charged. At the end of period 4, the full original principal is due along with the last period's interest. The effective cost drops to 16.9 percent as compared to the first loan. This is the case because the principal is not being repaid. More funds are available during the loan period with the interest-only loan. Thus, the added costs associated with fees and compensating balance on the full principal are not as great as with an amortizing loan.

Effective Cost, Standby Financing

In many cases, a borrower arranges financing that will not be fully used. Such an arrangement is called *standby financing*. In addition to borrowed funds, it provides a

Row Loan Data:	Col. B	Col. C	Col. D	Col. E	Col. F	Col. G
113	Amount		$100,000			
114	Periods		4			
115	Rate		15.0%			
116	Payout period		6			
117	Initial fee		0.5%			
118	Compensating balance		10%			
119	Calculating effective cost					
120		Period 0	Period 1	Period 2	Period 3	Period 4
121	Cash	$100,000	-$26,424	-$26,424	-$26,424	-$26,424
122	Fee	-$500				
123	Compensating balance	-$10,000				$10,000
124	Balloon payment					-$42,957
125	Cash flow	$89,500	-$26,424	-$26,424	-$26,424	-$59,381
126	**Effective cost**		17.3%			

Formula:

D126	=IRR(C125:G125)

Figure 8-6. Effective Costs with Fees and Balances.

backup source of funds for contingency or opportunity purposes. The effective cost of such financing is heavily affected by fees and compensating balances. This is also shown in Figure 8-7, where we assume that the borrower will use only 60 percent of the loan, but where a compensating balance is required on the full approved amount. The effective cost has risen to 18.4 percent.

CONCLUSION

Time value of money techniques can fit any financing schemes developed by lenders or borrowers. We simply adjust the receipts and payments of cash for the timing and compounding assumptions to calculate the effective cost of the financing.

	Col. B	Col. C	Col. D	Col. E	Col. F	Col. G
Row Loan Data:						
133	Amount		$100,000			
134	Periods		4			
135	Rate		15.0%			
136	Payout period		6			
137	Initial fee		0.5%			
138	Compensating balance		10%			
139	**Interest-Only Payments, 100 Percent Usage**					
140		Period 0	Period 1	Period 2	Period 3	Period 4
141	Cash	$100,000	-$15,000	-$15,000	-$15,000	-$15,000
142	Fee	-$500				
143	Compensating balance	-$10,000				$10,000
144	Balloon payment					-$100,000
145	Cash flow	$89,500	-$15,000	-$15,000	-$15,000	-$105,000
146	**Effective cost**		16.9%			
147	**Interest-Only Payments, Not Full Usage**					
148		Period 0	Period 1	Period 2	Period 3	Period 4
149	Usage	60.0%				
150	Cash	$60,000	-$9,000	-$9,000	-$9,000	-$9,000
151	Fee	-$500				
152	Compensating balance	-$10,000				$10,000
153	Balloon payment					-$60,000
154	Cash flow	$49,500	-$9,000	-$9,000	-$9,000	-$59,000
155	**Effective cost**		18.4%			

Figure 8-7. Effective Cost, Interest-Only Payments.

CHAPTER 8 APPENDIXES

How to Understand Risk in Borrowing or Lending Arrangements

1. Amount Due on a Single-Payment Note

A loan has the following data. What is the amount due on this single-payment note with each compounding assumption?

Loan Data

Amount	$300,000
Days of loan	75
Days in year	365
Rate	10.0%

Answers

Annual Compounding

	Periods	Rate	Loan	Due
Data	0.21	10.0%	$300,000	
Solution				$305,933

Compounding by Days in Year/Days of Loan

	Periods	Rate	Loan	Due
Data	1	2.1%	$300,000	
Solution				$306,164

Daily Compounding

	Periods	Rate	Loan	Due
Data	75	0.03%	$300,000	
Solution				$306,227

2. Effective Cost of a Single-Payment Note

A single-payment note has the following data. What is the effective cost with each compounding assumption?

Loan Data

Amount	$300,000
Days of loan	120
Days in year	365
Amount due	$307,890

Answers

Annual Compounding

	Periods	Rate	Loan	Due
Data	0.33		$300,000	$307,890
Solution		8.2%		

Compounding by Days in Year/Days of Loan

	Periods	Rate	Loan	Due
Data	1.00		$300,000	$307,890
Solution		8.0%		

Compounding Daily

	Periods	Rate	Loan	Due
Data	120.00		$300,000	$307,890
Solution		7.9%		

3. Calculating the Periodic Payment on a Loan

A loan has the following data. What is the periodic payment?

Loan Data

Amount	$300,000
Periods of loan	24
Periods in year	4
Annual rate	14.0%

Answer

	Periods	Rate	Loan	Payment
Data	24	3.50%	$300,000	
Solution				$18,682

4. Preparing an Amortization Schedule for a Loan

A four-year variable-rate loan has the following data. Complete the amortization schedule.

Loan Data

Amount	$300,000
Periods of loan	8
Interest rates:	
Year 1	15%
Year 2	13%

Year 3	11%
Year 4	12%

Answer

	Period 1	Period 2	Period 3	Period 4
Periods remaining	8	7	6	5
Rate	15.0%	13.0%	11.0%	12.0%
Payment	$66,855	$62,892	$59,428	$60,930
Interest portion	$45,000	$36,159	$27,655	$26,357
Principal portion	$21,855	$26,733	$31,773	$34,573
Ending balance	$278,145	$251,412	$219,640	$185,066

5. Calculating a Balloon Payment

Using the following data, calculate the balloon payment at the end of the four periods.

Loan Data

Amount	$300,000
Periods	4
Rate	15.0%
Payout period	7

Answer

	Period 1	Period 2	Period 3	Period 4
Payment	$72,108	$72,108	$72,108	$72,108
FV, principal				$524,702
FV, payments				$360,063
Balloon payment				$164,639

Formulas:

FV, principal	Loan Bal*(1+Periodic Rate)^Periods
FV, payments	Payment*(((1+Periodic Rate)^Periods-1)/Payment)
Balloon payment	FV Principal - FV Payments

6. Effective Cost of Loan with Fees and Balloon Payment

A loan has the following data. What is the effective cost of the loan with the impact of fees and a compensating balance?

Loan Data

Amount	$300,000
Periods	4
Rate	7.0%

Payout period		5
Initial fee		1.0%
Compensating balance		10.0%

Answer

	Period 0	Period 1	Period 2	Period 3	Period 4
Cash	$300,000	-$73,167	-$73,167	-$73,167	-$73,167
Fee	-$3,000				
Compensating Balance	-$30,000				$30,000
FV, principal					$393,239
FV, payments					-$324,858
Balloon					-$68,381
Cash flow	$267,000	-$73,167	-$73,167	-$73,167	-$111,548
Effective cost	8.6%				

Formulas:

FV, payments	Loan Bal*(1+Periodic Rate)^Periods
Balloon	Payment*(((1+Periodic Rate)^Periods-1)/Payment)
Cash flow	FV Principal-FV Payments
Effective cost	Spreadsheet function =IRR(cash flow stream)

7. Effective Cost of Loan with Interest-Only Payments

A loan has the following data. It requires interest-only payments. What is the effective cost of the loan?

Loan Data

Amount	$300,000
Periods	4
Rate	11%
Payout period	9
Initial fee	1.0%
Compensating balance	10.0%

Answer

Interest-only payments, 100 percent usage:

	Period 0	Period 1	Period 2	Period 3	Period 4
Cash	$300,000	-$33,000	-$33,000	-$33,000	-$33,000
Fee	-$3,000				
Compensating balance	-$30,000				$30,000
Balloon payment					-$300,000
Cash flow	$267,000	-$33,000	-$33,000	-$33,000	-$303,000
Effective cost	12.6%				

Formula:

Effective cost	Spreadsheet function =IRR(cash flow stream)

8. Effective Cost of Loan Without Full Usage

For the loan in the previous exercise, what is the new effective cost if the usage drops to 60 percent?

Answer

	Period 0	Period 1	Period 2	Period 3	Period 4
Cash	$180,000	-$19,800	-$19,800	-$19,800	-$19,800
Fee	-$3,000				
Compensating balance	-$30,000				$30,000
Balloon payment					-$180,000
Cash flow	$147,000	-$19,800	-$19,800	-$19,800	-$169,800
Effective cost	13.9%				

Formula:

Effective cost	Spreadsheet function =IRR(cash flow stream)

How to Compare Sources of Long-Term Financing

Weldon Manufacturing Company is seeking financing for a new operation. The major costs to be capitalized totaled just over $9 million, as follows:

Item	Installed Cost
Machinery	$6,300,000
Support equipment	1,600,000
Facility renovation	1,600,000
Total	$9,500,000

The company budgeted 10 percent for contingencies.
    Weldon identified three sources of financing.

- A bond offering for four years. The bond would require annual interest payments at a coupon rate of 15.5 percent. Investment bankers would receive 2 percent of the offering as a commission.
- A bank loan with variable-rate interest payments at prime, compounded quarterly and paid quarterly. The bank would charge a $100,000 fee upon approval, and Weldon Manufacturing would have to maintain a 10 percent compensating balance in a transactions account. The period would be four years with a seven-year payout. Prime would probably average 14 percent over the loan period.
- A variable-rate loan from a Transamerica financing subsidiary at 3 percent above the one-year Treasury bill rate, compounded and paid annually. The loan period would be four years with an eight-year payout. The Treasury bill rate for the next year is expected to average 11 to 13 percent.

To calculate the periodic cost for quarterly compounding, the firm used a spreadsheet with 16 columns and the built-in IRR function.

Question: Which method is preferred?

Answer. Because of the lower interest rate, the bank financing is the lowest-cost alternative. (See the solutions that follow.) The lower rate offsets the fee and compensating balance requirement.

Solutions

Data

Project cost	$9,500
Contingency	10%

Financing 1: Bond

Bond Data

Periods	4
Rate	15.5%
Payout period	4
Fee	2%
Compensating balance	0%

Bond Face Value

Project	$9,500
Contingency	$950
Fee	$209
Bond face value	$10,659

Effective Cost

	Period 0	Period 1	Period 2	Period 3	Period 4
Bond	$10,659				
Annual interest		-$1,652	-$1,652	-$1,652	-$1,652
Compensating balance	0				0
Balloon payment					-$10,659
Cash flow	$10,659	-$1,652	-$1,652	-$1,652	-$12,311
Effective cost	15.5%				

Formula:

Effective cost	Spreadsheet function =IRR(cash flow stream)

Financing 2: Bank Loan

Loan Data

Project	$9,500
Contingency	10%
Years of loan	4
Periods in year	4
Payout period in years	7
Annual rate	14%
Initial fee	$100
Compensating balance	10%

Loan Balance

Desired financing	$10,450
Compensating balance	$1,045
Borrow the fee	$100
Loan balance	$11,595

Periodic Payment

Periods	28
Periodic rate	3.5%
Periodic payment	$656

Formula:

Periodic payment	(Loan Bal*Periodic Rate)/(1-(1/(1+Periodic rate)^Periods))

Balloon Payment

Payment	$656
Loan periods	16
FV, principal	$20,106
FV, payments	$13,763
Balloon payment	$6,342

Formulas:

FV, principal	Loan Bal*(1+Periodic Rate)^Periods
FV, payments	Payment*(((1+Periodic Rate)^Periods-1)/Payment)
Balloon payment	FV Principal–FV Payments

Effective Cost

Hint: To calculate periodic cost, use a spreadsheet with 16 columns and the built-in IRR function. The 16 columns would use the following numbers.

	Period 0	Period 1	Period 2	Period 3	Period 4
	$11,595	-$656	-$656	-$656	-$656
		Period 5	**Period 6**	**Period 7**	**Period 8**
		-$656	-$656	-$656	-$656
		Period 9	**Period 10**	**Period 11**	**Period 12**
		-$656	-$656	-$656	-$656
		Period 13	**Period 14**	**Period 15**	**Period 16**
Cash		-$656	-$656	-$656	-$656
Balloon payment					-$6,342
Cash with balloon					-$6,998

The effective cost is calculated by multiplying the periodic cost by the number of periods in a year.

Periodic cost	-3.5%
Periods in year	4
Effective cost	-14.0%

Financing 3: Floating-Rate Financing

Loan Data

Periods	4
Rate	15%
Payout period	8

Annual Payment

Project	$9,500
Contingency	$950
Financing needed	$10,450
Payment	$2,329

Formula	(Loan Bal*Periodic Rate)/(1-(1/(1+Periodic Rate)^Periods))

Balloon Payment

Loan period	4
FV, principal	$18,277
FV, payments	$11,628
Balloon payment	$6,649

Formulas

FV, principal	Loan Bal*(1+Periodic Rate)^Periods
FV, payments	Payment*(((1+Periodic Rate)^Periods-1)/Payment)
Balloon payment	FV Principal-FV Payments

Effective Cost

	Period 0	Period 1	Period 2	Period 3	Period 4
Cash	$10,450	-$2,329	-$2,329	-$2,329	-$2,329
Balloon payment					-$6,649
Cash flow	$10,450	-$2,329	-$2,329	-$2,329	-$8,977
Effective cost	15.0%				

Formula

Effective cost	Spreadsheet function =IRR(cash flow stream)

Chapter
9
Risk and Required Return

The relationship between risk and return is developed in a framework called the *capital asset pricing model*. The model offers a theory and a methodology for evaluating any investment decision in which capital is committed for the purpose of earning future profits. The model was first proposed domestically in the United States by Sharpe, Lintner, Miller, and Modigliani, and then by others in the 1960s, and is fully developed today.

In its purest form, the capital asset pricing model is a comprehensive theory of risk and return relationships in perfect markets. It makes such assumptions as rational behavior on the part of all investors; a highly competitive environment for investing, where all investors know the risks and expected returns of all investments; no fees, commissions, or taxes; and no risk of bankruptcy. Within the confines of these restrictive assumptions, a risk-return relationship is developed in considerable detail. In perfect markets, such as those assumed by the model, there is no quarreling with capital asset theory. It is a conceptually correct approach to risk and return.

In most settings, however, we are seeking the required return in imperfect markets. Not all information is known. Not all investors are rational, nor do they all have equal access to all markets. Bankruptcy is a daily possibility and occurrence. How does the capital asset theory hold up under such circumstances? The answer is, remarkably well.

In this chapter, we will examine the nature of risk. Then, we will cover risk and required return in the framework of the capital asset pricing model. Finally, we will identify some of the risks facing investing firms.

NATURE OF RISK

Risk may be defined as the likelihood that the actual return from an investment will be less than the expected return. Stated differently, it is the variability of return from the investment. As an example, consider two possible projects, as shown in Figure 9-1:

- *Project A.* This is a machine with a 60 percent likelihood of a 10 percent expected return. There is a 20 percent chance of a 9 percent return, if operating costs rise

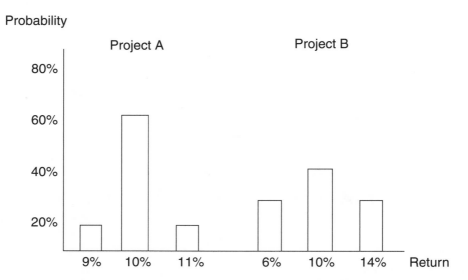

Figure 9-1. Comparison of Dispersion of Returns of Two Investments.

unexpectedly, or a 20 percent chance of an 11 percent return, if operating costs drop unexpectedly.

- *Project B.* This machine is similar and also offers a 10 percent expected return. However, if the level of economic activity is strong, a 30 percent likelihood, the overall return would rise to 14 percent. If economic activity is weak, also a 30 percent likelihood, the overall return would drop to 6 percent.

The two alternatives, shown in Figure 9-1, involve different levels of risk, even though both machines have a 10 percent expected return. Project B is riskier because of the greater variability of return.

Calculation of Expected Return

Project A	20% × 9% + 60% × 10% + 20% × 11% = 10%
Project B	30% × 6% + 40% × 10% + 30% × 14% = 10%

Probability Distributions

The term *probability* refers to an estimate of the frequency of the occurrence of future outcomes. Statisticians and others create *probability distributions* that show a range of such outcomes. Some key terms are:

- *Mean or expected value.* This is the "most likely" or "best" estimate of the return from an investment.
- *Discrete probability distribution.* This is a distribution that has a limited number of identifiable values.
- *Continuous probability distribution.* This is a distribution that can take on all possible numerical values over the range between the highest and lowest values.

- *Normal or bell-shaped distribution.* This is a continuous distribution that has been found to describe accurately many types of frequency data, such as estimates of return from investing in capital and financial assets.

Suppose we have an asset that cost $100,000. We are expecting a rise in its market value to $108,000 in one year. We will receive another cash inflow of $4,000 at the end of the year. The expected return from this portfolio is 12 percent, as follows:

$$E(\text{Return}) = (\$108,000 - \$100,000 + \$4,000)/\$100,000 = 12\%$$

Dispersion of the Return

We expect a 12 percent return from our investment. We can also estimate the likelihood of this return. Suppose we have data from prior investing and have determined that 12 percent is achieved 40 percent of the time. In addition, 20 percent of the time, similar portfolios produced either 8 or 16 percent returns, and 10 percent of the time, returns were 4 or 20 percent. With this information, we have five possible profit levels, as shown in Figure 9-2. This is a discrete probability distribution. As it is a normal probability distribution, it still has a 12 percent expected return.

$$E(\text{Return}) = \$4,000 \times 10\% + \$8,000 \times 20\% + \$12,000 \times 40\% + \$16,000 \times 20\% + \$20,000 \times 10\% = \$12,000 = 12\%$$

Normal Probability Distribution

To illustrate normal probability distributions, consider Figure 9-3. Both investments offer a 14 percent likely return, but the returns for Investment A range from 10 to 16 percent, while Investment B offers a dispersion of returns between 6 and 20 percent.

The probability distribution highlights the fact that expected return is not a point estimate—that is, a single number that can usually be achieved. Rather, it is the center point

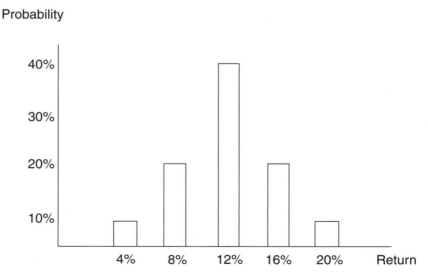

Figure 9-2. Discrete Probability Distribution.

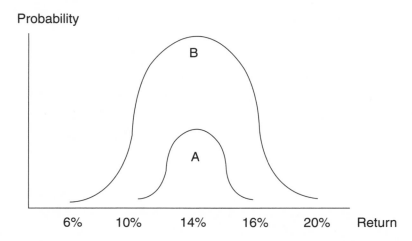

Figure 9-3. Continuous Probability Distributions for Two Investments.

of a range of possible returns. The actual return will rarely be exactly what we estimate. Still, a relationship exists. In low-risk ventures, we will be closer to our estimate than we will be in high-risk ventures. Stated differently, low-risk ventures have tighter probability distributions than high-risk ventures.

Standard Deviation

A *standard deviation* is a measure of the dispersion of returns in a normal probability distribution. A small standard deviation indicates an investment with less risk than similar investments with larger standard deviations.

The standard deviation is particularly useful because *six standard deviations make up virtually the entire range from an investment.* Thus, three standard deviations below the expected return will be the lowest likely return, and three standard deviations above the expected return will be the highest likely return. Figure 9-4 shows the entire range of returns, with the standard deviations on the *y* axis. Alternatively, we can show the same diagram for a specific proposal. As an example, assume that an investment proposal offers an expected return of 15 percent with a standard deviation of 4 percent. What is the entire range of possible returns? The answer is 3 to 27 percent, as shown in Figure 9-5.

Likelihood of Returns

The standard deviation can be used to determine the likelihood of achieving returns other than the expected return. This works because we know the probability of the occurrence of returns within given distances from the expected return. As an example, Figure 9-4 shows that approximately 68 percent of all returns occur within plus or minus one standard deviation from the expected value. Half of all possibilities occur above the midpoint and half occur below it, so 34.13 percent occur within one standard deviation above the midpoint and another 34.13 percent occur within one standard deviation below the midpoint. If a return is close to the expected return, it is more likely to occur than a return

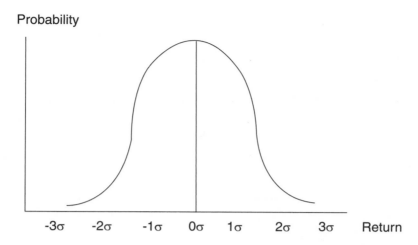

Figure 9-4. Likelihood of Occurrence of Returns by Standard Deviation Groupings.

that is further away, as indicated by the fact that 34.13 percent occur between the expected value and one standard deviation, only 13.59 percent occur between one and two standard deviations, and less than 3 percent occur beyond two standard deviations from the midpoint.

Standard Normal Distribution Table

The relationships shown in Figure 9-4 can be handled more precisely with the use of a standard normal distribution table, such as the one given in Figure 9-6. As an example of the use of this table, consider a firm that is forecasting a return of $1,400,000 with a standard deviation of $200,000. What is the probability of a return greater than $1,250,000? The answer starts with the value $1,250,000, which is found at minus 0.75 standard deviation from the expected value. Using the table, we go to 0.7 in the left-hand column and across to the column headed by 0.05. At the crossing of 0.7 and 0.05, we find the value

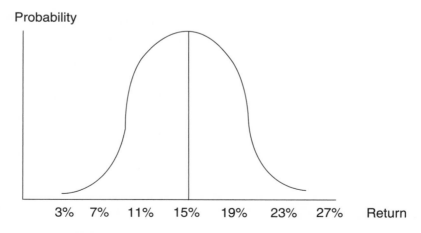

Figure 9-5. Entire Range of Returns for a Project.

0.273. This means that there is a 27.3 percent chance of a return between $1,250,000 and $1,400,000. Also, there is a 50 percent chance of a return greater than $1,400,000. Thus, the chance of a return greater than $1,250,000 is 0.273 + 0.50, or 77.3 percent.

Example. A firm is considering an investment with an expected value of $90,000 and a standard deviation of $10,000. What is the chance of a return greater than $105,000?

	0.00	0.01	0.02	0.03	0.04	0.05	0.06	0.07	0.08	0.09
0.0	0.500	-0.004	-0.008	-0.012	-0.016	-0.020	-0.024	-0.028	-0.032	-0.036
0.1	-0.040	-0.044	-0.048	-0.052	-0.056	-0.060	-0064	-0.068	-0.071	-0075
0.2	-0.079	-0.083	-0.087	-0.091	-0.095	-0.099	-0.103	-0.106	-0.110	-0.114
0.3	-0.118	-0.122	-0.126	-0.129	-0.133	-0.137	-0.141	-0.144	-0.148	-0.152
0.4	-0.155	-0.159	-0.163	-0.166	-0.170	-0.174	-0.177	-0.181	-0.184	-0.188
0.5	-0.192	-0.195	-0.199	-0.202	-0.205	-0.209	-0.212	-0.216	-0219	-0.222
0.6	-0.226	-0.229	-0.232	-0.236	-0.239	-0.242	-0.245	-0.249	-0.252	-0.255
0.7	-0.258	-0.261	-0.264	-0.267	-0.270	-0.273	-0.276	-0.279	-0.282	-0.285
0.8	-0.288	-0.291	-0.294	-0.297	-0.300	-0.302	-0.305	-0.308	-0.311	-0.313
0.9	-0.316	-0.319	-0.321	-0.324	-0.326	-0.329	-0.332	-0.334	-0.337	-0.339
1.0	-0.341	-0.344	-0.346	-0.349	-0.351	-0.353	-0.355	-0.358	-0.360	-0.362
1.1	-0.364	-0.367	-0.369	-0.371	-0.373	-0.375	-0.377	-0.379	-0.381	-0.383
1.2	-0.385	-0.387	-0.389	-0.391	-0.393	-0.394	-0.396	-0.398	-0.400	-0.402
1.3	-0.403	-0.405	-0.407	-0.408	-0.410	-0.412	-0.413	-0.415	-0.416	-0.418
1.4	-0.419	-0.421	-0.422	-0.424	-0.425	-0.427	-0.428	-0.429	-0.431	-0.432
1.5	-0.433	-0.435	-0.436	-0.437	-0.438	-0.439	-0.441	-0.442	-0.443	-0.444
1.6	-0.445	-0.446	-0.447	-0.448	-0.450	-0.451	-0.452	-0.453	-0.454	-0.455
1.7	-0.455	-0.456	-0.457	-0.458	-0.459	-0.460	-0.461	-0.462	-0.463	-0.463
1.8	-0.464	-0.465	-0.466	-0.466	-0.467	-0.468	-0.469	-0.469	-0.470	-0.471
1.9	-0.471	-0.472	-0.473	-0.473	-0.474	-0.474	-0.475	-0.476	-0476	-0.477
2.0	-0.477	-0.478	-0.478	-0.479	-0.479	-0.480	-0.480	-0.481	-0.481	-0.482
2.1	-0.482	-0.483	-0.483	-0483	-0.484	-0.484	-0.485	-0.485	-0.485	-0-486
2.2	-0.486	-0.486	-0.487	-0.487	-0.488	-0.488	-0.488	-0.488	-0.489	-0.489
2.3	-0.489	-0.490	-0.490	-0.490	-0.490	-0.491	-0.491	-0.491	-0.491	-0.492
2.4	-0.492	-0.492	-0.492	-0.493	-0.493	-0.493	-0.493	-0.493	-0.493	-0.494
2.5	-0.494	-0.494	-0.494	-0.494	-0.495	-0.495	-0.495	-0.495	-0.495	-0-495
2.6	-0.495	-0.496	-0.496	-0.496	-0.496	-0.496	-0.496	-0.496	-0.496	-0.496
2.7	-0.497	-0.497	-0.497	-0.497	-0.497	-0.497	-0.497	-0.497	-0.497	-0.497
2.8	-0.497	-0.498	-0.498	-0.498	-0.498	-0.498	-0.498	-0.498	-0.498	-0.498
2.9	-0.498	-0.498	-0.498	-0.498	-0.498	-0.498	-0.499	-0.499	-0.499	-0.499
3.0	-0.499	-0.499	-0.499	-0.499	-0.499	-0.499	-0.499	-0.499	-0.499	-0.499

Figure 9-6. Standard Normal Distribution Table.

Answer. 6.68 percent. First, $105,000 is 1.5 standard deviations above $90,000. The value in Figure 9-6 at 1.50 is 0.433. Subtracting this from the 0.50 chance of a return greater than the expected value gives us 0.50 - 0.433 or 6.7 percent chance of a return greater than $105,000.

Expression of the Standard Deviation

An advantage of the standard deviation as a measure of dispersion is that it can be expressed in the same measurement units as the expected return. If the return is given in dollars, the standard deviation can be given in dollars. Or if the return is a percent, the standard deviation can be expressed as a percent. This allows a direct comparison of competing proposals.

As an example, suppose a proposal has an expected return of 10 percent with a standard deviation of 2 percent, while a second proposal offers an expected return of 12 percent with a standard deviation of 3 percent. Figure 9-7 shows a comparison of the two proposals, with the entire range of possible returns for each.

In evaluating the two proposals in the figure, one offers a lower expected return with a smaller standard deviation and, thus, less risk. But the higher return from the second proposal may offset the larger dispersion of returns. This kind of comparison is facilitated by using the standard deviation as a measure of risk.

Estimating the Standard Deviation

Three basic approaches can be used to estimate the standard deviation:

- *Historical calculation.* One approach makes use of the dispersion from previous investment proposals. From the firm's records on prior investments in similar projects, data can be developed on the closeness of actual results to the original forecast. If estimates for investments in past periods were fairly close, a small standard deviation would be expected. Larger dispersions on past projects would warrant a

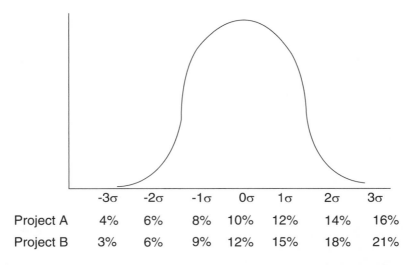

	-3σ	-2σ	-1σ	0σ	1σ	2σ	3σ
Project A	4%	6%	8%	10%	12%	14%	16%
Project B	3%	6%	9%	12%	15%	18%	21%

Figure 9-7. Direct Comparison of Two Proposals Using the Standard Deviation.

larger estimated standard deviation. The mathematical process for determining the standard deviation from past proposals is beyond the scope of this chapter.

- *The 99 Percent Estimation Technique.* The analyst gathers individual estimates of the entire likely range of returns from a proposal. Once the full range is estimated, it represents six standard deviations by definition. One-sixth of the range is a standard deviation.

    Example. After consulting with the operating department, the accounting department, and several of the firm's managers, an analyst concludes that the lowest return from an investment is likely to be a loss of 20 percent and the highest could be a profit of 25 percent. What is the standard deviation?

    Answer. 7.5 percent. The entire range is from -0.20 to + 0.25, or 45 percent. Dividing this by 6, we get 7.5 percent.

- *The two-thirds estimation technique.* This is based on the fact that approximately two-thirds of the time (68.26 percent actually), the return from a proposal will be within a range of one standard deviation (plus or minus) from the expected return. This is part of the definition of standard deviation.

    After consulting with other members of the firm, the analyst could estimate the range of returns that is likely to happen two-thirds of the time. Once this range is forecast as accurately as possible, we have a range of one standard deviation above and below the expected return. Half of this range will be a standard deviation.

CAPITAL ASSET THEORY

The capital asset theory matches risk with return. The rate of return from a capital investment is a concept that has different meanings to different investors. Some companies seek near-term cash inflows and give less value to more distant returns. Such a firm might invest in a project where high profits are possible today, but the future is uncertain. Other investors are concerned primarily with long-term market penetration and growth. They would seek investments that offer the promise of long-term, stable, higher-than-average growth of sales and earnings. Still others measure return using financial ratios. They might seek to invest in a company that has a high return on investment or return on equity.

However return is measured, the expected return from any investment proposal will be linked in a fundamental relationship to the degree of risk in the proposal. In order to be acceptable, a high-risk proposal must offer a higher forecasted return than a lower-risk proposal.

Market Line

A *market line* may be defined as the general pattern of risk and return in an investing market. Such a line is shown in Figure 9-8. With respect to this diagram, we might note some characteristics of the line, namely:

- *It is upward sloping.* The line slopes upward from the left axis of the diagram. This reflects the general pattern of more risk, more return.

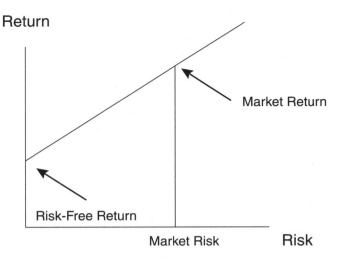

Figure 9-8. The Market Line.

- *Risk is on the* x *axis.* The horizontal, or *x*, axis takes the independent variable. The vertical, or *y*, axis takes the dependent variable. From this diagram, we can see that the rate of return is dependent upon the degree of risk in a proposal. Thus, risk is an independent variable; return, a dependent variable.
- *There is a risk-free rate of return.* The point where the market line touches the *y* axis is the risk-free rate of return. In the major industrial countries, this is the return on government securities, which, if held to maturity, offer no risk of default on either principal or interest. This is the minimum acceptable return for any investment.
- *There is a market portfolio.* This is a group of assets weighted at the same dollar value as all assets in the market. The *market return* is the expected return on the market portfolio. It is the average return, if you will, on all the assets traded in the market.
- *It is a straight line.* A number of empirical studies indicate that the trade-off between risk and return is a linear relationship; that is, a straight line is the correct way to draw the market line.

Two Components of Risk

Within the overall definition of risk as dispersion of return, two components may be identified:

- *Business risk.* This is the chance that the firm will not compete successfully using the assets that it purchases. As an example, the firm may acquire a machine that does not operate as expected or does not produce salable products, or it may face other operating or market difficulties that cause losses. Any operational problems are classed as business risk.
- *Financial risk.* This is the chance that an investment will not generate sufficient cash flows to cover interest and principal payments on its debt or to provide adequate profits to the owners. If the firm falls short of its return goal, it may be able to cover its operating expenses but not the financing costs of the original investment.

The two components of risk are implied in the market line. The market portfolio offers both business and financial risk. Figure 9-8 also shows an assumed identification of business and financial risk in the capital asset framework.

Inefficient Markets

In an efficient or perfect market, all assets are traded with the proper relationship of risk and return. Therefore, all stocks, bonds, and capital assets would be located somewhere on the market line. In an inefficient market, however, some assets offer a better return than others at a given risk level. In practice, efficient markets are not likely for many investments. This is particularly the case when we cross national boundaries. The same artificial constraints that create additional risks also produce inefficiencies. Some assets offer a better return than others at a given risk level. An inefficient market, which could apply either domestically or internationally, is shown in Figure 9-9, where Investments A through E do not fall on the market line.

Investor Indifference Curves

In Figure 9-9, we can see the assets that are available in the marketplace. They are only one-half of the investment decision. The other half involves the firm's attitude toward risk; that is, which asset will be selected from all the available choices. Conceptually, we can formalize the investor's view of risk through the use of indifference curves.

An *indifference curve* is a graphic representation of the trade-offs in value between risk and return. As an example, suppose a firm wants no risk if it can achieve a 6 percent return. If it accepts low risk in a proposal, it wants a 9 percent return. Medium risk commands a 12 percent return. From these data, we can draw the indifference curve shown in Figure 9-10.

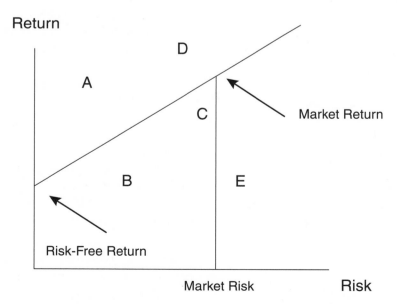

Figure 9-9. The Market Line with Inefficiencies.

The investing firm will trade off risk and return as shown by the curve. Suppose, for example, that the firm can accept a low-risk proposal with a 10 percent return but can get only 5 percent on government securities. Which investment would be undertaken? The answer is the 10 percent alternative because this has a greater utility than a 5 percent no-risk investment. But if an 8 percent no-risk bond had been available, it would have been chosen over the low-risk investment. If both a 6 percent no-risk bond and a 9 percent low-risk proposal were available, the firm would be indifferent between the two, as both would be equally acceptable.

RISK AND REQUIRED RETURN

To complete the conceptual relationship between risk and return, we join the concepts of the market line and the indifference curve. The optimal investment will be found at the point where the indifference curve touches an investment alternative. This is shown in Figure 9-11. When the indifference curve reaches a proposal, we have a risk level that is satisfactory to the firm. We also have an investment that offers an appropriate return for that risk level. This is an acceptable investment.

How Should We Determine the Required Return?

The process of determining the required return involves the calculation of the appropriate level of return to compensate the firm for the risk it is undertaking. If a firm is considering a high-risk proposal, it should get a high return. A low-risk proposal would offer a lower return in most situations. This is the correct basis for determining the required return on an investment.

It also considers the desire of the firm, as expressed in its attitude toward risk and return in different international markets. Some firms seek minimal risk in all investments.

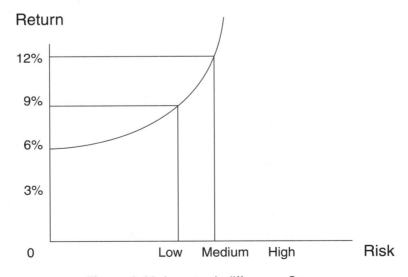

Figure 9-10. Investor Indifference Curve.

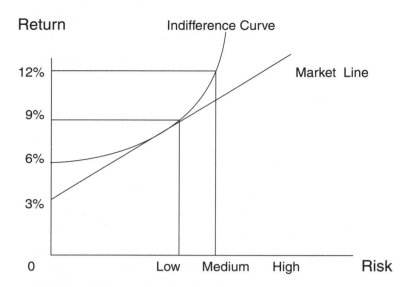

Figure 9-11. Indifference Curve and Intersection with Market Line.

Others pursue markets that offer higher risks and higher likely returns. Stated differently, the firms do not have the same indifference curves.

Having said that, we can identify three categories of investments in terms of the trade-off between risk and return:

- *Efficient.* This type of investment is found on or above the capital market line. In Figure 9-9, Investments A and D are efficient.
- *Acceptable.* These investments both are efficient and meet the firm's desirable matching of risk and return. If a firm wants less risk, Investment A in Figure 9-9 is acceptable. If it wants a chance for a higher return at a higher risk level, Investment D is acceptable.
- *Inefficient.* These investments are below the market line, as is true of Investments B, C, and E in Figure 9-9. In terms of risk and return, these investments are not acceptable.

Calculating the Required Return

To illustrate the process of determining the required return, let us use the standard deviation as the risk measure. Then, the formula for the required return on an investment is:

$$E(\text{Return})_{\text{required}} = E(\text{Return})_{\text{risk-free}} + [\text{Excess(Return)}_{\text{market}}] \times (\sigma_{\text{asset}}/\sigma_{\text{market}})$$

where Excess(Return)$_{\text{market}}$ is the *excess return on the market portfolio*, calculated by subtracting the risk-free return from the market return.

In this formula, the measure of risk is the relationship between the asset's standard deviation and the standard deviation of the market portfolio. If an asset has a higher standard deviation, and, hence, a higher dispersion of return, than the market, the required return will exceed the required return for the market.

Example. An asset has a standard deviation of 0.043 at a time when the market standard deviation is 0.052. The risk-free rate of return is 7.8 percent, and the market return is 12.3 percent. What is the required return on the asset?

Answer. The required return is 11.5 percent, as follows:

$$E(\text{Return})_{required} = 0.078 + (0.123 - 0.078) \times (0.043/0.052) = 0.115$$

Plotting the Market Line

We can plot the market line by locating two points: (1) the risk-free rate of return and (2) the return on the market portfolio. Once we have the two points, we can draw the line. We can also determine the level of low, medium, and high risk. Let us illustrate the process.

Assume that a company has decided that the market portfolio offers a medium level of risk. Thus, $\sigma_{market}/\sigma_{market}$, which equals 1, is plotted at "medium." The risk-free asset, with a low risk level, is plotted at $\sigma_{risk-free}/\sigma_{market}$, or 0. The relationships are:

Ratio	Level of Risk
0	Low
0.5	Medium low
1.0	Medium
1.5	Medium high
2.0	High

For this investor, the market line can be drawn as shown in Figure 9-12. In this example, the likely return on the market portfolio is 16 percent and the standard deviation is 12 percent. A government bond offers a likely return of 8 percent, with a zero standard deviation.

A Solved Problem

Once we have located the market line, we can evaluate investment decisions. For example, suppose Investment X offers a 20 percent return and has a standard deviation of 14 percent, and Investment Y offers a 10 percent return with a standard deviation of 8 percent.

The required returns are:

X $E(\text{Return})_{required} = 0.08 + (0.16 - 0.08) \times (0.14/0.12) = 0.173$

Y $E(\text{Return})_{required} = 0.08 + (0.16 - 0.08) \times (0.08/0.12) = 0.133$

Based on our analysis, Investment X is acceptable because the likely return of 20 percent exceeds the required return of 17.3 percent. Investment Y is not acceptable, since the required return of 13.3 percent exceeds the likely return of 10 percent.

FINANCIAL AND OPERATIONAL RISKS

The capital asset pricing model spends considerable time on the identification of risk. In this section, we will cover different kinds of risks in greater detail.

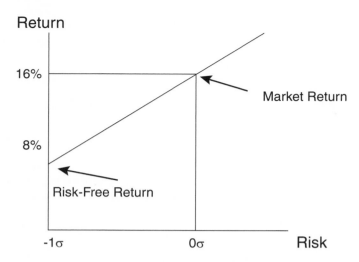

Figure 9-12. A Market Line Using the Standard Deviation as a Risk Measure.

Business Risk in Unregulated Companies

We have already identified *business risk* as the chance of loss if an asset cannot be employed in such a way as to earn a profit. Examples are:

- *Operating failures.* This is a situation in which a company cannot perform as promised or deliver specified goods on time.
- *Weak market.* This occurs when products or services cannot be sold at prices sufficient to cover costs.
- *High costs.* Some companies have excessive fixed or variable costs as a result of inefficient or obsolete operations. Alternatively, high costs may result from the inability to expend capital to purchase current technology.
- *Inflation.* This refers to rises in the cost of goods or services.

Financial Risk

We have already defined *financial risk* as the chance that a firm will not be sufficiently profitable to repay the providers of its capital. Major sources of financial risk are:

- *Level of debt.* Some companies have large mortgages on real assets and other unsecured obligations. As a general statement, high debt levels compared to asset values and cash flows represent a high risk.
- *Level of interest.* Some companies have high interest costs on most or all of their debt obligations compared to other companies. A high aggregate level of interest compared to competitors represents high risk.
- *Length of time for debt.* Some companies have mortgages on assets that extend for virtually the entire service lives of the mortgaged assets. A longer average maturity of debt increases risk.
- *Inadequate cash to pay dividends.* The holders of common stock expect to earn a return on their investment, either in the form of cash dividends or through increases

in the value of the stock. If the level of return available from alternative assets rises above the return offered by a company's stock, the cash available to pay dividends may not meet the expectations of investors.

Foreign Exchange Risk

Fluctuating foreign exchange rates can affect the profit of companies that receive a large portion of their business from international operations. Two situations are common:

- *Rise in expenses.* A company may pay a portion of its manufacturing expenses in a currency that is rising in value compared to other currencies. This will cause a rise in costs to produce goods.
- *Decline in revenues.* Conversely, a company may sell goods or services for a currency that is declining in value. This will cause a drop in revenues.

Risk Factors Affecting Profitability

From the perspective of profitability, firms can focus on five risk factors:

- *Costs.* Does the firm have control over the expenses needed to create its products or services and generate its revenues?
- *Price adequacy.* Is the firm able to generate a sufficient selling price for its goods or services?
- *Utility of assets.* Does the firm maintain idle or obsolete assets that are not useful in generating sales?
- *Sales volume.* Is the firm able to achieve a sufficient volume of sales?
- *Financing expenses.* Does the firm have excessive debt or high-cost debt, resulting in high interest payments?

Categories of Insurable Risk

A *pure risk* is the chance of an unexpected or unplanned loss without the accompanying chance of a gain. This is also called an *insurable risk.* Four categories of such risks can be identified:

- *Personal risk.* This refers to the possibility of economic or emotional losses that might be suffered by individuals as they live their daily lives. Examples are the possibility of death, injury, disability, illness, and unemployment.
- *Property risk.* This covers the possibility of economic losses that would result if tangible property were to be damaged, destroyed, or stolen. Such losses can be direct, as when a building is destroyed by a hurricane. Or they can be indirect, as when a company loses sales because its factory has been shut down by a fire.
- *Liability risk.* This involves the economic losses that could occur if someone accuses another person or organization of causing a loss or damage and then pursues reimbursement through various legal means.
- *Performance risk.* This area deals with possible economic losses that could occur if a person or organization failed to provide goods or services as promised. Examples

would be the failure to pay a debt according to the terms of a loan agreement or allegations that a contractor had failed to construct a house according to the specifications of a blueprint.

CONCLUSION

Over a long period of time, economists and others developed theories for understanding risk. They also proposed models that help analysts link the level of risk in business operations and investments with the return that compensates investors for taking risks and pursuing opportunities. Financial risk management is highly dependent upon a complete understanding of the capital asset theory linking required return, likely return, and the cutoff point for investments.

CHAPTER 9 APPENDIXES

How to Measure Uncertainty and Assess Required Return

1. Measuring the Entire Range of Forecasted Returns
An investment proposal has the following data. What is the entire range of possible returns?

Expected return	19%
Standard deviation	11%

Answer

-3σ	-2σ	-1σ	0σ	1σ	2σ	3σ
-14%	-3%	8%	19%	30%	41%	52%

2. Determining the Likelihood of Returns
An investment proposal has the following data. What is the chance of a return greater than 18%?

Expected return	14%
Standard deviation	8%

Answer

Standard deviation from mean	0.5
Value from table	0.192
Chance of greater return	0.308

3. Likelihood of Returns
An investment proposal has the following data. What is the chance of a return of at least 15%? What is the chance of a return of at least 20%?

Expected return	18%
Standard deviation	2%

Answer

	15%	20%
Standard deviation from mean	-1.5	1.0
Value from table	0.433	0.341
Chance of greater return	0.933	0.159

4. Likelihood of Returns

An investment proposal has the following data. What is the chance of a return between 15% and 25%?

Expected return	20%
Standard deviation	10%

Answer

	15%	25%	15% to 25%
Standard deviation from mean	-0.5	0.5	
Value from table	0.192	0.192	
Chance of return			0.384

5. Calculating Required Return

An investment proposal has the following data. What is the required return on the asset?

Expected return, market portfolio	15%
σ_{market}	12%
σ_{asset}	8%
Risk-free return	5%

Answer

$E(\text{Return})_{risk\text{-}free}$	5.0%
$\text{Excess}(\text{Return})_{market}$	10.0%
$\sigma_{asset}/\sigma_{market}$	66.7%
Required return	11.7%

Formula:

$$E(\text{Return})_{required} = E(\text{Return})_{risk\text{-}free} + [\text{Excess}(\text{Return})_{market}] \times (\sigma_{asset}/\sigma_{market})$$

6. Calculating Required Return

An investment proposal has the following data. What is the required return on the asset?

Expected return, market portfolio	12%
σ_{market}	15%
σ_{asset}	25%
Risk-free return	7%

Answer

$E(\text{Return})_{\text{risk-free}}$	7.0%
$\text{Excess(Return)}_{\text{market}}$	5.0%
$\sigma_{\text{asset}}/\sigma_{\text{market}}$	166.7%
Required return	15.3%

7. *Finding Acceptable Investments in Terms of Risk and Return*

A company has established the following ratios of standard deviations of an asset to the market:

$\sigma_{\text{asset}}/\sigma_{\text{market}}$	Level of Risk
0.0	Low
0.5	Medium low
1.0	Medium
1.5	Medium high
2.0	High

The company has two investment proposals with the following data. Given the ratios of standard deviations of an asset to the market, what is the risk level of each investment? Which investments are acceptable?

Expected return, market portfolio	10%
σ_{market}	8%
Risk-free return	6%
Expected return, Asset R	14%
$\sigma_{\text{asset R}}$	14%
Expected return, Asset S	9%
$\sigma_{\text{asset S}}$	8%
R $\sigma_{\text{asset}}/\sigma_{\text{market}}$	1.75
S $\sigma_{\text{asset}}/\sigma_{\text{market}}$	1.00
R risk level	Medium high to high
S risk level	Medium

Answer

	R	S
$E(\text{Return})_{\text{risk-free}}$	6.0%	6.0%
+ $\text{Excess(Return)}_{\text{market}}$	4.0%	4.0%
$\sigma_{\text{asset}}/\sigma_{\text{market}}$	175.0%	100.0%
Required return	13.0%	10.0%
Likely return	14.0%	9.0%
Is it acceptable?	Yes	No

How to Assess the Required Return on a Complex Investment

Background. As a result of an increasing emphasis on audio and visual communications by businesses and other organizations, considerable growth is expected for business television. The Budapest International Teleport project is designed to respond to the needs in this market.

Business television allows teleconferencing involving individuals or organizations all over the world. Using a ground uplift unit to reach a satellite transponder, a ground station transmits a signal that can be picked up by receivers in other parts of the world. After a number of locations are linked in the system, individuals can talk to and see each other. This allows meetings, conferences, and other exchanges of information in an informal or formal setting, with participants remaining in their home countries.

The Project. The Budapest International Teleport Ltd. was founded to provide television service to private or public customers with interests in Eastern Europe. It will provide the equipment and network management necessary to implement point-to-multipoint video communications. Its services will be divided into three categories:

- *Public-event one-way television.* The company will create a portable network that is in place to transmit a specific program. An example might be the broadcast of the soccer World Cup to television stations in many countries.
- *Contract network two-way television.* This will consist of permanent networks to supply ongoing programming for customers who have a need for frequent teleconferences with a large number of individuals. An example might be the weekly meetings of a worldwide sales force, where new products are introduced and participants can discuss features.
- *Private-event two-way television.* This will consist of a portable network to transmit a program and allow viewers to ask questions or discuss their reactions. An example might be the annual meeting of a corporation, where shareholders at different locations can request information from management.

Capabilities. Budapest International Teleport plans to design and market business television systems in these three market segments. It will have the equipment to perform the site survey, design the hardware and software configuration, manage a permanent installation, manage temporary and permanent networks, test the equipment, and run events.

The company will be established in the capital city of Hungary in facilities purchased as part of a program to attract investors. The entity will have a separate legal existence, protected by a new law passed by the government. No taxes will be levied for the first seven years. The location is ideal for providing uplink connections that can service the United States and Canada, all of Europe, the western areas of the former USSR, and much of the Middle East and Africa. Arrangements can be made for extended coverage to the rest of the world.

The company is being positioned to provide responsive service and maximum performance to customers by:

- Hiring an experienced business television staff.
- Building a modern network control center just outside of Budapest. The center, which is nearing completion, has the capability to access all North American and European satellites.
- Creating desirable network characteristics, including transmission monitoring, trouble resolution, and encryption control.
- Assembling an online database providing immediate information on alternative transmission modes and customer requirements.
- Operating five transportable earth stations completely equipped with redundant transmission equipment, with such units to be located in Ohio, California, England, Warsaw, and Moscow.
- Managing a projection and staging unit that can provide technical support for audio, multiimage, lighting services, and video systems. This unit would be stationed in California.

Marketing Strategy. The company will aggressively pursue opportunities involving the dissemination of information in areas where forecasts by independent researchers indicate considerable growth in the near future. These include:

- Executive communications
- New product announcements
- Technical and other training
- Sales or motivational events
- Entertainment events
- Sporting events
- Continuing education
- Intercompany communications

Competition exists in the markets identified for Budapest International Teleport. Competitors include subsidiaries of AT&T, MCI, ITT, RCA, Holiday Inn, American Express, VideoStar, the Houston Teleport, the Atlanta Teleport, the New York Teleport, Luxembourg TeleSystems, London Omni-Network, and Deutsche-Tel Systems.

Business will be pursued by commission agents located initially in New York, Atlanta, San Francisco, Chicago, Toronto, London, Paris, Vienna, Warsaw, Bahrain, and Moscow. Contracts have already been signed to use 65 percent of both the NetSync circuits and the Telco-CX circuits that will be installed during the first year. The clients and their estimated percentage of usage are as follows:

Client	Percent
The United Nations (various agencies)	7%
Auto Union Partners GMBH	9%
Italia Consortium	11%
Church of Christian Fundamentals	3%
Russian Ukrainian Investors	6%

Client	Percent
Polanska Telecommunications	5%
General Motors Corporation	2%
Skandia Hotel Systems	4%
Sun Light Cruise Lines	3%
Egyptian Telecommunications	15%

Ownership. The Budapest International Teleport will be owned and operated by a joint venture between a U.S. corporation and U.K. Investors, a group of private individuals seeking investments. Each partner will purchase 50 percent of the common stock. Long-term debt will be used to purchase or build the assets of the company, which will be approximately $60 million on the day of the start-up. Working capital will be funded primarily by payables and other current liabilities. Cash flow from operations will fund growth and expansion.

Estimated Revenues. The company estimates that it will receive revenues from four sources, as follows:

- *Circuits.* Customers will pay to use the various transmission facilities, either on annual retainer contracts or on a per-usage basis.
- *Facilities rental.* The company will lease its permanent facilities in Hungary or its transportable units on a short-term basis and charge rental fees based on time and usage.
- *Technical services.* The company's technicians will perform installation, maintenance, and other contract services for other telecommunications companies.
- *Brokerage.* The company will steer some business to other telecommunications providers and collect a fee for this service.

During its first year of operation, the company will charge competitive rates. The cost of providing telecommunications services in Eastern Europe is still dropping. Lower revenues are forecast after the first year as the company meets competition and expands its business. A further per-circuit decline in revenues is forecast after Year 2.

Estimated Expenses. The joint venture will incur fixed and variable expenses. The circuit costs, by and large, are fixed but are estimated in financial plans as a percent of revenues for each year. Other costs are a mix of fixed and variable. Insurance has been estimated as a separate item. Depreciation is set at 15 percent, which reflects an estimate of the rate of obsolescence. Interest on debt is forecast to be 8 percent for the first three years of the venture. No taxes are paid on earnings. Each year, 40 percent of the profits will be repatriated to the partners.

Required.

- Identify the largest risks found in the Budapest Teleport Project.
- What should be the required return on the project at a time when the following is true?
  - U.S. 10-year government bonds offer a return of 8 percent annually.
  - The forecasted return on the market portfolio appears to be 12 percent annually

Possible Answer for Budapest's Largest Risks. One answer is:

1. Challenges from obsolescence of technology
2. Possible operating problems in different markets
3. Inflation of expenses not matched with rising prices
4. Nonrenewal of contracts
5. Inability to earn adequate profits to pay interest on debt
6. Inability to earn adequate profits to repay principal on debt
7. Inability to convert foreign exchange
8. Contingent losses that are not insured

Required Return. The appetite for risk determines the answer.

The project has a high level of risk, as the new company faces technological, political, and a variety of other risks.

With common stock at 12 percent before taxes, a return of 15 to 18 percent before taxes seems to be indicated.

Part 5 | Nature of a Capital Investment Decision

Without any doubt, capital budgeting is the most powerful area of financial risk management. Proportional to the size of the firm, decisions to invest capital in new areas can make or break a company. Decisions are made with long-term expectations when much information is not fully known and changing circumstances can invalidate business plans and budgets. If we do it right, our capital budget leads to good decisions based on the best information and solid techniques for analyzing risk. If we do it wrong, trouble lies ahead.

Fortunately, we do have tools to help us in managing this aspect of financial risk. In the two chapters in this part, we measure the two sides of a capital budgeting decision. They are:

- *Cash flows*. The cash flow stream is the critical element of any capital budgeting analysis. How much do we have to invest? When do we have to invest it? What risks may arise prior to the start of operations? Then, what do we get back? When do the inflows occur? How certain are they? Finally, what will we have at the end of a planning horizon? What will our project be worth in four, five, or seven years? We ask this question even for projects planned for unlimited time periods.
- *Cash returns*. What is the likely return from the investment? Does the project match our appetite for risk? Does the expected return match or exceed the required return, given the inherent risk that the firm is accepting with the investment?

In this part of our story, we build a powerful model for assessing a capital budgeting proposal. At the same time, the tool simplifies the picture so that the analyst can focus on risk rather than on complexity. An example is the introduction of the midyear factor for discounting cash flows. It allows monthly cash inflows in the appearance of full years and increases the accuracy of the tools we use to calculate likely returns.

Upon completion of this part, the reader will have a practical, real-world tool for assessing the financial risk from capital investments.

Chapter
10

Capital Budgeting
Cash Flows

Capital budgeting is the decision-making process used by companies to evaluate long-term investments in large capital assets. It also covers decisions to acquire other firms, either through the purchase of their common stock or through the purchase of a group of assets that can be used to conduct an ongoing business. Capital budgeting describes the firm's formal planning process for the acquisition and investment of capital and results in a capital budget that is the firm's formal plan for the expenditure of money to purchase fixed assets.

Organizations make investment decisions within the framework of a strategic vision that should be leading the organization to achieve financial goals. The framework for capital budgeting is that a project must have certain characteristics:

- *Desirable.* The project should represent a worthwhile goal for the investment of funds. It must achieve a financial, reputational, or other goal within the risk appetite of the firm.
- *Feasible.* The goals of the project should be realistic. That is, the objectives must be realizable within the capabilities and resources that can be allotted to the project.
- *Focused.* The capital budget itself should provide guidance for decision making. It starts with the outlay that begins the project and concludes at the end of a planning horizon with a forecasted financial value.
- *Directional.* The numbers should show a pathway to follow from the launch of the project to maturity of financial outcomes.
- *Flexible.* Discussions of cash flows and returns should include adjustments that might be needed if assumptions do not work out or conditions change.

All this is well and good and is part of capital budgeting, but first the company must have the financial tools to develop cash flow streams that can be understood by management. Then, the cash flows must be adjusted for the time value of money so that the risk in the timing of cash flows and likely returns is clearly understood by decision makers. In this chapter, we cover the framework of capital budgeting and the careful creation of cash flow streams. In the next chapter, we cover the calculation of returns.

FOUNDATION OF CAPITAL BUDGETING

The preparation of a capital budget and decisions to invest in real estate or purchase other capital assets represent a long-term commitment by any private company. In this section, we will examine the concepts that assist in making such commitments.

Significance of Capital Budgeting

The commitment of funds to fixed asset investments is significant to the firm for a number of reasons:

- *Substantial dollar amounts.* These investments are generally made in large projects involving tens or even hundreds of millions of dollars. In terms of dollars alone, capital budgeting decisions are significant to even the largest corporations.
- *Long time periods.* When financial securities are purchased, a decision that is made today can easily be reversed tomorrow. Stock bought on an exchange can be sold, reversing the transaction. This is not the case with the purchase of capital assets. The company is making a long-term decision that is not likely to be reversed in a short period of time.
- *Loss of liquidity.* Money invested in capital assets is not readily available for other purposes. The loss of liquidity adds to the significance of capital budgeting activities.
- *Over- and undercapacity.* If the budget is drawn carefully, it usually improves the timing and quality of asset acquisitions. If it is done poorly, it can cost the firm large sums of money because it leads to overcapacity or undercapacity, sometimes at the same time. The firm may have idle assets to produce a product that is not in demand, but also have a shortage of the machinery and facilities needed to produce a much-demanded, high-profit product.

Motives for Investment

A corporation evaluates capital budgeting proposals for several reasons, including:

- *High profits.* Capital investments offer the prospect of high risk and high return. One motive for investing is to earn a high profit.
- *Growth.* By purchasing capital assets that offer potentially high returns, a corporation can accelerate its growth.
- *Diversification.* Many companies operate in cyclical businesses. A company can reduce the risk of large losses in one area by acquiring other lines of business.

Ranking of Proposals

Once the capital budget is nearing completion and different projects have been identified, the firm must select the projects it will finance. Among the problems that arise are the following:

- *Mutually exclusive projects.* If the firm accepts one project, it may rule out another. These are called *mutually exclusive projects.*

- An example of this kind of project would be the need to transport supplies from a loading dock to the warehouse. The firm may be considering two proposals—forklifts to pick up the goods and move them, or a conveyor belt connecting the dock and the warehouse. If the firm accepts one proposal, it eliminates the need for the other.

- *Contingent projects.* The utility of some proposals is contingent upon the acceptance of others. For example, a firm may be considering the construction of a new headquarters building and a new employee parking lot. If it decides not to build the headquarters building, the need for the lot is gone. At the same time, if the firm builds the headquarters building and not the lot, the employees will have no place to park. These are contingent proposals.

- *Capital rationing.* Companies normally have more proposals than they can fund properly. In this case, only the most desirable projects receive approval. Capital rationing occurs when the firm has more acceptable proposals than it can finance. In this situation, the firm should rank the projects from highest to lowest priority. Then a cutoff point is selected. Proposals above the cutoff will be funded; those below will be rejected or delayed. The cutoff point is selected after carefully considering the number of projects being considered, the goals of the firm, and the availability of capital to finance the capital budget.

Priority for Capital Investment

An insurance company is seeking to become a major player in providing medical malpractice coverage for hospitals. It has two intermediate goals: to provide coverage to physicians and to provide it to nurses. A full-scale effort has been made with respect to both. The Austin office has succeeded with physicians. Kansas City is faltering with nurses.

The company has additional resources to support the marketing strategy. Austin proposes going directly after the final goal. Kansas City wants resources to solve the nursing problems first.

What should the company do?

Answer

This is a question that tests the firm's appetite for risk. The cash required can be determined for both strategies, but the discussion will need to turn to risk.

Two Sides to a Capital Budgeting Decision

A capital budgeting decision involves two independent analyses, as follows:

- *Likely return.* This involves a forecast of the probable or expected return from the investment. The analysis begins with an expenditure of cash and a stream of cash inflows returning to the firm. Then, the analyst either calculates a rate of return or determines whether an investment meets or exceeds a required return.

- *Required return.* This involves the issue of whether the likely return is satisfactory, given the level of risk in the investment. If an investment is sufficiently risky as to require a 20 percent annual return after taxes, the proposal must offer a likely return of at least 20 percent.

In this framework, we are dealing with the techniques to determine the likely return. We will assume that the required return is appropriate to the level of risk inherent in the proposal.

Accounting Role in Capital Budgeting

Capital budgeting decisions are made on the basis of cash flows. Accounting calculations should be limited to three areas:

- *Tax effects.* A corporation may have to pay taxes based on reported profits from a proposed venture. If so, tax effects on cash flow should be included in the analysis.
- *Balance sheet effects.* Adding capital assets or accounting losses from investments will affect the balance sheet of a publicly traded company. Investments should be evaluated for their impact on the balance sheet.
- *Future earnings.* Similarly, a publicly traded company seeks to achieve stability of its earnings over time. Investments should be evaluated in terms of their impact on net income.

Planning Horizon

A *planning horizon* is a time period used for the evaluation of a capital investment. Normally 5 to 7 years is used for real estate or acquisitions. Predicting the future for 7 years is difficult enough; doing it for 15, 20, or 30 years, the time periods for many long-term investments in capital projects, is virtually impossible.

The proper approach to calculating the likely return is to assume that an asset is purchased in Year 0 and sold at the end of the planning horizon. This allows the analyst to account for all cash flows over the life of an investment. The ending value reflects the analyst's best estimate of the cash that could be realized from the asset if it were sold at the end of the planning horizon.

Depreciation Tax Shields

A major cash flow factor for capital investments involves the use of depreciation as a tax shield for income. *Depreciation* is an accounting device that allows a firm to charge off a portion of its investment as an expense over time. It is a *tax shield*, defined as a noncash expense that reduces the level of taxes paid by a firm.

Depreciation appears as an expense in the company's accounting records, but it does not involve the use of cash. It reduces reported profits but increases cash inflows, as shown in Figure 10-1. The effect of depreciation is also to increase the likely return on a real estate investment.

A number of approaches are used to determine the depreciation on assets in different countries of the world. Two major categories can be identified:

- *Accelerated depreciation.* This occurs when the tax regulations allow a company to speed up the rate of depreciation on an asset, taking larger amounts in earlier years.

	With $400,000 Depreciation	Without $400,000 Depreciation
Revenues	$1,600,000	$1,600,000
Less cash expenses	-600,000	-600,000
Less depreciation	-400,000	0
Taxable income	$600,000	$1,000,000
Taxes at 25%	-150,000	-250,000
After-tax income	$450,000	$750,000
Plus revenue shielded	+400,000	
After-tax cash flow	$850,000	$750,000

Figure 10-1. Effect of Depreciation on After-Tax Cash Flow.

Since depreciation reduces taxes, earlier depreciation charges speed up the cash flows from an investment proposal.

• *Straight-line depreciation.* This is a method of calculating depreciation in which the cost of a fixed asset is spread equally over its expected service life or some number of years specified in the tax code. The formula for calculating straight-line depreciation is:

Annual Depreciation = Original Book Value/Years

Because of the increased cash flow with accelerated depreciation, most firms use it in determining the depreciation schedule for capital assets if it is available. We will use straight-line depreciation so that we do not have to cover different methods of accelerated depreciation.

Question. An asset is depreciable using straight-line depreciation over five years to a zero book value. Its original book value is $1 million. What are the annual amounts of depreciation?

Answer. The schedule is:

Year	Starting Book Value	Rate	Annual Depreciation
1	$1,000,000	1/5	200,000
2	800,000	1/5	200,000
3	600,000	1/5	200,000
4	400,000	1/5	200,000
5	200,000	1/5	200,000
6	0		0

Funds Tied Up

The purchase of a fixed asset may also involve other cash expenditures. *Funds tied up* refers to any cash that must be used to support a capital investment. Cash may be needed to provide liquidity in the management of a commercial property or may be needed to provide working capital for the operators of a fixed asset.

In handling funds tied up, the analyst must determine whether the money will be returned when the investment is liquidated. If so, the correct technique for handling cash tied up is to treat it as an outflow when the assets are purchased and an inflow at the end of the planning horizon. If the cash is a permanent contribution to a fixed asset and will never be recovered, the correct technique is to treat it only as an outflow at the start of the time period. An example would be an increase in the level of spare parts that will not be recovered when a machine is scrapped at the end of its service life.

In some cases, an investment will generate a cash inflow to the company. The purchase of a high-technology asset that can be operated more efficiently may free cash that was previously tied up supporting an older asset. In this case, a cash inflow would be recognized when the asset is purchased.

Impact of Debt

The purchase of an asset may involve the use of debt for a portion of the financing. This is commonly the case because investors seek to borrow at one rate and earn a higher rate on the use of the asset.

When analyzing the impact of debt, the first step is to determine the portion of the purchase price that will be financed from debt sources. Then, an average interest rate over the period of the planning horizon must be assumed. This is true even though interest rates will vary for most loans. The analyst makes the best estimate of the likely average rate and uses it to calculate the periodic payment.

Once the payment has been calculated, it is separated into principal and interest components. Each component plays a role in the capital budgeting analysis:

- *Role of interest.* If a company must pay taxes on its earnings, the interest is normally tax-deductible each period. The tax savings must be included in the cash flow analysis.
- *Role of principal repayment.* The principal repayment reduces the outstanding debt balance. At the end of the planning horizon, the remaining debt must be paid off. The determination of the level of debt remaining requires the use of each year's principal repayment.

The balance of the outstanding principal is deducted from the residual value at the end of the horizon even though the company may not plan on selling the asset at that time. This process is mathematically needed in order to have an accurate calculation of the return on the project.

Residual Value

A *residual value* is defined as the estimated value of an asset at the end of the planning horizon. Two such values may be identified:

- *Book residual value.* This is the accounting value calculated by deducting accumulated depreciation from the original cost.
- *Cash residual value.* This is the net amount of money that the firm will receive if it sells the asset and pays any costs of liquidating the investment.

When evaluating fixed assets, book and cash values at the end of the planning horizon must be compared. Three situations are possible:

- *Cash exceeds book residual value.* When this happens, the property is being sold for more money than its accounting value. The difference is a gain. If the company pays income taxes, they must be paid on the gain.
- *Book exceeds cash residual value.* When this happens, the property is being sold below its accounting value. The difference is a loss. A tax credit may be available to the company.
- *Cash equals book value.* In this situation, no tax effect occurs.

CASH FLOWS

The likely return on a capital investment is calculated using time value of money techniques. They build upon a cash flow stream. In this section, we will develop such a stream.

After-Tax Cash Flow Stream

A *cash flow stream* may be defined as a listing of all cash outlays for and inflows from a capital investment, matched with the time periods in which they occur. As an example, assume that an asset requires a total outlay of $10 million, $6 million at the start of a year and $4 million at the end when the asset becomes operational. Year 0 is defined as the start of operations. The first payment therefore occurs at Year –1. Once in operation, the asset yields annual inflows of $1 million for four years, and it is still worth $10 million at the end of Year 4. The cash flow stream would be:

	Year -1	Year 0	Year 1	Year 2	Year 3	Year 4
Cash Flows	-$6,000	-$4,000	+$1,000	+$1,000	+$1,000	+$11,000

Forecasting Residual Values

The residual value can be presented as a matter-of-fact component of a cash flow stream. In reality, it is one of the most difficult numbers to identify and one of the most critical for evaluating the amount of return. Three issues arise:

- *Market demand in the future.* The residual value at the end of a planning horizon depends upon the likely cash flows after the planning horizon. If the planning horizon is four years, the residual value is based upon projections from Year 5 onward. This is a highly uncertain forecast.
- *Rate of change in the industry.* If the project occurs in an industry that changes slowly, the future may be somewhat predictable. If we are dealing with telecommunications or information technology, the forecast of residual value may be tenuous at best.
- *Does a secondary market exist?* When dealing with the purchase of physical assets, the financial risk manager needs to recognize that assets must be upgraded or replaced as new developments arise in technology or other requirements. If the aging assets can be sold in a secondary market, the risk of obsolescence is reduced, as is the possibility that the project will have no residual value other than a scrap value.

A Solved Problem

To illustrate the process of creating a cash flow stream, let us consider a company that seeks to build a factory that would generate operating profits over a five-year planning horizon, The construction would involve two payments, one year apart. The first would be $20 million; the second would be $15 million. In addition, legal and accounting fees of 2 percent would be paid. The capitalized costs of installing equipment would be $1 million, payable with the second payment. Debt would be used to finance 70 percent of the purchase price and capitalized costs. The loan would require annual payments over ten years and carry a 9 percent annual interest rate. The building and equipment would be depreciated using the straight-line method over a nine-year period to a book value of zero. In five years, it would have a cash residual value equal to 70 percent of the original depreciable cost. The new operation would require additional working capital of $450,000 to be tied up during the planning horizon. A tax rate of 25 percent applies. What is the after-tax cash flow stream?

To solve this problem, the calculations in each of the following steps are needed:

- *Net cash outlay.* This consists of all money that is spent to begin a capital budgeting project.
- *Amortization schedule.* This is needed for the calculation of annual cash flows and the gain or loss at the end of the planning horizon.
- *Depreciation schedule.* This is needed for the tax calculation.
- *Tax calculation.* This provides the annual taxes so that after-tax cash flows can be determined.
- *Project cash flows.* These are the after-tax cash flows from operating the asset.
- *Residual cash flows.* This provides the cash effects from selling the asset at the end of the planning horizon.
- *After-tax cash flow stream.* This brings all the cash effects together in a final cash flow stream.

We will cover each of these steps in order.

Net Cash Outlay. The *net cash outlay* consists of the purchase price and other disbursements in order to purchase an asset. A net cash outlay is calculated in Figure 10-2, as follows:

- *Purchase price.* The asset will cost $35 million, paid in two payments one year apart. The first payment of $20 million is shown as occurring in Period –1; the remainder is paid in Period 0.
- *Debt portion.* A company may borrow a portion of the project cost when acquiring an asset. If this is done, the debt portion must be deducted from the project cost when calculating the net cash outlay. In our example, debt will equal 70 percent of the $35 million purchase price.
- *Brokerage and fees.* The purchase of an asset commonly involves fees for legal, accounting, and other activities. In our example, these are assumed to be 2 percent of the purchase price.

	Year -1	Year 0
Project cost	-$20,000	-$15,000
Percent bank financing	70%	70%
Bank financing	$14,000	$10,500
Legal and other fees	2%	2%
Fees	-$400	-$300
Capitalized costs		-$1,000
Funds tied up		-$450
Annual cash needed	-$20,400	-$16,750
Outlay each period	-$6,400	-$6,250
Required return	15%	
Present values	-$7,360	-$6,250
Net cash outlay		**-$13,610**

Figure 10-2. Net Cash Outlay.

- *Cost of funds tied up.* For the purpose of determining present value, Period 0 is defined as the start of the investment period. Any payments made prior to this time must be brought forward as the cost of tying up funds for the company, which is also the required return on investments.
- *Capitalized costs.* If a company purchases an asset that requires substantial transportation or installation costs, the government may require these disbursements to be added to the book value of the asset. This is called *capitalizing costs*. Then, depreciation will be allowed in future periods on the increased cost of the asset. In our example, $1 million of such costs will be capitalized.
- *Funds tied up.* Running the operations of a company requires setting aside cash to cover bank balances, receivables, inventory, and other working capital needs. In the figure, $450,000 of such funds will be tied up in Period 0 and released at the end of the planning horizon.
- *Net cash outlay.* This is calculated by:
  Project cost (outflow)
  Less debt (inflow)
  Plus fees (outflow)
  Plus capitalized costs (outflow)
  Plus funds tied up (outflow)
  Equals net cash outlay (outflow)

Amortization Schedule. We have already seen the term *amortization* as referring to the process of allocating loan principal over a specific period of time. If the schedule covers the entire loan period and shows the principal reduced to zero, the schedule is *fully amortizing*. If it shows a planning horizon that is shorter than the loan period, it is a *partial amortization schedule*, and there will be a loan balance in the final year. If it is assumed that the asset can be sold for a residual value in the final year, it must also be assumed that the ending loan balance is repaid.

Figure 10-3 shows an amortization schedule for the sample investment. Key features of the figure are:

- *Starting debt.* This initial debt was calculated in Figure 10-2.
- *Amortization schedule.* The schedule shows a 10-year loan with annual payments. The interest rate is 9 percent.
- *Periodic payment.* The payment is calculated by the @PMT built-in function in the electronic spreadsheet. If the analyst inserted a formula instead of using the built-in function, it would be:

$$PMT = (PV*Int)/(1-1/(1+Int)^\wedge n)$$

$$(26,040*0.09)/(1-1/(1+0.09)^\wedge 10) = \$4,058$$

- *Interest and reduction of principal.* The figure shows each period's starting balance, payment, interest, reduction of principal, and the remaining loan balance after the period.
- *Zero ending balance.* At the end of the 10 periods, the loan balance is zero. Thus, the schedule fully amortizes the loan.

	Year -1	Year 0
Bank financing	$14,000	$10,500
Interest accrued 11%	$1,540	
Total owed in Year 0	$15,540	$10,500
Starting loan balance		$26,040
Periodic interest rate		9%
Periods of financing		10

	Year 1	Year 2	Year 3	Year 4	Year 5
Starting balance	$26,040	$24,326	$22,458	$20,421	$18,202
Payment	4,058	4,058	4,058	4,058	4,058
Interest	2,344	2,189	2,021	1,838	1,638
Principal repayment	1,714	1,868	2,036	2,220	2,419
Ending balance	$24,326	$22,458	$20,421	$18,202	$15,782

	Year 6	Year 7	Year 8	Year 9	Year 10
Starting balance	$15,782	$13,145	$10,271	$7,138	$3,723
Payment	4,058	4,058	4,058	4,058	4,058
Interest	1,420	1,183	924	642	335
Principal repayment	2,637	2,874	3,133	3,415	3,723
Ending balance	$13,145	$10,271	$7,138	$3,723	$0

Figure 10-3. Amortization Schedule.

Depreciation Schedule. In order to calculate tax effects, we must determine the depreciation schedule that applies to the asset. Figure 10-4 displays depreciation as follows:

- *Depreciable cost.* This is the amount that may be depreciated for accounting purposes. In our example, it is the sum of the purchase price, fees, and capitalized costs. For the purpose of calculating depreciable cost, the early payments are not brought forward using time value of money techniques. Note that the depreciable cost is also the starting book value of the asset.
- *Ending value.* Some depreciation methods require the owner to depreciate an asset only down to some ending value. This may be called a *scrap value, book residual value,* or some other name. In our examples, we will assume a zero ending value after the depreciation period.
- *Depreciation method and period.* If the company must pay taxes, the government has regulations that specify the depreciation schedule. In our example, we will assume that the asset is depreciated over 10 years using straight-line depreciation. The formula is:

Annual Depreciation = Depreciable Cost/Years

It gives the annual depreciation as shown in the figure.

Tax Calculation. Figure 10-5 shows the after-tax cash flows from the sample proposal. Some major components are:

- *Additional revenues and cash expenses.* Companies invest in a capital budgeting proposal in order to earn additional profits. The revenues and cash expenses are the first two lines of the tax calculation.
- *Depreciation.* This is needed to obtain the operating profits from the project.

Project cost	$35,000
Fees	$700
Capitalized cost	$1,000
Years of depreciation	10

	Year 1	Year 2	Year 3	Year 4	Year 5
Starting book value	$36,700	$33,030	$29,360	$25,690	$22,020
Depreciation	-3,670	-3,670	-3,670	-3,670	-3,670
Ending book value	$33,030	$29,360	$25,690	$22,020	$18,350

	Year 6	Year 7	Year 8	Year 9	Year 10
Starting book value	$18,350	$14,680	$11,010	$7,340	$3,670
Depreciation	-3,670	-3,670	-3,670	-3,670	-3,670
Ending book value	$14,680	$11,010	$7,340	$3,670	$0

Figure 10-4. Depreciation Schedule.

- *Interest.* The portion of a project financed by debt will require interest payments. These are deductible for tax purposes.
- *Tax rate.* This applies to any profits from the proposal after depreciation and interest are deducted. It can also provide a tax savings on other income of the firm, if the asset loses money in any year.
- *Taxes.* The pretax profit times the tax rate gives us the tax savings or loss.

Project Cash Flows. The operating profit, cash shielded by depreciation, and tax savings are inflows. The interest, principal repayments, and tax payments, if any, are outflows. Taken together, Figure 10-6 displays the after-tax cash flow.

Residual Cash Flows. The cash effects of assuming that the asset will be sold in the final year of the planning horizon are determined separately, as shown in Figure 10-7. Major items are:

- *Planning horizon.* The company has decided to use five years as the period of the analysis.
- *Cash value of the project.* The project will have an estimated net cash value in the final year. In our example, it is assumed to be 70 percent of the original depreciable cost.
- *Gain on sale.* The difference between the cash and book values is a gain on the sale of the asset. Taxes must be paid on the gain.
- *After-tax residual value.* The cash from the sale plus any funds freed less the taxes and remaining principal on the debt gives us the after-tax residual value.

After-Tax Cash Flow Stream. Figure 10-8 displays the cash flow stream, the final step of the process. It consists of the net cash outlay calculated in Figure 10-2, the annual cash flows calculated in Figure 10-6, and the after-tax residual value calculated in Figure 10-7.

	Year 1	Year 2	Year 3	Year 4	Year 5
Revenues	$70,000	$74,000	$78,000	$82,000	$86,000
Cash expenses	-58,000	-61,000	-64,000	-67,000	-70,000
Depreciation	-3,670	-3,670	-3,670	-3,670	-3,670
Operating income	$8,330	$9,330	$10,330	$11,330	$12,330
Interest	-2,344	-2,189	-2,021	-1,838	-1,638
Pretax profit	$5,986	$7,141	$8,309	$9,492	$10,692
Taxes 25%	-1,497	-1,785	-2,077	-2,373	-2,673

Figure 10-5. Tax Calculation.

	Year 1	Year 2	Year 3	Year 4	Year 5
Operating income	$8,330	$9,330	$10,330	$11,330	$12,330
Depreciation	3,670	3,670	3,670	3,670	3,670
Loan repayment	-4,058	-4,058	-4,058	-4,058	-4,058
Taxes paid	-1,497	-1,785	-2,077	-2,373	-2,673
After-tax cash	$6,446	$7,157	$7,865	$8,569	$9,269

Figure 10-6. Project Cash Flows.

	Year 5
Residual tax calculation	
Original depreciable cost	$36,700
Cash value of project at 70%	$25,690
Less book value	-18,350
Gain on sale	$7,340
Taxes 25%	$1,835

After-tax residual calculation	
Cash from sale	$25,690
Plus tied up funds freed	450
Less remaining debt	-15,782
Less taxes	-1,835
After-tax residual	$8,523

Figure 10-7. Residual Cash Flows.

Cash Flows and Venture Capitalists

In addition to capital budgets prepared by business firms, cash flow streams are a critical component of business plans submitted to venture capitalists. As venture capitalists are highly selective when choosing investments, and as they realize that their money will be illiquid for three or more years, they examine the cash flow stream and the assumptions underlying it carefully.

Entrepreneurs will be expected to provide investors with detailed cash flow streams at as many as six stages of financing:

- *Seed money.* This is a low-level of financing to test the viability of producing a product or service or entering a market. This funding may be provided by an angel investor, an affluent individual who provides capital for business start-ups in return for a share of the company's stock.
- *Start-up.* This involves funds to produce the product or service and set up the marketing phase.
- *First round.* This provides a cash infusion to launch the product or service when production is in place and potential customers are identified.
- *Second round.* This provides additional funding if sales are ramping up, but the firm has not reached the breakeven point.
- *Third round.* Also called mezzanine financing, this is an infusion of cash to allow rapid expansion.
- *Fourth round.* Also called bridge financing, this pays the costs of finding a larger corporation to purchase the company or covers the fees of selling stock to the public.

CONCLUSION

The key to evaluating a capital investment starts with a careful development of a cash flow stream. It starts with the net cash outlay and finishes with the residual value. The

	Year 0	Year 1	Year 2	Year 3	Year 4	Year 5
Net cash outlay	-$13,610					
After-tax cash flows		$6,446	$7,157	$7,865	$8,569	$9,269
After-tax residual						$8,523

Figure 10-8. After-Tax Cash Flow Stream.

next step is to use time value of money techniques to evaluate the return from the investment. This process is described in the next chapter.

CHAPTER 10 APPENDIX

How to Create a Capital Budgeting Cash Flow Stream

A capital proposal has the following data. Using these data, we will create a cash flow stream.

Data

	Year -1	Year 0	Year 1
Project cost	$45,000	$30,000	
Bank financing	60%	60%	
Bank interest	9%		
Fees	2%	4%	
Required return	16%		
Capitalized costs		$2,500	
Years of depreciation		8	
Funds tied up		$1,600	
Interest on permanent financing			8%
Periods of financing			8
Tax rate			20%

	Year 1	Year 2	Year 3	Year 4
Revenues	$110,000	$121,000	$133,100	$146,410
Expenses	$88,000	$96,800	$106,480	$117,128
Cash Value at End as Percent of Project Cost				80%

Net Cash Outlay.

	Year -1	Year 0
Project cost	-$45,000	-$30,000
Bank financing	60%	60%
Bank financing	$27,000	$18,000

	Year -1	Year 0
Fees	2%	4%
Fees	-$900	-$1,200
Capitalized costs		-$2,500
Funds tied up		-$1,600
FIXED		
Outlay each period	-$18,900	-$17,300
Required return	16%	
Present values	-$21,924	-$17,300
Net cash outlay		-$39,224

Amortization Schedule.

	Year -1	Year 0
Bank financing	$27,000	$18,000
Interest accrued 9%	$2,430	
Total owed in Year 0	$29,430	$18,000
Starting loan balance		$47,430
Periodic interest rate		8%
Periods of financing		8

	Year 1	Year 2	Year 3	Year 4
Starting balance	$47,430	$42,971	$38,155	$32,954
Payment	8,254	8,254	8,254	8,254
Interest	3,794	3,438	3,052	2,636
Principal repayment	4,459	4,816	5,201	5,617
Ending balance	$42,971	$38,155	$32,954	$27,337

Depreciation Schedule.

Project cost	$75,000
Fees	$2,100
Capitalized costs	$2,500
Years of Depreciation	8

	Year 1	Year 2	Year 3	Year 4
Starting book value	$79,600	$69,650	$59,700	$49,750
Annual depreciation	(9,950)	(9,950)	(9,950)	(9,950)
Ending book value	$69,650	$59,700	$49,750	$39,800

Tax Calculation.

	Year 1	Year 2	Year 3	Year 4
Revenues	$110,000	$121,000	$133,100	$146,410
Cash expenses	-88,000	-96,800	-106,480	-117,128
Depreciation	-9,950	-9,950	-9,950	-9,950
Operating income	$12,050	$14,250	$16,670	$19,332
Interest	-3,794	-3,438	-3,052	-2,636
Pretax profit	$8,256	$10,812	$13,618	$16,696
Taxes 20%	-1,651	-2,162	-2,724	-3,339

After-Tax Cash Flows.

	Year 1	Year 2	Year 3	Year 4
Operating income	$12,050	$14,250	$16,670	$19,332
Depreciation	9,950	9,950	9,950	9,950
Loan repayment	-8,254	-8,254	-8,254	-8,254
Taxes paid	-1,651	-2,162	-2,724	-3,339
After-tax cash	$12,095	$13,784	$15,643	$17,689

Residual Value.

	Year 4
Residual Tax Calculation	
Original depreciable cost	$79,600
Cash value of project at: 80%	$63,680
Less book value	-39,800
Gain on sale	$23,880
Taxes 20%	-4,776

After-Tax Residual Calculation	
Cash from sale	$63,680
Plus tied up funds freed	1,600
Less remaining debt	0
Less taxes	-4,776
After-tax residual	$60,504

After-Tax Cash Flow Stream.

	Year 0	Year 1	Year 2	Year 3	Year 4
Net cash outlay	-$39,224				
After-tax cash flows		$12,095	$13,784	$15,643	$17,689
After-Tax Residual					$60,504

Chapter
11
Capital Budgeting Returns

Once the cash flow stream for a capital budgeting proposal has been developed, we are ready to evaluate the likely return. In this chapter, we will compare three methods of measuring return: the payback method, the net present value method, and the internal rate of return method.

PAYBACK METHOD

The *payback period* is the length of time needed to regain the original cash outlay for an investment proposal. The calculations are in currency units and are not adjusted for the time value of money. The payback method seeks to determine the payback period for a capital investment. A quicker return of the original outlay not adjusted for the time value of money means that a project is more desirable than one with a longer payback period.

As an example, Figure 11-1 shows cash flow streams for Projects A and B. The outlays are given in Year 0. The residual value is included in Year 4. The payback periods are 3 years for Project A and 3 1/3 years for Project B. Under the payback method, Project A would be more desirable.

Utility of the Payback Method

The payback method is the easiest and least precise of the cash flow methods and has been widely used for a long time. Its primary role in the evaluation of capital investments is as a

Year	Project A	Project B
0	-$18,000	-$26,000
1	+6,000	+7,500
2	+6,000	+7,500
3	+6,000	+7,500
4	+10,000	+18,000

Figure 11-1. Payback Periods for Two Cash Flow Streams.

supplemental tool. Although it should not be used alone, it offers some benefits, including the following:

- *Highlights liquidity.* The payback method shows, in effect, how quickly cash will return to the firm. This information can be useful if the firm might be short on cash in the near future and is seeking early returns to finance future proposals.
- *Useful in uncertain conditions.* If a company is operating in a highly uncertain environment, early cash returns can reduce the level of risk. As an example, consider a firm that is entering a new field where competitors are expected in a few years. The uncertainty of who will enter and how successful they will be places a premium on early returns. In this situation, payback is a useful concept.
- *Useful in foreign investments.* A company may not have full knowledge of conditions in foreign markets. Basically, it is dealing with a higher level of uncertainty than in its domestic market. Payback can be a measure of how quickly returns will accrue as a hedge against changing conditions for the proposal where assets will be located in another country.

Weaknesses of the Payback Method

Although it has utility as a supplemental tool, the payback method suffers from some weaknesses, including the following:

- *Too much emphasis on liquidity.* One problem is that the payback method focuses too heavily on the liquidity aspects of a proposal. If payback is the main criterion for project selection, liquidity will receive priority over profitability. This would not be correct for most long-term investments.
- *Fails to recognize variations in cash flow.* Another problem is that payback does not distinguish variations in cash flow during the payback period. As an example, one project may have cash inflows of $300,000 for Year 1, $400,000 for Year 2, and $500,000 for Year 3. A second project may have inflows of $500,000, $400,000 and $300,000 for Years 1 to 3, respectively. If both projects involved net cash outlays of $1.2 million, the payback period would be three years for each. But the second project would give more cash earlier and thus would be more valuable.
- *Cannot handle varying economic lives.* Perhaps the major difficulty in using payback is that it cannot properly evaluate investments with different economic lives. If two projects each cost $2.5 million and have a $500,000 annual cash inflow after taxes, the payback period would be five years for each. If one project had an estimated life of seven years and the other had a nine-year life, the additional cash flow in Years 8 and 9 for the longer-lived project would not be reflected in the payback method. This could lead to an incorrect decision if payback were the only method of evaluation.

PRESENT VALUE TECHNIQUES

Given the weaknesses and limitations of the payback method, most investment analysis is performed using present value approaches to calculating return because they successfully handle two problems:

- *Varying periodic cash flows.* In a capital budgeting analysis, it is not likely that the cash flows will be identical each year. A proposal may involve the outlay for a project followed by different cash flows each year. Present value techniques allow the analyst to calculate the rate of return for varying annual, quarterly, or monthly cash flows.
- *Different time periods.* Proposals may also involve varying time periods. Present value techniques allow comparing returns in such a situation.

Present Values

The analysis of a proposal begins with the formula for time value of money. In a present value format:

Present Value = Future Value/(1 + Interest Rate)^n

where the interest rate is the discount factor and n is the number of periods.

The discount factor is the key to measuring the rate of return. When future values are discounted to a present value using a discount rate, the future values can be viewed as inflows while the present value can be viewed as an outflow. The discount factor that ties together the present value and future values is the rate of return on the investment.

This can be illustrated with a single investment for a one-year period. Suppose we can invest $1,000 on January 1 and receive $1,100 on December 31 of the same year. The return on the investment is calculated by discounting the future value of $1,100 back to $1,000 using a 10 percent discount factor, or:

$$1,000 = 1,100/(1 + 0.10)^1$$

As a more complex example of the use of this formula, let us consider the following cash flow stream:

	Year 0	Year 1	Year 2	Year 3	Year 4
Cash flows	-$10,000	+$1,000	+$1,000	+$1,000	+$11,000

The initial $10 million is already at the present value. Discounting the first $1 million with the formula PV = $1,000,000/(1 + 0.10)^1 gives a present value of $909,000. Discounting each cash inflow at 10 percent gives us the values:

	Year 0	Year 1	Year 2	Year 3	Year 4
Present value	-$10,000	+$909	+$826	+$751	+$7,513

If we add up the present values of the four future cash flows, they total exactly $10 million. When the sum of the future values equals the present value, the discount factor is also the rate of return on a cash flow stream.

INTERNAL RATE OF RETURN METHOD

The internal rate of return method calculates the actual rate of return provided by a specific stream of net cash benefits compared to the net cash outlay. It uses a trial-and-error approach to find the discount factor that equates the original investment to the net cash benefits. The discount factor, then, is the actual rate of return.

The internal rate of return formula sets the cash flow stream equal to zero, as follows:

$$0 = \sum_{t=1}^{n} \text{Cash Flow } (t)/(1+\text{IRR})^t$$

where IRR is the rate of return that makes the present value of net cash benefits (PVNCB) equal to the present value of the net cash outlay (PVNCO).

We are solving for IRR, which is both the discount factor and the rate of return. If, for example, we find that a 10 percent factor sets the benefits equal to the outlay, the internal rate of return for the investment is 10 percent.

As an example of this technique, we will calculate the internal rate of return for one of the four-year cash flow streams in Figure 11-1. The stream has an initial payment of $18,000, followed by an annuity of $6,000 for three years and a single payment of $10,000 in Year 4. The $18,000 is the net cash outlay; the $6,000 and $10,000 receipts are the net cash benefits.

We must estimate the rate of return and select a discount factor. This is essentially a trial-and-error process that is helped by experience. Let us try 10 percent as a factor:

Present Value at 10 Percent

Year	Cash Flow	Present Value
0	-$18,000	-$18,000
1	6,000	5,454
2	6,000	4,959
3	6,000	4,508
4	10,000	6,830
Net present value		**+$3,751**

In this example, we have solved for the *net present value*, which is the difference between the present value of the net cash benefits and the present value of the net cash outlay. A positive net present value of $375,000 is not close to zero. We must now try another factor. The question is, "Do we go up or down?" The rule is this:

In using present value tables, raising the discount factor lowers the present value. Lowering the discount factor raises the present value.

Thus, the discount factor of 10 percent is too low. Let us raise it to 18 percent in order to lower the present value of the benefits.

Present Value at 18 Percent

Year	Cash Flow	Present Value
0	-$18,000	-$18,000
1	6,000	5,085
2	6,000	4,309
3	6,000	3,652
4	10,000	5,158
Net present value		**+$204**

This is much closer, but it is still a little high. Try 20 percent to see if we can achieve a negative net present value.

Present Value at 20 Percent

Year	Cash Flow	Present Value
0	-$18,000	-$18,000
1	6,000	5,000
2	6,000	4,167
3	6,000	3,472
4	10,000	4,823
Net present value		**-$539**

We did it. We now know that the rate of return for the stream is between 18 and 20 percent, since we bracketed a zero net present value with these numbers. Since the $204,000 net present value at 18 percent is closer than the $539,000 at 20 percent, we know that the rate of return is closer to 18 percent than to 20 percent. We can repeat our calculations at, say, 18.5 percent if we want to refine our NPV further. For our purposes, we do not need to seek more accuracy. We can recognize that the rate of return is between 18 and 19 percent, probably around 18.5 percent. If we wanted to get the NPV to exactly zero, we would keep trying until we found a discount factor of 18.535 percent.

Acceptance Criterion—The Required Return

Once the internal rate of return for a proposal has been forecast, the company must determine whether the project is acceptable. At this point, the firm usually considers return as a single input into the final decision. In addition to profits, the firm evaluates liquidity, growth, diversification, company image, and other factors that affect the goal of maximizing wealth.

Perhaps the most important single factor in evaluating proposals is the level of risk inherent in the project. If a project offers a high risk that the return will not be achieved, the required return on the project will also be high. The trading off of risk and return is the process that the firm should use in determining the acceptability of its proposals.

Once the risk level of a proposal has been determined, the firm will select a cutoff point for that risk level. This is defined as the boundary between accepted and rejected investment proposals. The required return for the proposal's level of risk will be the cutoff point for the proposal. The determination of required return has already been covered in an earlier chapter. In our example, let us assume that we estimated the after-tax required return for the project to be 12 percent. Since the project offers a likely return between 18 and 20 percent, the project is acceptable.

NET PRESENT VALUE (NPV) METHOD

The net present value method is the second time value of money approach to evaluating the return from an investment proposal. It differs from the trial-and-error approach of the internal rate of return method. With the NPV method, we discount a project using the required return as the discount factor. If the net present value is positive, the proposal's forecast return exceeds the required return, and the proposal is acceptable. If the net present value is negative, the forecast return is less than the required return, and the proposal is not acceptable.

To illustrate the net present value method, let us consider the proposal we discussed in the previous section and assume that the required return on it is 15 percent. When we discount the cash flows at 15 percent, we get a net present value of $1,417.

Present Value at 15 Percent

Year	Cash Flow	Present Value
0	-$18,000	-$18,000
1	6,000	5,217
2	6,000	4,537
3	6,000	3,945
4	10,000	5,718
Net present value		**$1,417**

When discounted at the 15 percent required return, this proposal has a positive net present value. This would be expected, since we have already determined the forecast rate of return to be over 18 percent. Under the net present value method, proposals with positive net present values are acceptable, since they have forecast returns that are higher than the required return. Proposals with negative net present value are not acceptable.

Difference Between the IRR and NPV Methods

The internal rate of return and net present value methods can give different results in the ranking of proposals. This is the case because the two methods make different assumptions about the reinvestment of proceeds. In effect, the IRR method assumes that future cash receipts are invested at the rate of return forecast for the project. The NPV method assumes that proceeds are invested at the required return. If the forecast return on the project exceeds the required return, the two methods can give a different ranking of proposals.

To understand what is happening with the two methods, let us compare the results when Projects A and B are being evaluated. Proposal A involves a $1 million net cash outlay and has only one future receipt of cash, $1.2 million in one year. Proposal B also involves a $1 million outlay and also has a single receipt of cash, $1.5 million in three years. Figure 11-2 shows that the internal rate of return on these two proposals is 20 percent for A and 14.47 percent for B.

Using the internal rate of return method, Proposal A would be more desirable than Proposal B, since a 20 percent return is higher than a 14.47 percent return. But what would happen if the after-tax required return were only 8 percent? Using the net present value method, Figure 11-3 shows that we get a higher net present value with Proposal B. With the net present value method, Proposal B is more desirable than Proposal A.

Proposal A: Present Value at 20 Percent

Year	Cash Flow	Present Value
0	-$1,000	-$1,000
1	1,200	1,000
2	0	0
3	0	0
Net present value		**$0**

Proposal B: Present Value at 14.47 Percent

Year	Cash Flow	Present Value
0	-$1,000	-$1,000
1	0	0
2	0	0
3	1,500	1,000
Net present value		**$0**

Figure 11-2. Comparison of Two Proposals.

Which is correct? The answer is that it depends on what happens to the $1.2 million that Proposal A will return at the end of Year 1. If this $1.2 million can be invested so that it produces more than $1.5 million by the end of Year 3, Proposal A would be more desirable. If it cannot achieve $1.5 million, Proposal B is more desirable. In other words, the firm would be better off receiving just under 15 percent for three years rather than 20 percent for one year and a lower percent for the next two years.

Most financial analysts correctly argue that the net present value method is more accurate for most capital budgeting proposals. It assumes the investment of future cash flows at the required return, not at the potentially higher forecast return for a single proposal. Generally, it would be rare for a forecast return to be much higher than a required return. Thus, it is probable that the investment of future cash flows at the required return is more accurate in most cases. But, should the firm have the rare case in which proceeds can be invested at the internal rate of return, the internal rate of return method is more accurate.

MIDYEAR DISCOUNT FACTORS FOR CASH FLOWS

The cash flows in this chapter are discounted using the formula:

$$\text{Present Value} = \text{Future Value}/(1 + \text{Interest Rate})^n$$

where n is the future year. Thus, the first-year cash flow is discounted for one full year.

A more accurate result would be to discount each year's cash flows by the midyear point. The first year's cash flow is halfway between Year 0 and Year 1. Hence, it could be

Proposal A: Net Present Value at 8 Percent

Year	Cash Flow	Present Value
0	-$1,000	-$1,000
1	1,200	1,111
2	0	0
3	0	0
Net present value		**+$111**

Proposal B: Net Present Value at 8 Percent

Year	Cash Flow	Present Value
0	-$1,000	-$1,000
1	0	0
2	0	0
3	1,500	1,191
Net present value		**+$191**

Figure 11-3. Second Comparison of Two Proposals.

discounted at 0.5 instead of 1. This assumes that operating cash flows occur equally in January and December, February and November, March and October, and so forth. On average, the flows occur in the middle of the year. The first year would be discounted at 0.5, Year 2 at 1.5, Year 3 at 2.5, and Year 4 at 3.5. The formula would be:

$$\text{Present Value} = \text{Future Value}/(1 + \text{Interest Rate})^{(n-0.5)}$$

An even more accurate result occurs when we recognize that not all cash flows for a month occur on the last day of the month. To make that adjustment, we need to recognize the factor that adjusts the formula to midmonth. Figure 11-4 shows the net present value discount factors that reflect monthly discounting for a four-year project.

The same situation does not hold true for the residual value. Figure 11-4 shows correctly that the residual cash is received at the end of Year 4 and should be discounted for the full four years.

Calculating Net Present Value with Midyear Factors

The determination of the net present value is a matter of discounting all cash flows to a present value using the required return for the level of risk inherent in a project. Figure 11-5 provides data for a capital budgeting project. Figure 11-6 uses these data to calculate NPV with the formula Present Value = Future Value/(1 + Interest Rate)^n.

Calculating Internal Rate of Return with Midyear Factors

Similarly, Figure 11-7 calculates IRR. In this case, we are using a trial-and-error technique. The analyst selects a discount factor and uses it to discount all cash flows. If the NPV is positive, the analyst raises the factor in the next trial. If the NPV is negative, the next trial uses a lower factor. When the NPV is zero, the discount factor is the internal rate of return on the project.

Impact of Midyear Discounting

The midyear approach is more accurate than year-end discounting and can affect the acceptance decision for a project. Figure 11-8 contains data to illustrate the situation.

The impact on net present value is shown in Figure 11-9, where the difference in discounting converts a positive NPV into a negative NPV.

The impact on internal rate of return is the same. Figure 11-10 shows a substantial drop in IRR as a result of the discounting method.

Cash Flow	Factor
Annual cash, Year 1	0.57
Annual cash, Year 2	1.62
Annual cash, Year 3	2.68
Annual cash, Year 4	3.74
Residual, Year 4	4.00

Figure 11-4. Midmonth Annual Discount Factors.

	Year 0	Year 1	Year 2	Year 3	Year 4
Net cash outlay	-$9,000				
Annual cash flows		$1,620	$1,782	$1,960	$2,156
Residual cash					$7,650
Required return, cash flows	16%				
Required return, residual					20%
Discount factors		0.57	1.62	2.68	3.74

Figure 11-5. Data for Capital Budgeting Project.

	Year 0	Year 1	Year 2	Year 3	Year 4
Net cash outlay	-$9,000				
Annual cash flows		$1,620	$1,782	$1,960	$2,156
Residual cash					$7,650
Required return, annual cash flows		16%	16%	16%	16%
Required return, residual					20%
Present value midyear factors		0.57	1.62	2.68	3.74
Present value, annual cash	-$9,000	$1,489	$1,401	$1,317	$1,238
Present value, residual					$3,689
Net present value	**$134**				

Figure 11-6. Net Present Value Calculation.

	Year 0	Year 1	Year 2	Year 3	Year 4
Net cash outlay	-$9,000				
Annual cash flows		$1,620	$1,782	$1,960	$2,156
Residual cash					$7,650
Discount factor to zero NPV					
Trial and error, try:	19.00%				
Present value midyear factors		0.57	1.62	2.68	3.74
Annual cash flows	-$9,000	$1,467	$1,344	$1,230	$1,125
Residual cash					$3,815
Net present value	$0				
Internal rate of return	**19.00%**				

11-7. Internal Rate of Return Calculation.

	Year 0	Year 1	Year 2	Year 3	Year 4
Cash flow stream					
Net cash outlay	-$9,000				
Annual cash flows		$1,620	$1,782	$1,960	$2,156
Residual cash					$7,650
Required return, annual cash flows		16%	16%	16%	16%
Required return, residual					20%

Figure 11-8. Data for Impact of Midyear Discounting.

	Year 0	Year 1	Year 2	Year 3	Year 4
End-of-year factors		1.00	2.00	3.00	4.00
Present value, net cash outlay and cash flows	-$9,000	$1,397	$1,324	$1,256	$1,191
Present value, residual					$3,689
Net present value					**-$143**
Midyear factors		0.57	1.62	2.68	3.74
Present value, net cash outlay and cash	-$9,000	$1,489	$1,401	$1,317	$1,238
Present value, residual					$3,689
Net present value	**$134**				

Figure 11-9. Impact on NPV with Midyear Discounting.

	Year 0	Year 1	Year 2	Year 3	Year 4
End-of-year factors		1.00	2.00	3.00	4.00
Discount factor to zero NPV					
Trial	15.00%				
Present value, net cash outlay and cash	-$9,000	$1,409	$1,347	$1,289	$1,233
Present value, residual					$3,689
Net present value					$0
Internal rate of return	**15.00%**				
Midyear factors		0.57	1.62	2.68	3.74
Discount factor to zero NPV					
Trial	19.00%				
Present value, net cash outlay and cash	-$9,000	$1,467	$1,344	$1,230	$1,125
Present value, residual					$3,815
Net present value	$0				
Internal rate of return	**19.00%**				

Figure 11-10. Impact on IRR with Midyear Discounting.

CONCLUSION

Financial risk managers know that investors seek returns that are appropriate for the inherent risk in a proposed venture. The term *return* is quite specific. It means that the analyst creates a cash flow stream considering all cash impacts over a fixed planning horizon. This includes the total amount of the outlay, considering any debt that offsets the cash provided; cash flows each year, including tax consequences; and an after-tax residual value calculation that mathematically closes down the cash flow stream. The after-tax cash flow is tested using payback, internal rate of return, or net present value techniques to determine whether the likely return meets or exceeds the required return.

CHAPTER 11 APPENDIXES

How to Calculate a Payback Period

A project has the following data. What is the payback period?

	Year 0	Year 1	Year 2	Year 3	Year 4
Annual cash flow	-$6,500	$1,500	$2,500	$3,000	$4,500
Total cash flow	-$6,500	-$5,000	-$2,500	$500	$5,000

Answer
Payback is in the third year.

How to Calculate Net Present Value and Internal Rate of Return

Example 1.

	Year 0	Year 1	Year 2	Year 3	Year 4
Midyear factors		0.57	1.62	2.68	3.74
Annual cash flow	-$19,000	$4,000	$5,000	$6,000	$7,000
Required return	10%				

Answer.

	Year 0	Year 1	Year 2	Year 3	Year 4
Present values	-$19,000	$3,788	$4,285	$4,647	$4,901
Net present value	**-$1,378**				
Trial	6.44%				
Present values	-$19,000	$3,860	$4,519	$5,076	$5,543
Net present value	$0				
Internal rate of return	**6.44%**				

Example 2.

	Year 0	Year 1	Year 2	Year 3	Year 4
Midyear factors		0.57	1.62	2.68	3.74
Annual cash flow	-$27,000	$5,000	$6,000	$7,000	$10.000
Required return	13%				

Answer.

Present values	-$27,000	$4,425	$4,699	$4,851	$6,133
Net present value	**-$6,892**				
Trial	1.5%				
Present values	-$27,000	$4,958	$5,857	$6,726	$9,458
Net present value	$0				
Internal rate of return	**1.5%**				

Example 3.

	Year -1	Year 0	Year 1	Year 2	Year 3	Year 4
Midyear factors			0.57	1.62	2.68	3.74
Cash flow	-$60	-$90	$30	$30	$30	$100
Required return		12%				

Answer.

Present values	-$67	-$90	$27	$24	$21	$64
Net present value		**-$22**				
Trial	8.0%					
Present value	-$65	-$90	$29	$26	$24	$75
Net present value		$0				
Internal rate of return		**8.0%**				

How to Calculate Likely Return from a Capital Budgeting Project

Danforth, Inc., is a small California bottling company, founded by Jacob Danforth at the turn of the century. It was founded at the site of a mineral spring, 40 miles from San Francisco, and still ships bottled water throughout a six-state area. Its cash sales have stabilized at $27 million compared to cash expenses of $15 million on its bottled-water operations.

There is considerable excitement in the office of Jerry Danforth, the president and grandson of the founder. The company has been offered a nine-year lease on a well-known mineral spring near the Nevada-California line. The water from this spring has certain medicinal properties that make it valuable to physicians nationwide. Ralph Walton, the company's financial manager, has just worked up figures on the possibility of taking over the lease.

Ralph estimates that an operation at the new mineral spring would increase sales from $27 to $45 million the first year. Cash expenses would rise from $15 to $27 million. The additional revenues and expenses would grow by 10 percent a year after the first year.

Walton's plan is to move the water by tank truck from the spring to the company's main bottling facilities. The problem is capacity. At the present level of sales, the firm cannot handle the additional bottling needs of the new spring. A check with a machinery foundry indicates that it will cost approximately $32 million to purchase, transport, and install new bottling machinery capable of handling the new spring. Of the amount, $12 million would be paid in Year −1 and the balance in Year 0. A bank would provide construction financing for 60 percent of the project and capitalized costs. The interest rate would be 11 percent. Permanent financing was also available for seven years with steady annual payments at 8 percent.

After four years, the machinery will have a cash value equal to 50 percent of the original cost. It will be depreciated over six years using the straight-line method.

Ralph Walton has mentioned that the new operation would tie up an additional $400,000 in inventories and $1.2 million in receivables during the life of the project. The firm has the funds to finance these amounts.

Ralph Walton thinks the firm should seriously consider the new project, and Jerry is also favorably inclined. But as Ralph left the office, Jerry was heard to call out, "I want to know our rate of return on the project first. If we're not making 17 percent after taxes on the cash flows and 21 percent on the residual value, forget it." The firm's tax rate is 20 percent.

Required. What are the net present value and internal rate of return on this project?

Data.

	Year -1	Year 0
Project cost	-$12,000	-$20,000
Percent bank financing	60%	60%
Fees	2%	2%
Capitalized costs		-$3,000
Funds tied up		-$1,600
Required return, annual cash flows	17%	
Required return, residual	21%	
Short-term interest rate accrued	11.00%	
Long-term interest		8.00%
Years of depreciation		6

	Year 0	Year 1	Year 2	Year 3	Year 4
Growth rate			10%	10%	10%
Project revenues		$19,000			
Project cash expenses		-$12,000			
Tax rate	20%				
Cash value, percent of project starting value					50%
Present value midyear factors		0.57	1.62	2.68	3.74

Net Cash Outlay.

	Year -1	Year 0
Project cost	-$12,000	-$20,000
Percent bank financing	60%	60%

	Year -1	Year 0
Bank loan	$7,200	$12,000
Fees	2%	2%
Fees	-$240	-$400
Capitalized costs		-$3,000
Funds tied up		-$1,600
Outlay each period	-$5,040	$13,000
Required return	17%	
Present values	-$5,897	$13,000
Net cash outlay		-$18,897

Amortization Schedule.

	Year -1	Year 0
Bank financing	$7,200	$12,000
Short-term interest accrued (11%)	$792	
Total owed in Year 0	$7,992	$12,000
Starting loan balance		$19,992
Long-term interest		8.00%
Periods of financing		7

	Year 0	Year 1	Year 2	Year 3	Year 4
Starting balance		$19,992	$17,751	$15,332	$12,718
Payment		3,840	3,840	3,840	3,840
Interest		1,599	1,420	1,227	1,017
Principal repayment		2,241	2,420	2,613	2,822
Ending balance		$17,751	$15,332	$12,718	$9,896

Depreciation.

	Year 0	Year 1	Year 2	Year 3	Year 4
Years of depreciation	6				
Project cost	$32,000				
Capitalized costs	$3,000				
Starting book value		$35,000	$29,167	$23,333	$17,500
Depreciation		5,833	5,833	5,833	5,833
Ending book value		$29,167	$23,333	$17,500	$11,667

Tax Calculation.

	Year 0	Year 1	Year 2	Year 3	Year 4
Growth rate			10%	10%	10%
Project revenues		$19,000	$20,900	$22,990	$25,289

	Year 0	Year 1	Year 2	Year 3	Year 4
Project cash expenses		-12,000	-13,200	-14,520	-15,972
Depreciation		-5,833	-5,833	-5,833	-5,833
Operating profits		$1,167	$1,867	$2,637	$3,484
Interest		-1,599	-1,420	-1,227	-1,017
Earnings before taxes		$-433	$447	$1,410	$2,466
Taxes (tax credit)	20%	$87	$-89	$-282	$-493

After-Tax Cash Flows.

	Year 0	Year 1	Year 2	Year 3	Year 4
Earnings before taxes		$-433	$447	$1,410	$2,466
Plus depreciation		5,833	5,833	5,833	5,833
Principal repayment		-2,241	-2,420	-2,613	-2,822
Taxes paid		87	-89	-282	-493
After-tax cash flow		$3,247	$3,771	$4,348	$4,984

Residual Tax Calculation.

	Year 4
Net cash value, 50% of original project cost	$17,500
Less book value	-11,667
Gain/loss on sale	$5,833
Taxes 20%	-$1,167

After-Tax Residual Calculation.

	Value
Cash from sale	$17,500
Plus tied up funds freed	1,600
Less taxes	-1,167
After-tax residual	$17,933

Cash Flow Stream.

	Year 0	Year 1	Year 2	Year 3	Year 4
Net cash outlay	-18,897				
Annual cash flow		3,247	3,771	4,348	4,984
After-tax residual					17,933

Required Returns.

Annual cash flows	17%
Residual	21%

Net Present Value Calculation.

	Year 0	Year 1	Year 2	Year 3	Year 4
Net cash outlay	-18,897				
Annual cash		3,247	3,771	4,348	4,984
Residual cash					17,933
Required return annual cash		17%	17%	17%	17%
Required return, residual					21%
PV mid-year factors		0.57	1.62	2.68	3.74
PV NCO and cash	-18,897	2,969	2,924	2,855	2,770
PV residual					8,366
NPV	987				

Internal Rate of Return Calculation.

	Year 0	Year 1	Year 2	Year 3	Year 4
Net cash outlay	-18,897				
Annual cash		3,247	3,771	4,348	4,984
Residual cash					17,933
Discount factor to zero NPV					
Trial and error, try:	21.45%				
PV mid-year factors		0.57	1.62	2.68	3.74
Annual cash	-18,897	2,906	2,752	2,583	2,409
Residual cash					8,243
Net present value	0				
IRR	21.45%				

Is the Project Acceptable? The NPV is positive, and the IRR indicates that the project meets the required returns. The final decision will be made with this as a single input.

How to Balance Conflicting Views in a Capital Budget Discussion

The Barrett Corporation is a medium-sized cable manufacturing company in northern Indiana, approximately 40 miles from Chicago. Founded in 1923, the company has expanded steadily and has developed solid contacts with utilities in a number of midwestern states. The company has several long-term contracts with firms, including subsidiaries of American Telephone and Telegraph.

Barrett's management has been particularly interested in taking advantage of the demand for soft, fully annealed copper wire, which is used in insulated conductors in communication and power systems. The executive committee of the firm has been discussing an expansion of wire drawing facilities to meet anticipated demand.

To gain the most recent information, Joe Halli, the firm's controller, went to the recent Wire Association Convention to review the various types of machines available. He paid particular attention to manufacturers with machinery that promised high production and consistent quality. After three days of discussion with a variety of production and industry experts, Joe called George Gray, a representative for a milling and machinery firm in Cincinnati. Joe asked George to send him some of the details on the machinery that they had discussed, and George agreed to do so. Two weeks later, Joe received a letter from George Gray (see Exhibit 11-1).

After reading the letter carefully and making some notes on it, Joe sent a memorandum to Nick Schafer, the firm's production manager, and Lew Wallis, the firm's senior production accountant. He asked both men to respond to the letter from George Gray and to answer some questions related to other aspects of the investment decision. Three days later, Joe received Nick's reply (see Exhibit 11-2).

Two days after receiving Nick's memorandum, Joe received a reply from Lew Wallis (see Exhibit 11-3). Before Joe had a chance to consider either of the positions, he got a second memorandum from Nick Schafer (see Exhibit 11-4).

After receiving the final memorandum, Joe called Lew Wallis. Lew said that he had helped Nick work out the figures on the annual revenues and expenses, and Lew indicated that the percentages and dollar figures were logical and probably correct. But Lew insisted that the purchase of new machinery still did not make sense because the machinery was simply too expensive.

That night, Joe took the memorandums home to evaluate the MX900. At the likely risk level, the project would have to earn a return equal to or greater than 9 percent after taxes on cash flows and 13 percent on any residual value exposure. And this would be after considering a 30 percent tax rate.

Exhibit 11-1. Memo from George Gray

Dear Mr. Halli,

In response to your inquiry, I am pleased to suggest a machine that would amply meet your needs for high-quality fully annealed copper wire.

I refer to the MX900 model, probably the finest full production wire drawing machine on the market today. The wire drawing machine and annealer are an integral unit with special electronic controls that allow the annealer to work during start-up procedures. Your production manager will well understand how this excellent machine offers lower operating costs due to less scrap and simplified operating procedures.

If you order one of these machines by January 1, and make the required deposit, I will personally guarantee that the machine will be set up and operating one year later. And I will be further able to guarantee that you will receive our current price less a 10 percent discount, an attractive offer indeed! The pricing is as follows:

Price	$5,000,000
Less 10% discount	-500,000
Net price	$4,500,000
Plus shipping/installing	400,000
Fully installed price	$4,900,000

Deposit (January 1) $1,900,000

Balance due (December 31) $3,000,000

As an item of interest, you should know that our prices have already risen by 5 percent on these machines and will rise another 8 percent on January 1. By ordering and paying your deposit prior to January 1, you in effect will be saving 23 percent compared to an order placed next year when I probably will not be able to offer any discount.

If you need any additional information, please do not hesitate to call me. I look forward to hearing from you in the near future.

Sincerely yours,

George Gray

Exhibit 11-2. Memo from Nick Schafer

TO: Joe Halli

FROM: Nick Schafer

We should seriously consider this machine. We could buy it and get rid of an old MX430, which we bought a few years ago from the same firm. It has no value. If we make the change, we do have to plan on tying up $250,000 of increased inventory once the machine is fully operational. This is important, but more important, the machine will save us money, so I think it would make sense to make a replacement with the MX900.

Exhibit 11-3. Memo from Lew Wallis

TO: Joe Halli

FROM: Lew Wallis

I got a copy of Nick's memo, and we had better think twice on this new machine. In a few years, this new machine would be a piece of junk. I made a couple of phone calls and learned that this new machine is just too sophisticated for long-term use. Do you know what my "experts" estimate the new machine would be worth in the future? Twenty-five percent of its original cost. Some cash value in four years, heh? But that's the price of buying fancy equipment. And everybody knows this. Even with straight-line depreciation over 10 years to a zero book value, this machine is not reasonable. The MX900 for over $5 million? You'll never convince me that it makes sense. I think Nick's just not thinking, and I *strongly* urge you to stay with our existing machine.

Exhibit 11-4. Memo from Nick Schafer

TO: Joe Halli

FROM: Nick Schafer

Hold it! Stop! Wait! Whatever happened to production efficiency? Lew's memo does not even touch on the rather impressive economics offered by each machine. I have done some quick figures and the MX900 will save us a bundle. I've figured in a few probabilities, and just look at the annual benefits with this machine:

	At Present	With MX900
Revenues	$13,000,000	$21,000,000
Expenses	7,000,000	13,500,000

These are big savings the first year. And they will grow by 5 percent annually in Years 2 to 4. Don't give up the ship.

Questions.
1. What is the net cash outlay for the new machine?
2. Prepare a cash flow stream for the new machine.
3. What is the internal rate of return on the new machine?
4. What is the net present value for the machine?
5. Is the project acceptable?

Solution.

Data. If you do not need some of the data, insert zero.

	Year -1	Year 0
Project cost	-$1,900	-$3,000
Percent bank financing	0%	0%
Fees	0%	0%
Capitalized costs		$0
Funds tied up		-$250
Required return, annual cash flows		9%
Required return, residual		13%
Short-term interest rate accrued	0%	
Long-term interest rate		0%
Years of depreciation		10

	Year 0	Year 1	Year 2	Year 3	Year 4
Growth rate			5%	5%	5%
Project revenues		$8,000			
Project cash expenses		$6,500			
Tax rate	30%				
Cash value, percent of project starting value					25%
Present value midyear factors		0.57	1.62	2.68	3.74

Net Cash Outlay.

	Year -1	Year 0
Project cost	-$1,900	-$3,000
Percent bank financing	0%	0%
Bank loan	0	0
Fees	0%	0%
Fees	0	0
Capitalized costs		0
Funds tied up		-$250
Outlay each period	-$1,900	-$3,250
Required return	9%	
Present values	-$2,071	-$3,250
Net cash outlay		-$5,321

Amortization Schedule.

	Year -1	Year 0
Bank financing	0	0
Short-term interest accrued	0%	0
Total owed in Year 0	0	0
Starting loan balance	0	
Long-term interest	0%	
Periods of financing	7	

	Year 0	Year 1	Year 2	Year 3	Year 4
Starting balance		0	0	0	0
Payment		0	0	0	0
Interest		0	0	0	0
Principal repayment		0	0	0	0
Ending balance		0	0	0	0

Depreciation Schedule.

	Year 0	Year 1	Year 2	Year 3	Year 4
Years of depreciation	10				
Project cost	$4,900				
Capitalized costs	0				
Starting book value		$4,900	$4,410	$3,920	$3,430
Depreciation		490	490	490	490
Ending book value		$4,410	$3,920	$3,430	$2,940

Tax Calculation.

	Year 0	Year 1	Year 2	Year 3	Year 4
Growth rate			5%	5%	5%
Project revenues		$8,000	$8,400	$8,820	$9,261
Project cash expenses		-6,500	-6,825	-7,166	-7,525
Depreciation		-490	-490	-490	-490
Operating profit		$1,010	$1,085	$1,164	$1,246
Taxes	30%	-303	-326	-349	-374

After-Tax Cash Flows.

	Year 0	Year 1	Year 2	Year 3	Year 4
Operating profit		$1,010	$1,085	$1,164	$1,246
Plus depreciation		490	490	490	490
Principal repayment		0	0	0	0
Taxes paid		-303	-326	-349	-374
After-tax cash flow		$1,197	$1,250	$1,305	$1,363

Residual Tax Calculation.

	Year 4
Net cash value 25%	$1,225
Less book value	-2,940
Gain/loss on sale	-1,715
Taxes 30%	-515

After-Tax Residual Calculation.

Cash from sale	$1,225
Plus tied up funds freed	+250
Less taxes	+515
After-tax residual	$1,990

Cash Flow Stream.

	Year 0	Year 1	Year 2	Year 3	Year 4
Net cash outlay	-$5,321				
Annual cash flow		$1,197	$1,250	$1,305	$1,363
After-tax residual					$1,990

Required Returns.

Annual cash flows	9%
Residual	13%

Net Present Value Calculation.

	Year 0	Year 1	Year 2	Year 3	Year 4
Net cash outlay	-$5,321				
Annual cash flows		$1,197	$1,250	$1,305	$1,363
Residual cash					$1,990
Required return, annual cash		9%	9%	9%	9%
Required return, residual					13%
Present value mid-year factors		0.57	1.62	2.68	3.74
Present value, NCO and cash	-$5,321	$1,140	$1,087	$1,036	$987
Present value, residual					$1,220
Net present value	$148				

Internal Rate of Return Calculation.

	Year 0	Year 1	Year 2	Year 3	Year 4
Net cash outlay	-$5,321				
Annual cash flows		$1,197	$1,250	$1,305	$1,363
Residual cash					$1,990
Discount factor to zero NPV					
Trial and error, try:	11.70%				
Present value mid-year factors		0.57	1.62	2.68	3.74
Annual cash flows	-$5,321	$1,124	$1,044	$970	$901
Residual cash					$1,278
Net present value					$0
Internal rate of return	11.70%				

Is the Project Acceptable? The NPV is positive, and the IRR indicates that the project meets the required returns. The final decision will be made with this as a single input.

Part 6 | Factors That Affect the Value of a Firm

The cutting edge of financial risk management is concerned with adding to the current value of the firm. If the firm's stock is selling today for $50 a share, how can we raise that value to $60? The question is more complex than it may seem. We must deal with three issues:

- *Valuation factors.* The first question we have to ask is, what determines value? Is it cash flow, profits, growth, or the liquidation value of idle assets or even all assets? The answer is that we assess value from multiple perspectives, isolating these perspectives at first and then bringing them together. The tools give an approximate assessment of financial relationships. Then, the analyst can view all factors together and make a judgment that goes beyond the individual measurements.
- *Impact of debt on the capital structure.* Everybody knows that it is risky to borrow and even worse to borrow too much. But what does that mean? Can a firm simply have too much debt? Can high interest rates be the source of future problems? Can the pursuit of financial leverage sink a firm if conditions change? The answer to all these questions, of course, is yes. The problem is to decide how to manage the financial risk when we lever the firm to increase return to the owners.
- *Possibility of external growth by acquisitions.* The fastest way to grow is through external acquisition of existing operations. This can also be a risky way to pursue a higher value for the firm's stock. If the business combination fails to work as forecasted, the value of the firm can drop dramatically.

In the next three chapters, we develop concepts and tools to assess the factors that determine value and establish a range of value for a firm. Then, we examine the impact of favorable financial leverage on that value. In this regard, financial risk management pursues two goals: Invest in projects that create value, and use debt properly in the financing of those projects. Do both when seeking external growth.

Chapter
12

Valuation of Common Stock

A major portion of the assets of corporations is invested in the equity securities of other corporations. An *equity security* is a legal and financial instrument that represents ownership in a firm. The ownership rights may be known in advance and are protected under various laws and legal precedents.

A *corporation* is a legal entity that is created under the law and is empowered to own assets, to incur liabilities, and to engage in business operations. A major advantage of the corporate form is the ease of transferring ownership. This is done through the sale of common stock.

In this chapter, we will examine the ownership of common stock. We will begin with the nature of financial securities and markets. Then, we will develop a foundation for different concepts of value. Next, the concepts will be applied specifically to common stock.

COMMON STOCK AND EQUITY MARKETS

Common stock is an equity security representing the residual ownership of a corporation. *Preferred stock* is an equity security that usually has limited claims on earnings but has priority over common stock with respect to earnings. Common stock is a more important investment for most companies. In this section, we will examine the nature of common stock and the securities markets in which such stock is traded.

Rights of Shareholders

Common stock provides certain rights to shareholders. These are:

- *Claim on residual earnings*. The holder of stock is guaranteed the right to participate in sharing the earnings of the firm after all other obligations are met. The value of this right, of course, is dependent upon the ability of the company to earn a profit.
- *Voting rights*. Common shareholders usually also have the right to vote at stockholders' meetings on issues affecting the fundamental policies of the corporation. Also, shareholders generally have the right to elect members of the board of directors.

However, an exception to this right can occur if the firm issues more than one class of common stock. The holders of one class of stock may have restricted voting rights.

- *Dividend rights.* A *dividend* is a portion of a firm's profits that is distributed to the holder of a share of stock. The firm's common shareholders are entitled to receive dividends, if and when they are declared by the board of directors and paid by the company.
- *Miscellaneous rights.* Common shareholders have other rights as well. They may inspect the company's books for the purpose of evaluating management and obtain a list of the names and addresses of other shareholders. They may transfer their ownership by selling the stock without the consent of the corporation. In a bankruptcy or liquidation, they have a claim on the company's remaining assets after all creditors' and preferred shareholders' claims have been paid.

Types of Dividends

A *dividend* is a share of the profits of a corporation that is distributed to holders of shares of stock. The firm's common shareholders are entitled to receive dividends, if and when they are declared by the board of directors. Dividends generally vary with the performance of the company. Basically, we can identify three kinds of dividends:

- *Cash dividends.* This is the most common form. These dividends are expressed in terms of dollars per share. Thus, if a firm declares a dividend of $5 per share, a shareholder who owns 1,000 shares will receive a check for $5,000.
- *Stock dividends.* With a stock dividend, the board votes to issue additional shares to current shareholders rather than paying them any money. A 10 percent stock dividend gives a stockholder 10 shares of stock for each 100 held. Stock dividends are less desirable than cash. They are better than no dividend at all, however, particularly if the market does not decrease the price of the stock in response to the dividend.
- *Property dividend.* Although this is quite rare, occasionally a company will distribute bonds, the stock of other companies, other securities, or merchandise to its stockholders. A dividend of a financial security may be quite valuable to certain investors. The distribution of small bottles of perfume by a perfume manufacturer is of little value.

Markets for Common Stock

Common stock is traded in carefully regulated securities markets. Once a corporation has issued stock, that stock can be bought or sold by investors in a *secondary market*, defined as a mechanism for trading common stock after it has been issued by a corporation. A *dealer* acts as a principal and buys and sells securities for its own account. A *broker* acts as an agent for others and receives a commission for facilitating the purchase and sale of stock. The same firm or individual may act as either a dealer or a broker in different transactions, as long as the role is disclosed to customers.

Common stock in the United States is traded in various secondary markets, including:

- *Over-the-counter market.* This is a computerized information system that operates primarily through the National Association of Securities Dealers Automated Quotation System (Nasdaq). It is an electronic linkage of thousands of brokers across the country that allows current price quotations to be displayed on a computer terminal upon request. Participants can then execute trades by pushing buttons on the keyboard.
- *New York Stock Exchange.* A *stock exchange* is a central location where members may buy or sell common stock. The New York Stock Exchange is the largest in the country. Stocks are traded by 1,300 members who agree to the rules and regulations of the exchange.
- *Other Electronic Trading.* Stocks are increasingly trading away from organized exchanges on globally connected systems operating 24 hours a day.

Regulation of the Securities Markets

The trading of common stock in the United States is closely regulated to protect individual investors. The *Securities and Exchange Commission (SEC)* administers the nation's securities laws with two goals in mind:

- *To make financial data public.* The SEC requires firms to provide financial and other information in standardized formats. If a firm will not disclose the required information, its common stock cannot be sold to the general public.
- *To minimize possible fraud.* The SEC monitors corporations to reduce the chance of misrepresentation, dishonesty, and fraud connected with the sale of common stock.

VALUATION CONCEPTS

When an investor is evaluating the purchase of common stock to hold in an investment portfolio, she must be knowledgeable with respect to investment values. In this section, we will examine different concepts of value.

Common Stock Values

The *value* of a security may be defined as its worth in money or other securities at a given moment in time. The value of an equity security can be expressed in various terms, including:

- *Going concern value.* This is applied to the common stock of a profitable and otherwise successful firm with prospects for indefinite future operations. The value is based upon future cash flows, profits, dividends, or the growth rate of the business.
- *Liquidation value.* This applies to the common stock of a firm that is ceasing operations. It assumes the sale of all assets, the payment of all liabilities, and the repurchase of any preferred stock. The remaining value is the liquidation value of the common stock.
- *Market value.* This is the value of stock based upon the assessment of all investors at a given moment in time. In effect, it is the current market price of the stock.

- *Book value.* This is the value based on the firm's accounting records. It is calculated by dividing the total of contributed capital and retained earnings by the number of shares outstanding.

Intrinsic Value

A stock's *intrinsic value* is the real worth of the security when the primary factors that create value are taken into consideration. In other words, it is the market value that would be justified by an analysis of the fundamental factors of stock value. It may be based on any or all of the following:

- *Physical assets.* The firm's cash, securities, real estate, and other assets have a market value. They can be sold to pay off debt and provide a dividend to shareholders. A firm may have intrinsic value because it has assets that can be sold.
- *Likely future earnings.* The future earnings of a firm can provide monies for the holders of common stock. This can be in the form of either cash dividends or growth in the market value of the stock. Many analysts view future earnings per share as being the single most important determinant of value on a going concern basis.
- *Likely future dividends.* The future dividends provide cash for investors. If a shareholder holds only a small percentage of a company's stock, the level of dividends may be the major focus of efforts to identify intrinsic value. This method is incomplete by itself, since retained earnings can cause a growth in market value and a capital gain when the stock is sold. Usually, both dividends and capital gains are considered when calculating intrinsic value.
- *Likely growth rate.* A firm with high prospects for significant increases in earnings in the future can have a value based on its growth rate. The stocks of firms that are growing rapidly tend to have higher intrinsic values than the stocks of slower-growing firms.

Intrinsic Value Analysis

Intrinsic value analysis is the process of comparing the real worth of a stock with its current market price. The primary goal is to identify two categories of stock:

- *Clearly undervalued stock.* This is defined as a stock whose value based on fundamental factors exceeds the current asking price in the market. This means that the security is worth more than its selling price. As soon as other investors discover the low price, the market will bid up the price. Thus, the investor seeks to identify and purchase such stock.
- *Clearly overvalued stock.* This is defined as a stock whose current market price exceeds the value calculated from fundamental factors. In this situation, the security is worth less than its selling price. As soon as other investors discover the high price, they will be reluctant to purchase the stock, and the price will fall. With overvalued stock, the investor seeks to identify and avoid it.

Limitations of Intrinsic Value Analysis

The analyst should recognize a number of limitations of intrinsic value analysis, including the following:

- *Marketplace slow to recognize value.* In many cases, stocks can trade above or below their intrinsic values for years.
- *Unpredictable acquisitions.* During a typical year, many surprise offers are made to purchase large blocks of the common stock of publicly traded firms. These offers are usually significantly higher than current market prices. They usually occur as a result of factors that are not easily uncovered by intrinsic value analysis.
- *Speculative firms.* Some firms operate in markets where future success is not easily predicted. Examples are companies that are developing new products for high-technology markets and oil exploration firms. The value of these stocks depends upon factors that are not easily analyzed with intrinsic value techniques.
- *High-growth firms.* A firm that is growing rapidly will generally be priced to reflect future expectations of rapidly growing sales and profits. The value of such firms is dependent upon a realization of the growth rate. Since rapid increases in sales and profits are difficult to sustain in most competitive environments, intrinsic value analysis is of limited help with high-growth firms.

Current Market Value Analysis

A second major analytical tool for evaluating common stock considers the prices of individual stocks and compares them to other indicators of market value. Called *current market value analysis*, this approach deals with market prices, not intrinsic values. It considers short-term factors such as:

- *Overall market level.* At certain times, common stock appears to be undervalued compared to bonds, other financial securities, real estate, or other investments. At such times, investors may seek to acquire a higher percentage of stock in their investment holdings. The logic is that stocks overall are undervalued. As soon as the market recognizes the disparity between stocks and other investments, stock prices will rise.
- *Industry comparisons.* Stocks in the same industry may trade at widely different prices that do not appear to be based upon fundamental factors. An investor may seek to purchase the stock of a firm whose price is lagging behind that of other stocks in the industry. The rationale, once again, is that the market will discover the discrepancy and the stock price will rise.
- *Cyclical lows.* The market prices of many stocks fluctuate in a cyclical pattern. The stock price may rise for a period of time, possibly with the support of institutional investors. Then, it may be sold to yield some profits for its holders. The result is a pattern of rising and falling prices. The investor may seek to purchase the stock at cyclical lows and sell it near cyclical highs.

VALUE OF COMMON STOCK

Present value techniques are used to determine the current value of common stock. In this section, we will examine different valuation approaches.

Required Return as Discount Factor

The *required return* on any investment may be defined as the minimum expected return that is needed if investors are to purchase and hold the asset. It reflects the level of risk offered by the investment. Higher-risk investments require a higher return.

In capitalization techniques for common stocks, the time value of money is the required return on the stock. It is used as the capitalization or discount factor in each analysis.

Capitalization Rate

This is a measure of the rate of return that investors demand before they will purchase a stock. It is the reciprocal of the price-earnings ratio. The formula is:

Capitalization Rate = Earnings per Share (EPS)/Market Price

We discussed the capitalization rate earlier when we discussed ratio analysis. Now we use it in a valuation framework as the required return for publicly traded common stock. A stock with $6 earnings per share and a current market price of $72 has a capitalization rate of 6/72, or 8.33 percent. This firm earns 8.33 percent on the value of its common stock. If investors did not require this return, they would pay more or less for the stock, and the rate of return would drop or rise.

Single-Period Model

The *single-period model* is a common approach to assessing the intrinsic value of common stock. It uses present value analysis and calculates the current value based on a one-year holding period for the stock.

As an example, assume that a stock is expected to have a market price of $110 in one year. Further assume that it will pay cash dividends of $3 per quarter during the year at a time when the required return is 10 percent compounded quarterly. The ending value and quarterly dividends are discounted separately. The present value is the sum of the present values of each quarterly dividend and the ending market price, as follows:

$$\$110/1.025^4 = \$99.65$$

$$\$3/1.025^1 = \$2.93$$

$$\$3/1.025^2 = \$2.86$$

$$\$3/1.025^3 = \$2.78$$

$$\$3/1.025^4 = \$2.72$$

Total present value $110.94

Capitalization of Earnings

This method of valuation assumes that all reported earnings are essentially cash. Either the company pays cash dividends or the value of the company's stock grows by the amount of retained earnings. In either case, the shareholder gains cash. Thus, the earnings per share (EPS) can be capitalized directly by the required return on the stock. The formula is:

$$\text{Present Value} = \text{EPS}/E(\text{Return})_{\text{required}}$$

As an example of a capitalization of earnings method of determining intrinsic value, consider a stock with an earnings per share of $10. At the risk level posed by the stock, the required return is 12 percent. The intrinsic value would be:

$$\$10/0.12 = \$83.33$$

Note: Earlier we used the normal price-earnings ratio as an indicator of the value of stock. Now we see that the capitalization of earnings technique is an identical measure of value, as it is the reciprocal of the price-earnings ratio.

Perpetual Dividends, No Growth

This model makes use of cash dividends to determine intrinsic value. It is useful for evaluating the stocks of mature corporations that pay out most or all of their earnings as dividends. These corporations may be expected to pay dividends perpetually, but will grow only slowly at best.

A *perpetuity* may be defined as a stream of cash to be paid or received indefinitely. The intrinsic value of a perpetuity is given by the formula:

$$\text{Present Value} = \text{Payment}/\text{Interest Rate}$$

where the payment is the periodic receipt or payment of cash in dollars.

The perpetual dividends, no growth formula gives results identical to those from the capitalization of earnings formula. This is true because earnings per share is assumed to be the same as dividends. The formula is:

$$\text{Present Value} = \text{DPS}/E(\text{Return})_{\text{required}}$$

where DPS is the current dividends per share.

As an example of the use of this formula, a stock may pay quarterly dividends of $3 per share at a time when money has a required return of 8 percent annually. Using perpetual dividends and no growth, the stock has an intrinsic value calculated by dividing the dividend by the quarterly required return, as follows:

$$\$3/0.02 = \$150$$

Perpetual Dividends, Constant Growth

This model assumes that earnings and dividends are growing at the same constant rate. It is also called the *Gordon model* [from Myron J. Gordon, *The Investment, Financing, and Valuation of the Corporation* (Homewood, Ill.: Irwin, 1962)]. It applies to firms that retain a portion of their earnings to finance their growth.

The basis for the formula is that future dividends are discounted to a present value using the required return. It may be expressed:

$$\text{Present Value} = \text{Sum of } \frac{1}{[1 + E(\text{Return})_{required}]} [DPS(1 + g)^t]$$

where $[DPS(1 + g)^t]$ is a stream of dividends from Period 1 to Period t. In this model, t periods equals infinity. The factor g is the constant growth rate.

This formula can be simplified algebraically so that it does not require solving for an infinite stream of constantly growing dividends. It becomes:

$$\text{Present Value} = DPS(1)/[E(\text{Return})_{required} - g]$$

As an example of the use of the formula, a firm has earnings per share of $2.50, a dividend payout of 50 percent, and a growth rate of 5 percent. The required return is 10 percent. The dividends per share is $1.25 ($2.50 × 0.50), and the intrinsic value is:

$$\$1.25/(0.1 - 0.05) = \$25$$

Factors in the Gordon Model

Three primary design factors can be observed in the workings of the perpetual dividends, constant growth model:

- *Shareholder's return—single variable.* The return to the shareholder consists solely of future dividends. Earnings returned by the firm are part of the growth factor that operates to increase dividends, but only future dividends are viewed as a return.
- *Growth rate based on market price.* The growth rate is calculated by using the percent of retained earnings based on the current market price. If a stock is selling for $50 and retains $2 per share, the growth rate is 4 percent.
- *Required return equals likely return.* The model assumes that the market is efficient, and thus that the required return on stock will equal the likely or expected return from the combination of cash dividends and growth in stock value resulting from retained earnings.

When the required return is assumed to be the same as the likely return, the Gordon model gives identical results to the capitalization of earnings model.

Gordon Model in Inefficient Markets

An *inefficient market* exists when the required return is not equal to the likely return from an investment. Once we understand the perpetual dividends, constant growth model, it can be used in situations where the likely return is not equal to the required return. Three situations are possible:

- *The required return is less than the likely return.* In this case, the firm has a higher relationship of likely earnings per share to market price than is required by investors. As an example, an 8 percent return might be required and the firm may expect to earn 10 percent. If dividends are declared and paid, the investor can earn only 8 percent on other investments of similar risk. Thus, raising dividends as a percentage of earnings should lower intrinsic value.

* *The required return equals the likely return.* When this is the case, the firm is doing about as well as required. The shareholder might not care about the level of dividends.
* *The required return exceeds the likely return.* In this situation, the firm is not doing as well as required. The intrinsic value will be lower than the value for an identical firm that is expected to achieve its required return. Although it starts with a lower value, the intrinsic value should rise if the dividends are increased. Raising dividends allows the shareholders to invest the money elsewhere at a higher return for the level of risk assumed.

Figure 12-1 shows the effect of different dividend payouts under the Gordon model. Firms A, B, and C all have the same required return of 10 percent. Firm A has a likely return of 8 percent, Firm B has a likely return of 10 percent, and Firm C has a likely return of 12 percent. The market price for each stock is $20. Thus, the earnings per share is expected to be $1.60 for Firm A at an 8 percent return, $2 for Firm B at a 10 percent return, and $2.40 for Firm C with its likely return of 12 percent.

	Firm A	Firm B	Firm C
Required return	10%	10%	10%
Likely return	8%	10%	12%
Market price	$20.00	$20.00	$20.00
Earnings per share	$1.60	$2.00	$2.40
Dividends per Share at Dividend Payouts of:			
30%	$0.48	$0.60	$0.72
50%	0.80	1.00	1.20
70%	1.12	1.40	1.68
100%	1.60	2.00	2.40
Formula: EPS × Dividend Payout			
Growth Rates at Dividend Payouts of:			
30%	6%	7%	8%
50%	4%	5%	6%
70%	2%	3%	4%
100%	0%	0%	0%
Formula: (1 - Dividend Payout) × EPS/Market Price			
Intrinsic Value with Dividend Payouts of:			
30%	$10.91	$20.00	$45.00
50%	13.33	20.00	30.00
70%	14.74	20.00	26.25
100%	16.00	20.00	24.00
Formula: DPS/[E(Return)$_{required}$ - Growth Rate]			

Figure 12-1. Intrinsic Values at Different Dividend Payout Levels.

The figure shows four possible dividend payouts (DPS/EPS): 30, 50, 70, and 100 percent. Dividends per share are calculated for each company and payout level. They range from $0.48 for Firm A at a 30 percent payout to $2.40 for Firm C at a 100 percent payout.

The growth rates are calculated in the next section of the figure. The firms do not grow at a 100 percent dividend payout. The growth rate is 8 percent for Firm C at a 30 percent payout.

The final section of the figure shows the intrinsic value using the Gordon model. The least valuable firm is Firm A, since it has the lowest likely return. Its value rises from $10.91 to $16 as it pays out more dividends, but the value is always below $20. Firm B has a $20 intrinsic value at all dividend levels, since its required return is equal to the likely return. Firm C is most valuable at all dividend levels, but the highest value occurs with the lowest dividend payout. This is because investors would want the firm to retain its earnings and earn 12 percent on a stock that requires only 10 percent for its risk level.

COMPARATIVE APPROACHES TO VALUATION

An investor commonly evaluates intrinsic value by comparing one stock with another. It may be argued that firms with similar operating characteristics and risk will have similar values. In this section, we will cover some comparative approaches to valuation.

Comparing Price-Earnings Multiples

A *price-earnings ratio* is calculated by dividing the market price of common stock by its earnings per share, or:

P/E Multiple = Market Price/EPS

An analyst can observe the price-earnings multiples of publicly traded companies and apply them to other stocks to determine a fair price to pay for stock. This technique might be used for stock that is not widely traded or stock that is held privately.

This technique can be valid within a restricted scope. If market conditions appear to be stable, it can be assumed that normal price-earnings relationships exist. These can reflect the intrinsic value of stocks.

As an example, consider Firm X, which is privately held and has earnings per share of $20. Firms Y and Z are similar firms that are publicly traded. Both Y and Z have P/E multiples of 15:1. The value of Firm X could be estimated at $300, as follows:

Intrinsic Value = 15 × $20 = $300

Comparing Book and Market Values

The *book value per share* of a company's common stock is calculated by dividing the total contributed capital and retained earnings on the balance sheet by the number of shares outstanding, or:

Book Value = Equity/Shares Outstanding

In most cases, the book value bears no direct relationship to the intrinsic value of common stock. At the same time, similar firms can have similar relationships of market value to book value. Assume that a publicly traded firm has a market price that is three times higher than its book value per share. A similar firm might be expected to have the same relationship.

As an example, assume that the common stocks of medium-sized commercial banks are currently trading at market prices that are 1.5 times their book values. A medium-sized privately held bank has a book value per share of $15. Its intrinsic value can be estimated at $22.50 ($15 × 1.5).

Comparing Values Based on Revenues

In some situations, companies' values are based on their ability to generate revenues. This is particularly the case for companies that may become takeover candidates. As an example, a cable television company may be valuable to companies that want to sell their own products using its facilities. The same is true for retail gas stations, which can be used to sell the gasoline of a refiner. The existence of a large revenue base will have value for some purchasers. If an investor is holding the stock when a takeover attempt occurs, the investor can gain a quick profit.

Values Based on Assets

In some situations, companies' values are based on undervalued assets. An example is an oil company that has a large volume of reserves. If a company has one billion barrels of oil in the ground at a time when crude oil sells for $30 a barrel, these assets can justify a high intrinsic value. A second example is a movie company that stores old films in its vaults. Although not currently being used, the films could become attractive to cable television operators and would be a basis for a takeover of the firm.

CONCLUSION

Many approaches can be used to analyze the value of common stock. In most cases, the value is created by cash flows, profits, or rises in asset values. These factors are measured using a framework of risk and required return. High growth rates can add the potential for steep rises in the value of stock. They are also risky, as excessive growth can destabilize an operation. As we use the tools of valuation, we also recognize the role of financial risk management to keep forecasts in perspective.

CHAPTER 12 APPENDIXES

How to Measure Intrinsic Value

Intrinsic Value with Single-Period Model.

Data

Value in one year	$40.00
Dividends per quarter	$1.25

Required return	14.00%
Periodic return	3.50%

Answer

	Year 0	Q1	Q2	Q3	Q4
Maturity value					$40.00
Dividends		$1.25	$1.25	$1.25	$1.25
Present values:					
Present value, maturity					$34.86
Present value, dividends		$1.21	$1.17	$1.13	$1.09
Intrinsic value	$39.45				

Return on Investment.

Data

	Year 0	Year 1
Initial cost	-$8,000	
Plus fees	-$200	
Ending value		$10,000
Less fees		-$300
Dividends		$500

Answer

Cash flow stream	-$8,200	$10,200
Return on investment		24.39%
Formula: (Future Value - Present Value)/Present Value = Return		

Capitalization of Earnings and Gordon Model Value.

Data

Earnings per share	$4.50
Required return	13.00%
Dividends per share	$1.80
Market price	$38.50

Answer

Capitalization of Earnings

Earnings per share	$4.50
Required return	13.00%
Intrinsic value	$34.62

Gordon Model

Earnings per share	$4.50
Dividends per share	$1.80
Dividend payout	40%
Retained earnings per share	$2.70
Divided by market price	$38.50
Growth rate	7.01%
Required return minus growth	5.99%
Divided into DPS	$1.80
Intrinsic value	$30.07

Difference in Valuation with Capitalization of Earnings and the Gordon Model.

Question. For the stock in the previous exercise, why is the intrinsic value different with the two valuation methods?

Answer. They are different because the firm is not earning exactly the required return. Since it earns less than the required return, the Gordon model reduces its value.

Required return	13.00%
Earnings per share	$4.50
Market price	$38.50
Actual return	11.69%

Intrinsic Value with Normal Market Price/Book Value Ratio.

Data

Earnings per share	$6.00
Book value of stock	$30.00
Normal P/E ratio	12
Normal market price/book value ratio	2.50

Answer
Between $72.00 and $75.00.

Earnings per share	$6.00
Normal P/E ratio	12
Value with P/E	$72.00
Book value	$30.00
Normal market price/book value ratio	2.50
Value with market price/book value ratio	$75.00

Intrinsic Value with Discounted Cash Flow Stream.

Data

Future value in 3 years	$60.00
Annual dividends	$8.00
Required return	15.00%
Periodic return	3.75%

Answer

	Year 0	Year 1	Year 2	Year 3
Maturity value				$60.00
Dividends		$8.00	$8.00	$8.00
Required return		15.00%	15.00%	15.00%
Cash flow stream		$8.00	$8.00	$68.00
Present value		$6.96	$6.05	$44.71
Intrinsic value	$57.72			

Intrinsic Value with Ratio of Market Price to Book Value.

Data

	Co. A	Co. B	Co. C
Market price	$50	$90	?
Book value	$30	$59	$45

Answer

Market price/book value	1.67	1.53
Average ratio, market price/book value		1.60
Present value of Co. C using average ratio		$72

How to Calculate the Value of a Firm's Common Stock

An investment analyst is considering the purchase of a block of the stock of Parker Printing Company. It trades in the market at a recent price of $60 a share. The analyst has a balance sheet, an income statement, and additional data as shown. Is the stock a good investment based on its likely intrinsic value?

Parker Income Statement (000s).

	Year 1
Sales and revenues	$580,000
Materials expenses	162,400
Labor expenses	121,800

	Year 1
Depreciation	26,100
Overhead	46,400
Cost of goods sold	356,700
Gross margin	$223,300
Selling expenses	87,000
General and administrative expenses	98,600
Operating income	$37,700
Interest on debt	9,300
Earnings before taxes	$28,400
Federal income taxes	7,100
Net income	**$21,300**
Dividends	$8,520
Change in retained earnings	$12,780

Parker Balance Sheet (000s).

	Year 0	Year 1
Cash	$14,700	$15,800
Accounts receivable	76,200	80,200
Inventories	76,000	80,000
Other assets	13,000	12,000
Equipment	141,500	148,000
Real estate	42,000	45,000
Total Assets	**$363,400**	**$381,000**
Accounts payable	$47,000	$45,000
Wages payable	3,200	4,000
Taxes payable	3,400	2,200
Secured long-term debt	88,000	84,000
Other long-term debt	77,000	88,220
Common stock	5,000	5,000
Additional capital	27,000	27,000
Retained earnings	112,800	125,580
Total Liabilities and Equity	**$363,400**	**$381,000**

Parker Additional Data.

Shares outstanding	5,000
Asking price	$60
Dividend payout	40%
Normal P/E multiple	12

Normal market price to book value	1.5
Assessed value of real estate	$150,000
Assessed value to market value	80%

Liquidation Percentages

Cash	100%
Receivables	90%
Inventories	50%
Other assets	50%
Fixed assets	50%

Earnings per Share

Net income	$21,300
Shares outstanding	5,000
Earnings per share	$4.26

Growth Rate

Dividend percentage	40%
Retained earnings percentage	60%
Retained earnings, dollars	$2.56
Divided by asking price	$60.00
Growth rate	4.26%

Capitalization of Earnings Value

Earnings per share	$4.26
Divided by required return	8.33%
Intrinsic value	$51.12

Gordon Model Value

Required return	8.33%
Growth rate	4.26%
Dividends per share	$1.70
Divide by required return - growth rate	4.07%
Intrinsic value	$41.83

Comparative Price-Earnings Value

Earnings per share	$4.26
Times normal P/E multiple	12
Intrinsic value	$51.12

Comparative Market Price/Book Value

Equity	$157,580
Shares outstanding	5,000
Book value	$31.52
Times normal market price/book value ratio	1.5
Intrinsic value	$47.27

Liquidation Value

	Asset	Factor	Value
Cash	$15,800	100%	$15,800
Receivables	$80,200	90%	$72,180
Inventories	$80,000	50%	$40,000
Other assets	$12,000	50%	$6,000
Fixed assets	$148,000	50%	$74,000
Real estate	$150,000	1.25	$187,500
Total value			$395,480
Less debt			-$223,420
Market value of stock			$172,060
Shares outstanding			5,000
Liquidation value			$34.41

Is the Stock a Good Value? On a going concern basis, the stock has intrinsic values in the $40 to $50 range. The liquidation value is below the low end of this range. At $60, the stock appears to be overpriced.

Chapter

13

Capital Structure of the Firm

CAPITAL STRUCTURE

An important job of the board of directors and the CEO is to establish the mix of funds that will be used to finance a firm's assets. *Capital structure* is defined as the combination of debt and equity that provides the financing for assets. Two expressions of capital structure are:

- *Balance sheet.* Accounting develops the book value of assets and matches it against total liabilities. The difference between assets and debt is equity, the accounting value of ownership. The breakout between debt and equity shows the capital structure for accounting purposes.
- *Market values.* Separately, capital structure can start with debt and equity. How much does a firm owe? What is the market value of its stock? The capital structure is measured in terms of market levels rather than by using accounting data.

The two methods of calculating capital structure have different roles. Accounting values are widely used by creditors to facilitate comparing different firms, with the expectation that they employ similar accounting practices. Most analysts consider this to be a valuable approach to understanding risk from excessive debt. It is not appropriate for the capital-structure decisions that must be made by the board and the CEO, however. Their primary concern should be the pursuit of a mixture of debt and equity that links risk and required return. This means that they should use market values as they manage capital structure.

Goals of Capital Structure Management

Managing a firm's capital structure involves pursuing the following goals:

- *Determine appetite for risk.* The firm makes decisions on products and markets, with varying risks and opportunities across different operating segments. The firm's appetite for risk may be defined as the potential adverse impact that the organization is willing to accept in order to achieve a return on its assets. Some organizations have a large appetite for risk, pursuing high returns accompanied by high levels of risk. Others are conservative and accept lower likely returns accompanied by lower levels of risk.

- *Optimize mixture of debt and equity financing.* Once the level of risk is established, the firm makes decisions concerning the level of debt in the capital structure. Larger amounts of debt or higher-cost debt raises the risk level and requires the firm to demand a higher required return.

WEIGHTED AVERAGE COST OF CAPITAL (WACC)

WACC is a traditional approach to understanding capital structure. It is a starting point for the calculation of the impact of using a combination of debt and equity in a capital structure. It consists of two components. We will cover each in turn.

Cost of Fixed-Return Securities

A fixed-return security is either debt or preferred stock. The difference in calculating the cost is that most systems allow companies to deduct interest from corporate income taxes. The cost of debt formula is:

$$K_i = \text{Interest}/D(\text{Market}) \times (1 - \text{Tax Rate})$$

where:

K_i = before-tax cost of debt

Interest = the annual interest paid on all debt

D(Market) = the dollar value of debt in the capital structure

Tax Rate = the income tax rate as a percent of net income

Figure 13-1 contains a calculation of the after-tax cost of debt.

For preferred stock financing with a fixed rate and no deduction of dividends for tax purposes, the formula simply omits the tax component and becomes:

$$K_{ps} = \text{Dividends}/PS(\text{Market})$$

where annual dividends are divided by average outstanding preferred stock.

Data	
Annual interest	$2,000
Average debt	$15,000
Tax rate	30.0%

Calculation	
Interest	$2,000
Divided by debt	$15,000
Times (1 - tax rate)	70.0%
K_i	9.3%

Figure 13-1. After-Tax Cost of Debt.

Cost of Common Stock

Determining the cost of common stock starts with assumptions:

- *Going concern basis.* A going concern is expected to operate successfully for an indefinite period of time. Thus, current values reflect future values.
- *Net income approximates cash flow.* The reported earnings using accounting techniques is roughly the same as cash flow from operations.

With these two assumptions, the cost of common stock, commonly called the cost of equity, is calculated by the formula:

$$K_e = NIAT/CS(\text{Market}) \quad \text{or} \quad K_e = EPS/\text{Market Price}$$

where

NIAT = net income after taxes

CS(Market) = market value of all common stock

EPS = earnings per share

Market Price = current market price of a share of common stock

Figure 13-2 contains a calculation of the after-tax cost of equity.

Weighted Average Model

Having calculated separately the cost of fixed-return securities and common stock, we can determine the firm's current cost of capital as a weighting of the capital structure components. First, we recognize that the total value of the firm is the sum of the value of debt, preferred stock, and common stock, expressed by the formula:

$$V(\text{Market}) = D(\text{Market}) + PS(\text{Market}) + CS(\text{Market})$$

For a firm without preferred stock, the formula is:

$$K_o = \%D(\text{Market}) \times K_i \times (1 - \text{Tax Rate}) + \%CS(\text{Market}) \times K_e$$

where %D(Market) is the percentage of debt and %CS(Market) is the percentage of common stock in the capital structure.

Figure 13-3 contains a calculation using the weighted average cost of capital.

Data

Net income after taxes	$9,000
Shares outstanding	20,000
Market price	$3.00

Calculation

NIAT	$9,000
Divided by CS(Market)	60,000
K_e	15.0%

Figure 13-2. After-Tax Cost of Equity.

Data

Debt	$15,000
Shares outstanding	20,000
Market price	$3.00
Cost of debt	9.3%
Cost of equity	15.0%
Tax rate	30.0%

Calculation

Debt	$15,000
Plus *CS*(Market)	60,000
V(Market)	$75,000
Debt	$15,000
Divided by *V*(Market)	$75,000
%*D*(Market)	20.0%
Times K_i	9.3%
Times (1 - tax rate)	70.0%
Plus %*CS*(Market)	80.0%
Times K_e	15.0%
K_o	13.3%

Figure 13-3. Weighted Average Cost of Capital.

Utility of Weighted Average Model

Weighted average cost of capital offers advantages and disadvantages as a model of return for a firm. Strengths of the model include the following:

- *Straightforward approach.* The model builds on the components of the capital structure and reflects the current return required by shareholders. In that sense, it shows the risk appetite of the owners of the business. If they were not satisfied with the return, they would sell the stock and invest elsewhere.
- *Responsive to changing conditions.* It reflects actions both within the firm and in the market for its securities. If the company adjusts its debt level or interest payments, the cost of debt changes. If the market price changes, that is also reflected in the required return.
- *Useful during "normal" times.* WACC produces reasonable results when a firm has a normal or satisfactory level of debt and is operating within forecasted profit and cash flow expectations.

The weighted average model also has some weaknesses:

- *Excessive low-cost debt.* It can be misleading when a firm has a high level of low-cost debt. Short-term financing can represent an important source of funds for firms experiencing financial difficulties. If it is in the form of payables, it may have no cost at all. An excessive reliance on payables, and overdue payables at that, raises the risk level for a firm even as it lowers the overall cost of capital. This can be misleading if shareholders do not recognize the exposure and pay lower prices for the stock.

- *Problem with low profits.* The model cannot handle periods of low operating income. If profit margins and returns on investment drop below the required returns, shareholders cease to value firms on a going concern basis. Instead, either a liquidation or a speculative value takes over. This is a situation of high risk for the firm and its shareholders, and the value of WACC disappears.

- *Not useful at the margin.* In finance, an area outside existing activities is considered to be "at the margin." The current cost of capital or required return is also the average return. New projects are considered to be outside current limits. The weighted average model does not work for new projects, as they must be evaluated on the merits of their own risk and return.

REQUIRED RETURN AT THE MARGIN

For new projects, the calculation of required return and capital-structure decisions are made ignoring the current weighted average cost of capital. The process is twofold:

- *Appetite for risk determines required return.* A project is first assessed for the required return given the risk level as formulated within the capital asset pricing model.
- *Added risk for debt.* The added exposure as a result of using debt financing is an adjustment to the required return.

We will deal with these issues in a framework of three theories of capital-structure management.

Theory 1: Fixed K_o

The first theory postulates that the overall required return is fixed as a constant percentage of all projects in a given risk class. The relationship is expressed by the formula:

$$E(\text{Return})_{required} = \text{Operating Income/Project Cost}$$

Under the fixed-K_o theory, we recognize the following:

- K_o *(fixed).* This is the required return.
- *EBIT.* Earnings before interest and taxes is an alternative term used to express the operating income.
- *V(Market).* The project cost is also the value in the market for the project.

Thus, the formula expressing the fixed-K_o theory becomes:

$$K_o(\text{fixed}) = \text{EBIT}/V(\text{Market})$$

Proponents of the fixed-K_o theory contend that the required return is constant for any risk level. If we know the required return and the likely EBIT, we can solve for the value of the project. If we know the required return and the cost of the project, we can solve for the needed EBIT. The formulas are:

$$V(\text{Market}) = \text{EBIT}/K_o(\text{fixed})$$

and

$$\text{EBIT} = V(\text{Market}) \times K_o(\text{fixed})$$

Figure 13-4 shows a calculation of value at market and required EBIT.

Solving for K_e if K_o Is Fixed

If the overall required return is fixed based on the project, we do not need to calculate it. For a firm with debt, we can solve for K_e. We begin with the formula:

$$K_e = \text{NIAT}/CS(\text{Market}) = \text{NIAT}/[V(\text{Market}) - D(\text{Market})]$$

Next, we replace $V(\text{Market})$ with $\text{EBIT}/K_o(\text{fixed})$ to get:

$$K_e = \text{NIAT}/[\text{EBIT}/K_o - D(\text{Market})]$$

In this formula, all the values including the fixed K_o are known. This allows us to solve for K_e. If the project earns the overall required return, shareholders will earn the after-tax return calculated by the formula. Figure 13-5 shows such a calculation.

Theory 2: Fixed K_e

The second theory argues that the required return on equity capital is the independent variable that determines the value of the firm. The fixed K_e is determined by the return required by the investing community when viewing all projects or firms in a risk class. The value of equity or required NIAT can be solved for directly by the formula:

$$CS(\text{Market}) = \text{NIAT}/K_e(\text{fixed})$$

or

$$\text{NIAT} = CS(\text{Market}) \times K_e(\text{fixed})$$

To get the total value of the firm, we just add the debt to the value of equity determined by the formula.

Data

	Project A	Project B
EBIT	$7,500	
Cost of the project		$4,500
K_o(fixed)	16.0%	16.0%

Calculation

	Project A	Project B
V(Market)	$46,875	
Required EBIT		$720

Figure 13-4. Value at Market and Required EBIT.

Data

EBIT	$12,000
Interest rate	6.0%
D(Market)	$20,000
Tax rate	20.0%
K_o(fixed)	14.0%

Calculation

EBIT	$12,000
Interest rate	6.0%
Times D(Market)	$20,000
Interest	$1,200
EBT	$10,800
Times (1 - tax rate)	20.0%
NIAT	$8,640
EBIT/K_o - D(Market)	$65,714
After-tax K_e	13.1%

Figure 13-5. Required Return on Equity.

Solving for K_o if K_e Is Fixed

If we accept the proposition that the required return on equity capital is fixed, we can solve for overall required return. We begin with the formula for K_o:

$$K_o = \text{EBIT}/V(\text{Market})$$

We modify the formula so that the market value of the firm is expressed as the sum of the values of individual components in the capital structure:

$$K_o = \text{EBIT}/[D(\text{Market}) + \text{NIAT}/K_e(\text{fixed})]$$

This formula can be used to solve for the required return, since all components are known. Figure 13-6 shows such a calculation.

If the project earns 10.3 percent, the equity holders will earn their required return.

Theory 3: Varying K_e with Debt Levels

The third traditional theory argues that the relationship of NIAT and CS(Market) is fixed for a risk class, but that refers to the average or normal level of debt and debt cost in the capital structure. If interest rates rise or debt is added above the norms, the K_e rises to reflect the added exposure.

The value of this theory is that it focuses the firm on the impact of increasing or decreasing the debt-equity ratio. It also highlights the limitations of favorable financial leverage. Figure 13-7 shows the impact of the rising K_e even as the firm increases its favorable financial leverage. The EBIT rises more than the interest, but the CS(Market) drops as investors perceive the higher debt-equity exposure.

Data

EBIT	$12,000
D(Market)	$20,000
Interest rate	6.0%
Tax rate	20.0%
K_e(fixed)	9.0%

Calculation

EBIT	$12,000
Interest	$1,200
EBT	$10,800
Taxes	$2,160
NIAT	$8,640
EBIT	$12,000
D(Market) + NIAT/K_e(fixed)	$116,000
Before-tax K_o	10.3%

Figure 13-6. Required Return on a Project.

CONTRIBUTION OF MILLER AND MODIGLIANI

In a June 1958 article in the *American Economic Review*, Merton Miller and Franco Modigliani proposed three distinct propositions to prove which theory of capital structure is correct. The article makes use of a complex but rigorous proof that two firms in the same risk class and with the same earnings before interest and taxes should not have different overall values in the market. They should have a higher return on equity if they make use of favorable financial leverage. Although the proof of the propositions is beyond the scope of this book, the logic is inescapable. Thus, we will examine each proposition in turn.

	Before	After
Debt	$0	$20,000
Interest rate	0.0%	8.0%
Return on investment	10.0%	
EBIT	$5,000	$7,000
Less interest	$0	-$1,600
EBT	$5,000	$5,400
K_e(varying)	10.0%	11.0%
CS(Market)	$50,000	$49,091

Figure 13-7. Impact of Rising K_e When Debt Is Added.

Proposition I

Proposition I may be expressed in two ways:

- *In terms of* V*(Market)*. The market value of any firm is independent of its capital structure and is given by capitalizing its expected return at a rate appropriate to its risk class. The formula would be $V(\text{Market}) = \text{EBIT} / K_o(\text{fixed})$.
- *In terms of overall required return*. The required return for any firm is independent of its capital structure and is equal to the required return for a pure equity stream of its risk class. The formula is:

$$K_o(\text{fixed}) = \text{EBIT}/V(\text{Market})$$

Proposition II

This may also be expressed in two ways:

- *In terms of yield*. The expected yield of a share of stock is equal to the appropriate capitalization rate K_o for a pure equity stream of its risk class, plus a premium related to the financial risk. The premium is equal to the debt-equity ratio at market times the spread between K_o and K_i.
- *In terms of required return on equity*. The formula is:

$$K_e = K_o + (K_o - K_i) \times [D(\text{Market})/CS(\text{Market})] \times (1 - \text{Tax Rate})$$

Figure 13-8 shows a calculation of the cost of equity capital under Proposition II.

The firm has the option to borrow additional funds to increase the financial leverage in its capital structure. When it does this, K_e rises because of a drop in $CS(\text{Market})$ to compensate for the risk of the higher ratio of debt to equity. Figure 13-9 shows this impact using the data in Figure 13-8.

Data

K_o	10.0%
D(Market)	$4,000
K_i	7.0%
Tax rate	25.0%
CS(Market)	$6,000

Calculation

K_o	10.0%
Plus $(K_o - K_i)$	3.0%
Times D(Market)/CS(Market)	66.7%
Times (1 - tax rate)	75.0%
K_e	11.5%

Figure 13-8. Cost of Equity Capital Under Proposition II.

Data

K_o	10.0%
Original D(Market)	$4,000
New D(Market)	$5,000
K_i	7%
Tax rate	25%
CS(Market)	$6,000

Calculation

K_o	10%
Plus (K_o-K_i)	3%
Times D(Market)/CS(Market)	150%
Times (1-tax rate)	75%
K_e	13.4%

Figure 13-9. Impact of Adding Debt Under Proposition II.

Proposition III

The logical conclusion to the Miller-Modigliani position is found in Proposition III, which states that the cutoff point for investment in the firm will be, in all cases, K_o and will be completely unaffected by the type of security used to finance the investment. In different words, the gain from borrowing cheap funds is offset by the market's discounting the common stock to reflect the added risk.

Proof of Proposition III

Miller and Modigliani proved Proposition III by demonstrating how investors would react to a firm's accepting projects lower than the K_o for the risk class of the investment. Figure 13-10 shows an investing organization such as a mutual or pension fund that is sufficiently large to consider capital-structure leverage in its own portfolio. It can choose between Firms X and Y in the same risk class.

- *Column 1. Firm X at required return.* If Firm X has no debt, the investor expects a 12 percent return because X has an actual return that equals the required return. No leverage risk exists, so this is the right return.
- *Column 2. Firm Y at required return.* If Firm Y accepts debt but invests to earn 12 percent, the favorable financial leverage gives the investor 16 percent on the investment. The additional return compensates for the risk of debt.
- *Column 3. Firm Y below* $K_{o(required)}$. If Firm Y ignores Proposition III, it can invest as long as it has favorable financial leverage. Investing at 11 percent when 12 percent is required gives equity investors a return of 14 percent. Is this enough?
- *Column 4. Investor accepts leverage.* The investor has a choice to borrow individually and buy the stock of Firm X. He still has only $100,000 at risk, but half of it is to a creditor. He now expects a 16 percent return on his investment in Firm X, but only

	Firm X Unlevered	Firm Y Levered	Firm Y Ignores Prop. III	Firm X Personal Leverage
Debt	$0	$50,000	$50,000	$50,000
Equity	$100,000	$50,000	$50,000	$50,000
Assets	$100,000	$100,000	$100,000	$100,000
$K_{o(required)}$	12%	12%	12%	12%
$K_{i(after-tax)}$	0%	8%	8%	8%
$K_{o(likely)}$	12%	12%	11%	12%
Operating income	$12,000	$12,000	$11,000	$12,000
Interest	$0	$4,000	$4,000	$4,000
Net income	$12,000	$8,000	7,000	$8,000
Equity investment	$100,000	$50,000	$50,000	$50,000
$K_{e(likely)}$	12%	16%	14%	16%

Figure 13-10. Miller and Modigliani Data for Two Firms.

14 percent from Firm Y with similar debt risk. We can adjust the amounts invested to reflect other considerations, but we will always come back to the realization that investors will sell the stock of Firm Y because a higher return exists at the same capital-structure risk level with Firm X.

Contribution of Miller and Modigliani

Miller and Modigliani made a significant contribution to understanding risk in the capital structure. Many managers believed that firms should always take advantage of favorable financial leverage. If you could borrow at 8 percent after taxes and earn 9 percent after taxes, it was a sound strategy. It was not. The firm was incurring excessive risk if the project did not earn the K_o for its risk class.

Stated another way, Miller and Modigliani proved that all projects must be on or above the market line in the capital asset pricing model formulation. The market line is not invalidated by managing the capital structure.

OPTIMAL CAPITAL STRUCTURE

The optimal capital structure for a firm may be defined as the relationship of debt and equity that matches the firm's appetite for risk. If a firm borrows and favorable financial leverage increases return at an acceptable risk level, the value of its common stock will rise.

K_i, K_e, and K_o with Rising Debt to Equity

Figure 13-11 shows how a rising debt-equity relationship affects the components of the capital structure. The cost of debt rises as new bondholders or lenders perceive the increased risk of providing more debt funds. The return on equity rises until the after-tax cost of debt matches the overall required return. If we accept Miller and Modigliani, the overall required return is not affected by changes in the capital structure.

Optimal Debt Level

Figure 13-12 shows the optimal level of debt as a function of the debt-equity relationship. The firm borrows as long as it believes that the added risk is overcome by favorable financial leverage that produces an increase in the market price of stock. At some point, investors will become concerned about the risk level and begin to avoid the stock. The optimal point is to stop borrowing when the maximum acceptable risk and return are reached.

Target Level of Debt

Figure 13-13 shows another view of the optimal capital structure. As the firm adds debt with favorable financial leverage, the K_e rises, as does the value of the common stock. At

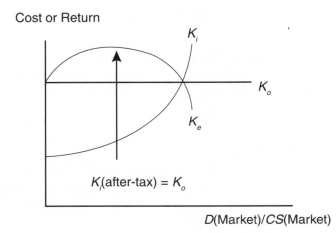

Figure 13-11. Impact of Rising Debt-Equity Relationship.

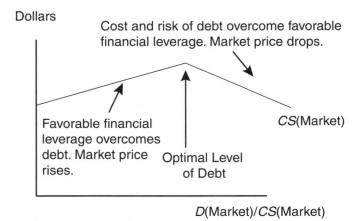

Figure 13-12. Optimal Level of Debt.

some perceived debt level, the risk becomes unacceptable, and borrowing should stop. This point can be the firm's target level of debt.

Capital Structure and Capital Asset Relationship

Figure 13-14 ties capital-structure relationships into the capital asset pricing model. The market line provides the separation between acceptable and unacceptable stocks or projects. The overall required return for a project appears as a K_o on the line. With favorable financial leverage, the K_e rises, but the equity holders are still on the market line. With additional risk, they are simply further up the line.

Optimal Capital Structure

Figure 13-15 moves the discussion into the reality that the theory explains capital structure, but real-world considerations bring in other factors. These factors include imperfect

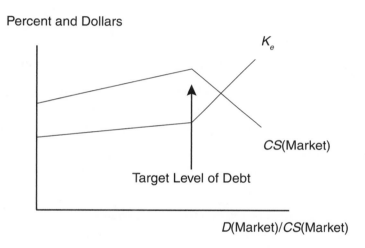

Figure 13-13. Target Level of Debt.

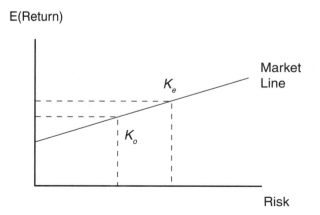

Figure 13-14. K_o and K_e Relationships to Market Line.

markets, uncertainty with respect to risks and return, and even irrational behavior by investors and financial institutions. As a result, the figure shows optimal capital structure as a range. In some situations, it may be appropriate to be conservative, and other situations may seem to justify more risk.

CONCLUSION

The risks of managing capital structure are fairly clear:

- K_o *is fixed.* The evidence is strong that investments should produce a return that is appropriate for the risk of the project.
- K_e *compensates for risk.* If the firm borrows, favorable financial leverage should bring a higher return on equity to compensate for the risk of adding debt.
- *Appetite for risk determines optimal structure.* Every firm and project can have a different optimal structure as a result of the different risk appetites of investors.

CHAPTER 13 APPENDIX

How to Determine the Required Return Under Different Investment Theories

Standard for Whether a Firm Has Achieved Its Optimal Capital Structure. The added profits from debt must match the owners' appetite for risk, and the stock price must not be being penalized by investors because they perceive excessive risk.

Role of Financial Leverage in Capital-Structure Management. It can increase return to equity owners by using low-cost debt to finance assets at a lower interest rate than the return on investment from financed assets.

Miller and Modigliani Conclusion on Overall Required Return. No firm should accept a project that does not offer a return on investment that is appropriate relative to the return from financing the project totally with equity.

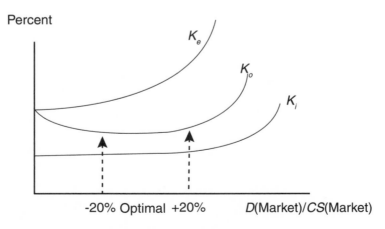

Figure 13-15. Optimal Capital Structure as a Range.

After-Tax Cost of Debt.

Data

Annual interest	$9,000
Average debt	$75,000
Tax rate	30.0%

Calculation

Interest	$9,000
Divided by debt	$75,000
Times (1 - tax rate)	70.0%
K_i	8.4%

After-Tax Cost of Equity.

Data

Net income after taxes	$12,000
Shares outstanding	14,000
Market price	$7.00

Calculation

NIAT	$12,000
Divided by CS(Market)	$98,000
K_e	12.2%

Weighted Average Cost of Capital.

Data

Debt	$170,000
Shares outstanding	14,000
Market price	$15.00
Cost of debt	9%
Cost of equity	18%
Tax rate	20%

Calculation

Debt	$170,000
Plus CS(Market)	$210,000
V(Market)	$380,000
Debt	$170,000
Divided by V(Market)	$380,000

%D(Market)	44.7%
Times K_i	9.0%
Times (1 - tax rate)	80.0%
Plus %CS(Market)	55.3%
Times K_e	18.0%
K_o	13.2%

Market Value and Required EBIT.

Data

	Project A	Project B
EBIT	$9,000	
Cost of the project		$3,200
K_o(fixed)	14%	17%

Calculation

V(Market)	$64,286	
Required EBIT		$544

Required Return on Equity.

Data

EBIT	$9,000
Interest rate	6%
D(Market)	$20,000
Tax rate	20%
Pretax K_o(fixed)	14%

Calculation

EBIT	$9000
Interest rate	6.0%
Times D(Market)	$20,000
Minus interest	$1,200
EBT	$7,800
Times tax rate	20.0%
Net income after taxes	$6,240
EBIT/K_o - D(Market)	$44,286
After-tax K_e	14.1%

Required Return on an Overall Project.

Data

EBIT	$7,500
D(Market)	$10,000
Interest rate	6.0%
Tax rate	20.0%
K_e(fixed)	14.3%

Calculation

EBIT	$7,500
Interest	$600
EBT	$6,900
Taxes	$1,380
NIAT	$5,520
EBIT	$7,500
D(Market) + NIAT/K_e(fixed)	$48,483
Before-tax K_o	15.5%

Firm's Cost of Equity Capital.

Data

K_o	15%
D(Market)	$11,000
K_i	9%
Tax rate	30%
CS(Market)	$24,000

Calculation

K_o	15.0%
Plus (K_o - K_i)	6.0%
Times D(Market)/CS(Market)	45.8%
Times (1 - tax rate)	70.0%
K_e	16.9%

Impact on K_e When Debt Is Added to the Capital Structure.

Data
See prior exercise.

Calculation

K_e rises.

Original debt	$11,000
New debt	$2,000
New D(Market)	$13,000
K_o	15.0%
Plus (K_o - K_i)	6.0%
Times D(Market)/CS(Market)	54.2%
Times (1 - tax rate)	70.0%
K_e	17.3%

Required Returns on Equity.

Data

	Project X	Project Y
Return on investment	12%	12%
D(Market)	0	$30,000
CS(Market)	$100,000	$70,000
Annual interest rate	0%	7%
Tax rate	20%	20%

Calculation

V(Market)	$100,000	$100,000
Return on investment	12%	12%
EBIT	$12,000	$12,000
Annual interest	$0	-$2,100
EBT	$12,000	$9,900
Taxes	-$2,400	-$1,980
Net income after taxes	$9,600	$7,920
CS(Market)	$100,000	$70,000
K_e	9.6%	11.3%

Chapter

14

Valuation of Business Combinations

A *business combination* is the uniting of two firms into a single economic unit. It may be achieved by the purchase of assets or common stock, and it may be paid for with cash or by issuing securities. It is one of the most critical issues in the valuation of firms, as the two parties must agree on the values of both firms.

BUSINESS COMBINATIONS

The term *growth* refers to increases in the size and activities of a firm. Three measures are common:

- *Increase in sales*. This shows that a firm is maintaining its competitive position by increasing the size or number of markets for its goods and services. Revenue growth helps achieve stability.
- *Increase in profits*. This shows the firm's ability to convert growth in sales and operations into increasing returns to shareholders. Growth in profits is measured by operating income or earnings per share.
- *Increase in assets*. This is the least desirable method of measuring growth. Although firms increase their assets to provide capacity for production and sales, assets may rise without a corresponding increase in sales or earnings. An increase in assets could be a sign of inefficiency rather than growth.

External Growth

This occurs when a firm takes over the operations of another firm. Since the acquired company has sales and assets of its own, the first company does not have to generate the new business from scratch. The term *acquisition* refers to the taking over of assets or securities in the process of external growth.

External growth offers a number of benefits:

- *Rapid expansion.* Acquisition is the quickest path to growth. The acquiring firm eliminates the lead time for ordering and installing machinery, producing products or services, and achieving sales.
- *Immediate cash inflows.* Since the firm is taking over an operating business, it will realize almost immediate inflows from the customers of that business.
- *Reduction of risk.* Entering a new market involves a calculated risk. Will new products sell in sufficient volume to be profitable? Will managers make the proper decisions in the new operating environment? By entering a field through an established and experienced management team, the acquiring firm reduces the chances for failure.
- *Economies. Start-up costs* are the initial expenses when a firm begins operating. It may involve training a new sales force or paying legal fees. These costs can be held to a minimum by purchasing an operating firm.

Reasons for Seeking Growth

Firms combine with other firms or seek acquisitions to achieve:

- *Diversification.* This reduces the risk of failure. If a firm produces a single product, a drop in demand for that product or the entry of a competitor can cause problems. Since demand and competitive factors are difficult to predict, diversification is a safeguard against disaster.
- *Stability.* A company with a large volume of sales is more stable than a firm with smaller revenues. High volume allows production economies and other cost savings. Also, high sales reflect a deeper penetration of markets. If a firm dominates a market, it is better able to withstand problems in that market.
- *Operating economies.* Large firms are able to achieve economies that are not available to small firms. Examples are purchasing blocks of advertising, purchasing supplies in bulk, and negotiating discounts.
- *Profits from turnaround situations.* When a firm is operating below its potential profit levels, a new management team could remove inefficiencies. This can result in a dramatic rise in profits. Such a firm offers a *turnaround situation.* A company in such a situation may become the target of acquiring firms. Its stock will be selling at a low price, a bargain if profits can be restored to higher levels.

Kinds of Business Combinations

Three types of combinations are important:

- *Horizontal union.* This is the joining of two firms that are in the same area of business. An example is the combining of two book publishers.
- *Vertical union.* This is the joining of two firms that are involved in different stages of the production or distribution of the same product. An example is the combining of a furniture manufacturer and a chain of office supply stores.
- *Conglomerate union.* A *conglomerate* is a firm that has external growth through acquisitions where the companies are not related either vertically or horizontally.

A typical conglomerate might have operations in manufacturing, electronics, insurance, and other businesses.

Holding Companies

A *holding company* owns a controlling interest in the voting stock of one or more other corporations, which are called *subsidiaries*. As little as 10 to 15 percent of a company's stock may be sufficient ownership to control the firm. If the holding company actively engages in the management of the subsidiary, the holding company is also called a *parent company*.

The holding company structure is desirable for a number of reasons:

- *Ease of ownership.* A holding company can purchase the stock of another company without difficulty. No formal approval is required by either firm's stockholders.
- *Lower cost.* If stock is purchased in small installments over time, the price may not be affected. In contrast, if shareholders of the soon-to-be subsidiary learned that another firm was seeking control, the price would rise.
- *Leverage and control.* Because a company can be controlled with a small percentage of the voting stock (assuming that the rest is widely held), a holding company allows control of many assets with a small investment.
- *Diversification.* A holding company can purchase the stock of different firms, thus diversifying its investments.
- *Avoiding foreign corporation status.* A *domestic corporation* is one that is chartered by the state or country in which it operates. A *foreign corporation* is one that is chartered outside the area. Since domestic corporations have lower taxes and other privileges, this status is preferred.

Availability of Financing

An acquiring firm needs adequate and reasonable financing to pay for an acquisition. Two approaches are:

- *Pay cash.* The acquiring firm may have the cash or may be able to raise it through the sale of debt or equity securities.
- *Issue corporate stock.* The acquiring firm can give its stock to the shareholders of the acquired firm.

PYRAMIDING

Pyramiding is controlling several companies through a small investment in each. As little as 10 percent of voting stock may be sufficient for control. Actual pyramids are complicated structures managed with complex legal, financial, and communications arrangements. We will examine a model of a pyramid rather than an actual operating structure.

Sample Pyramid

A firm has $5 million in cash and can borrow another $5 million. It may use its $10 million cash to buy all the stock in Companies 1 and 2, which serve as intermediaries.

Once it owns these companies, they may borrow $5 million each. This will give the original firm, now a parent company, control of assets valued at $20 million. Further assume that each intermediary company buys stock in subsidiaries, Firms 3, 4, 5, and 6. If these firms borrow $5 million each, the parent will be controlling firms with $40 million in assets as a result of its initial $5 million investment. The pyramid structure is shown in Figure 14-1.

In this pyramid, the subsidiaries are operating companies that own assets and produce revenues. The intermediaries are holding companies, with no assets other than the stock in other companies. The profits earned by the operating companies are passed through the holding companies to the parent.

Risks and Leverage in Pyramids

Significant financial leverage may be achieved in a pyramid structure. In the pyramid in Figure 14-1, $5 million in equity supports borrowing $35 million and thus finances $40 million in operating assets. This produces profits when its return on investment exceeds its interest rate. It produces losses when the reverse is true.

Financial Leverage in a Pyramid

Financial leverage exists when a firm borrows at one rate and invests at another rate. It is favorable when the return on investment exceeds the interest rate. It is unfavorable when the reverse is true. Financial leverage plays an important role in pyramids.

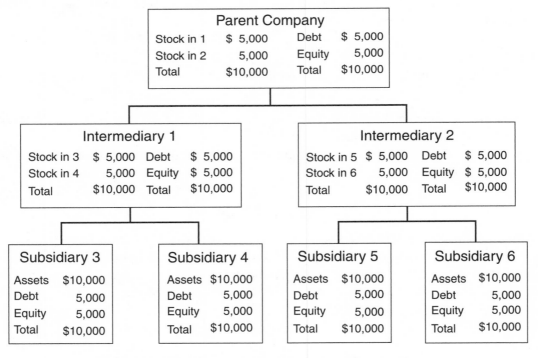

Figure 14-1. Corporate Structure Using Pyramiding.

Figure 14-2 shows a pyramid with favorable financial leverage. A 10 percent interest rate applies to $35 million of debt. The structure has a 15 percent return on investment in the operating subsidiaries. No taxes apply. The large profit at the parent level is the result of the leverage.

Figure 14-3 shows the risk of the pyramid scheme. Now return on investment has dropped to 5 percent, and the leverage has turned unfavorable. The parent has to cover all interest at the intermediary and parent levels because the subsidiaries need all their operating profit to cover their own debt. The pyramid might start to collapse.

The opportunities for leverage are high in pyramids, but so are the risks. Slight improvements in profit margins or asset turnover can be converted into large increases in after-tax earnings. Similarly, small decreases can affect the parent's ability to meet its interest payments.

Data

Return on investment	15%
Interest rate	10%
Total assets (in subsidiaries)	$40,000

	Parent
Debt	$5,000
Equity	$5,000
100% dividends from intermediaries	$3,000
Interest on debt	-$500
Earnings before taxes	$2,500

Intermediaries	1	2
Debt	$5,000	$5,000
100% dividends from subsidiaries	$2,000	$2,000
Interest on debt	-$500	-$500
Pretax profit	$1,500	$1,500

Subsidiaries	3	4	5	6
Assets	$10,000	$10,000	$10,000	$10,000
Debt	$5,000	$5,000	$5,000	$5,000
Operating profit	$1,500	$1,500	$1,500	$1,500
Interest on debt	-$500	-$500	-$500	-$500
Pretax profit	$1,000	$1,000	$1,000	$1,000

Figure 14-2. Favorable Financial Leverage in a Pyramid.

Data

Return on investment	5%
Interest rate	10%
Total assets (in subsidiaries)	$40,000

	Parent
Debt	$5,000
Equity	$5,000
Payment of interest for subsidiaries	-$1,000
Interest on debt	-$500
Loss in the structure	-$1,500

Intermediaries	**1**	**2**
Debt	$5,000	$5,000
100% dividends from subsidiaries	$0	$0
Interest on debt	-$500	-$500
Pretax profit	-$500	-$500

Subsidiaries	**3**	**4**	**5**	**6**
Assets	$10,000	$10,000	$10,000	$10,000
Debt	$5,000	$5,000	$5,000	$5,000
Operating profit	$500	$500	$500	$500
Interest on debt	-$500	-$500	-$500	-$500
Pretax profit	$0	$0	$0	$0

Figure 14-3. Unfavorable Financial Leverage in a Pyramid.

TAKEOVER STRATEGIES

When a firm decides to seek external growth, it begins to search for suitable candidates for acquisition. The search process may focus on a number of key characteristics:

- *Companies with net operating losses.* To be in a position to make acquisitions, a firm normally must be highly profitable. If the acquired firm has a recent history of operating at a loss, the tax code may allow the acquiring company to apply the past losses as a tax carryback or carryforward to reduce its taxes. This can be a key factor in the desirability of a combination.
- *Cash-rich companies.* A company may have accumulated a large amount of excess cash that would be useful to the acquiring firm, since it can help finance additional growth.
- *Synergistic prospects.* *Synergism* is the concept that some combinations have a total greater than the sum of the parts; that is, 2 + 2 = 5. If we combine two firms with

the proper operating characteristics, it may be possible to realize synergistic effects. One firm may have strong research and development, while the other has strong marketing. Together they would develop new products and bring them forcefully to the customer, resulting in profits that neither could achieve alone.

- *Companies with turnaround prospects.* A prime takeover candidate is the firm with low operating profits as a result of poor management or other controllable factors. By turning it around, the acquiring firm can achieve higher profits.

Spotting a Turnaround Situation

Guidelines to help a firm identify a turnaround situation include the following:

- *Recent drop in profits for individual firms, but not for the industry as a whole.* If a firm is experiencing internal problems, it may suffer a drop in operating profits. When the overall industry does not suffer such a drop, it is a good sign that the firm's profit decline results from an internal, and thus possibly controllable, factor.
- *Industries to be affected favorably by forecasted economic changes.* Economic forecasts are shifts in demand and changes in production for major industries. Each year brings forecasts of reduced production in some industries and increases in others. By analyzing these forecasts, a firm can identify industries with growth prospects in the short to medium term and can seek turnaround candidates in these industries.
- *Laggard firm in the industry.* Industries have successful and unsuccessful firms. Less profitable firms may have weak management. Taking over a laggard firm and replacing its management may bring a rapid increase in profits.
- *Break in management ranks.* Normally, a firm's top management works together and presents a united front to the outside world. Occasionally, however, some members of management break away. This may indicate that these managers see a better way to run the firm but are blocked by the controlling managers. The new ideas of the minority managers may be able to increase profits greatly. These situations call for further investigation.
- *Poorly performing firm with strength complementary to one's own strength.* The acquiring firm may have strength in marketing, while another firm may have strong products. A combination of these two firms would have both production and marketing expertise and could achieve solid increases in profits in a short period of time.

Determining the Purchase Price for a Turnaround Candidate

The technique of estimating future earnings per share can help in estimating the purchase price for a company that is not performing up to its potential. To illustrate this technique, financial data for Lenox Products are given in Figure 14-4. At present, the operating and financial characteristics indicate the following:

- *Lenox's P/E value is only $2 per share.* Thus, its current market price of $10 appears to be based more on the value of its assets than on its profits.
- *Lenox has excess cash.* It could pay a $5 dividend per share ($10 million/2 million shares). Half its assets are cash, an excessive amount for operations.

Projected Balance Sheet

	Present	Future
Cash	$10,000	$1,000
Other assets	10,000	29,000
Total Assets	$20,000	$30,000

	Present	Future
Debt	$1,000	$11,000
Equity	19,000	19,000
Total Debt and Equity	$20,000	$30,000

Other Financial Data

	Present	Future
Sales	$20,000	$60,000
Net income	$400	$6,000
Shares outstanding	2,000	2,000
Earnings per share	$0.20	$3.00
Return on Equity	2.1%	32%
Market value, one share:		
At normal P/E ratio of 10:1	$2	$30
Present market price of stock	$10	

Figure 14-4. Financial Data for Lenox Products.

- *Lenox has small profits.* Its EPS is only $0.20. Its return on equity is 2.1 percent ($400/$19,000).

If our firm acquires Lenox, we would take certain actions. Their financial impacts are forecast in the future column in the figure:

- We would eliminate the excess cash and invest it in other assets. Also, we would take advantage of favorable financial leverage by borrowing $10 million and increasing our debt-equity ratio to an acceptable .63/1.
- We would use the additional capital to purchase new equipment, which could increase production and provide more units to sell.
- We would use our own excellent marketing team to sell Lenox products, a step that should dramatically increase sales from $20 to $60 million.
- The new equipment and larger sales volume would result in more acceptable profit levels, as reflected in the $3 EPS and the 32 percent return on equity ($6 million/ $19 million).

With Lenox, the current market price of $10 makes the stock overpriced based on profits. Considering future profits, the stock is not overpriced. What is the intrinsic value? The answer is some price below $30, depending upon the degree of risk that we shall not be able to achieve the turnaround At $12 to $15 per share, the firm offers a chance for a sizable increase in the value of the common stock if projected figures are attained.

Opposition to an Acquisition

In many cases, management decides that another company should not acquire the firm. Many reasons may be given to explain the management's feelings:

- *Failure to understand the target firm's problems.* The management may feel that the acquiring firm does not understand the real difficulties that the existing management is facing. This lack of understanding may cause even greater problems once the acquisition has been completed.
- *Future plans not in the interest of the target firm's shareholders.* The acquiring firm may be planning to operate the target firm as a subsidiary in a new or restricted role. The target firm's operations may be modified or partially eliminated to fit in with the parent firm's other activities. This reduction of growth in production and sales might be viewed as harmful to the remaining shareholders of the target firm.
- *Low tender price or exchange ratio.* We have already noted that a firm that is about to be acquired is not realizing its full potential. If it were, the price could be too high for a takeover. Management may feel that conditions will soon improve and that the target firm's stock will rise rapidly. Thus, it may object to a takeover at the bargain price implied in the tender offer.
- *Acquiring firm's plan for new management.* Perhaps the most common objection of the existing management is that a new management will be installed after the takeover. The acquiring firm usually makes a major effort to identify the "deadwood" in the old management and may even replace it entirely. If the old management were strong, the firm would be doing better.

Resisting an Acquisition

A firm may employ various tactics to avoid being taken over by another firm, including the following:

- *Encourage stockholders to vote against the takeover.* Management can send notices to all shareholders, recommending that they refuse to cooperate with the acquiring group.
- *Block efforts to solicit tenders.* Management can refuse to release the mailing list of stockholders or otherwise make it difficult for the acquiring group to contact shareholders.
- *Involve a government agency.* If a government agency shows interest in the acquisition, it will make the effort more difficult. An agency could investigate antitrust considerations or find another reason to be involved.
- *Place controlling stock in friendly hands.* The firm resisting the takeover may issue stock in return for assets to a corporation that will vote on the side of management. The additional outstanding stock will make it more difficult for an unfriendly company to gain voting control.

- *Begin an unfavorable publicity campaign.* The very fact that management is openly willing to resist can have a detrimental effect. The acquiring company may feel that the unfavorable publicity is more harmful than the beneficial effects from the takeover.

CONCLUSION

External growth offers an attractive path for rapidly expanding a business or establishing a stronger market position. It just has to be done right. Financial risk managers know that business combinations offer both risk and opportunity. First, the tools of financial analysis provide an understanding of the relationships among risks, opportunities, and returns. Then, qualitative factors are considered. After considering the entire range of issues, the firm makes a decision to pursue an acquisition or withdraw from it.

CHAPTER 14 APPENDIXES

How to Assess the Value of a Complex Potential Acquisition Candidate

Northern Technologies Co. (NTC) is a potential acquisition candidate. It is a small high-technology firm with new and exciting products. All five of the company's business units have substantial international sales.

The company uses the profit margin as the driving force in determining its financial goals. It calls the ratio *return on sales* to focus everyone on the concept as a profit goal. The asset turnover (assets to sales) is relatively stable across business units, so the only way to improve return on investment is to focus on profit margin. The company's goal for next year is a return on sales of 9 percent

An analyst has reviewed the financial performance of NTC and submitted the following comments. Do you agree with them?

Analyst's Comments.

> NTC's revenues and profits are diversified in terms of both operating units and geography.
> Its after-tax profits have been growing. Its sales have not grown as much.
> It spends 5 percent of its revenues on R&D. This is important for a firm with 75 percent of its revenues coming from product sales.
> Dividends and retained earnings are reasonable.
> It uses its cash to replace assets, pay dividends, and repurchase common stock. The repurchase indicates that it has few opportunities to invest in new projects.
> The balance sheet contains no obvious flaws.
> The company is making progress on its target goal for return on sales.
> It is a balanced, well-managed company.
> The next step is to perform a present value analysis after gathering information on changes in the company's operating environment.

NTC Balance Sheet.

	Year -2	Year -1
Assets		
Cash and cash equivalents	$900	$1,127
Accounts receivable (net of doubtful accounts)	3,682	3,717
Inventories and contracts in progress	2,954	3,342
Future income tax benefits	950	946
Other current assets	466	479
Total current assets	**$8,952**	**$9,611**
Customer financing assets	$321	$296
Future income tax benefits	552	615
Fixed assets	4,420	4,371
Other assets	1,713	1,852
Total Assets	**$15,958**	**$16,745**
Liabilities and Shareowners' Equity		
Short-term borrowings	$294	$251
Accounts payable	2,084	2,186
Accrued liabilities	4,183	4,856
Long-term debt currently due	98	97
Total current liabilities	**$6,659**	**$7,390**
Long-term debt	$1,649	$1,437
Future pension and postretirement benefit obligations	1,399	1,247
Future income taxes payable	130	155
Other long-term liabilities	1,233	1,298
Minority interests in subsidiary companies	469	478
Series A convertible preferred stock outstanding	892	880
Deferred compensation	(494)	(446)
Total long-term debt	**$5,278**	**$5,049**
Common stock	$2,249	$2,345
Treasury stock	(1,168)	(1,626)
Retained earnings	3,252	3,849
Currency translation and minimum pension liability	(312)	(262)
Total shareowners' equity	**$4,021**	**$4,306**
Total Liabilities and Shareowners' Equity	**$15,958**	**$16,745**

NTC Income Statement.

	Year -3	Year -2	Year -1
Revenues:			
Product sales	$16,670	$17,972	$18,247
Service sales	4,131	4,652	5,026
Financing revenues and other income	396	178	239
	$21,197	**$22,802**	**$23,512**
Costs and Expenses:			
Cost of products sold	$13,773	$14,793	$14,625
Cost of services sold	2,559	2,807	3,112
Research and development	978	963	1,122
Selling, general, and administrative	2,536	2,651	2,872
Interest	275	244	221
	$20,121	**$21,458**	**$21,952**
Income before taxes and minority interests	$1,076	$1,344	$1,560
Income taxes	384	464	523
Minority interests in subsidiaries' earnings	107	130	131
Net income	**$585**	**$750**	**$906**

Earnings per share of common stock	$2.20	$2.85	$3.45
Cash dividends	$238	$252	$265
Dividends per share	$0.95	$1.03	$1.10

NTC Statement of Cash Flows.

Cash flows from operating activities	Year -3	Year -2	Year -1
Net income to net cash flows from operations:	$585	$750	$906
Depreciation and amortization	840	844	853
Minority interests in subsidiaries' earnings	107	130	131
Change in:			
Accounts receivable	-756	149	1
Inventories and contracts	290	2	-364
Other current assets	161	-179	-23
Accounts payable and accrued liabilities	6	177	618
ESOP deferred compensation	119	45	18
Other net	5	126	45
Net cash flows from operating activities	**$1,357**	**$2,044**	**$2,095**

Cash flows from investing activities			
Capital expenditures	-$759	-$780	-$794
Increase in customer financing assets	-248	-138	-137

Cash flows from operating activities	Year -3	Year -2	Year -1
Decrease in customer financing assets	545	373	185
Acquisition of business units	-125	-204	-317
Disposition of business units	282	103	177
Other net	16	-8	84
Net cash flows from investing activities	**($289)**	**($654)**	**($802)**

Cash flows from financing activities			
Issuance of long-term debt	$25	$30	
Repayment of long-term debt	-207	-299	-273
Decrease in short-term borrowings	-379	-92	-93
Common stock issued for employee stock plan	73	101	96
Dividends paid on common stock	-238	-252	-265
Common stock repurchase	-270	-221	-459
Dividends to minority interests and other	-102	-111	-91
Net cash flows from financing activities	**($1,098)**	**($874)**	**($1,055)**

Effect of foreign exchange rate changes	-5	-2	-11
Net increase (decrease) in cash equivalents	-35	514	227
Cash and cash equivalents, beginning of year	421	386	900
Cash and cash equivalents, end of year	$386	$900	$1,127
Interest paid net of amounts capitalized	$237	$220	$187
Income taxes paid net of refunds	$248	$461	$480

NTC Business Segments.

Total Revenues

	Year -3	Year -2	Year -1
Unit 1	$4,644	$5,287	$5,595
Unit 2	4,919	5,456	5,958
Unit 3	2,683	3,061	3,233
Unit 4	5,846	6,170	6,201
Unit 5	3,218	2,947	2,651
Corporate items and eliminations	(113)	(119)	(126)
Total	$21,197	$22,802	$23,512

Operating Profits

	Year -3	Year -2	Year -1
Unit 1	$421	$511	$524
Unit 2	278	354	422
Unit 3	182	180	196

	Year -3	Year -2	Year -1
Unit 4	380	530	637
Unit 5	282	209	234
Corporate items and eliminations	1	2	(21)
Total	$1,544	$1,786	$1,992
Financing revenues and other income net	(17)	(23)	(23)
Interest expense	(275)	(244)	(221)
General corporate expenses	(176)	(175)	(188)
Income before taxes and minority interests	$1,076	$1,344	$1,560

Capital Expenditures

	Year -3	Year -2	Year -1
Unit 1	$101	$115	$132
Unit 2	134	151	169
Unit 3	151	140	138
Unit 4	226	240	248
Unit 5	130	106	86
Corporate items and eliminations	17	28	21
Consolidated total	$759	$780	$794

Identifiable Assets

	Year -3	Year -2	Year -1
Unit 1	$2,068	$2,613	$2,712
Unit 2	2,776	2,959	3,387
Unit 3	1,818	1,875	1,856
Unit 4	4,221	4,215	4,261
Unit 5	1,720	1,425	1,416
Corporate items and eliminations	3,021	2,871	3,113
Consolidated total	$15,624	$15,958	$16,745

Depreciation and Amortization

	Year -3	Year -2	Year -1
Unit 1	$103	$108	$116
Unit 2	136	134	145
Unit 3	106	122	128
Unit 4	323	314	296
Unit 5	140	127	123
Corporate items and eliminations	32	39	45
Consolidated total	$840	$844	$853

NTC Geographic Areas.

Total Revenues

	Year -3	Year -2	Year -1
U.S. operations	$13,545	$13,968	$14,007
International operations:			
Europe	4,119	4,769	4,977
Asia-Pacific	2,461	3,024	3,395
Other	2,210	2,463	2,668
Corporate items and eliminations	(1,138)	(1,422)	(1,535)
Total	$21,197	$22,802	$23,512

Operating Profits.

	Year -3	Year -2	Year -1
U.S. operations	$746	$773	$965
International operations:			
Europe	399	457	461
Asia-Pacific	200	235	272
Other	204	321	310
Corporate items and eliminations	(5)	(16)	
Total	$1,544	$1,786	$1,992

Identifiable Assets.

	Year -3	Year -2	Year -1
U.S. operations	$7,912	$7,110	$7,252
International operations:			
Europe	2,199	2,540	2,749
Asia-Pacific	1,524	2,078	2,171
Other	1,022	1,357	1,454
Corporate items and eliminations	2,967	2,873	3,119
Total	$15,624	$15,958	$16,745

NTC Valuation Solution.

Sources of Revenues

NTC revenues come from five major business units.

	Year -3	Year -2	Year -1
Unit 1	$4,644	$5,287	$5,595
Unit 2	4,919	5,456	5,958
Unit 3	2,683	3,061	3,233

	Year -3	Year -2	Year -1
Unit 4	5,846	6,170	6,201
Unit 5	3,218	2,947	2,651
Total	$21,310	$22,921	$23,638

Percentages:			
Unit 1	21.8%	23.1%	23.7%
Unit 2	23.1%	23.8%	25.2%
Unit 3	12.6%	13.4%	13.7%
Unit 4	27.4%	26.9%	26.2%
Unit 5	15.1%	12.9%	11.2%
Total	100.0%	100.0%	100.0%

NTC revenues come from all over the world.

	Year -3	Year -2	Year -1
U.S. operations	$13,545	$13,968	$14,007
International operations:			
Europe	4,119	4,769	4,977
Asia-Pacific	2,461	3,024	3,395
Other	1,022	1,357	1,454
Total	$21,147	$23,118	$23,833
Percentages:			
U.S. operations	64.1%	60.4%	58.8%
International operations:			
Europe	19.5%	20.6%	20.9%
Asia-Pacific	11.6%	13.1%	14.2%
Other	4.8%	5.9%	6.1%
Total	100.0%	100.0%	100.0%

Operating Profits

Each business unit contributes to operating profits.

	Year -3	Year -2	Year -1
Unit 1	$421	$511	$524
Unit 2	278	354	422
Unit 3	182	180	196
Unit 4	380	530	637
Unit 5	282	209	234
Total	$1,543	$1,784	$2,013

	Year -3	Year -2	Year -1
Percentages:			
Unit 1	27.3%	28.6%	26.0%
Unit 2	18.0%	19.8%	21.0%
Unit 3	11.8%	10.1%	9.7%
Unit 4	24.6%	29.7%	31.6%
Unit 5	18.3%	11.7%	11.6%
Total	100.0%	100.0%	100.0%

Each area of the world contributes to operating profits.

	Year -3	Year -2	Year -1
U.S. operations	$746	$773	$965
International operations:			
Europe	399	457	461
Asia-Pacific	200	235	272
Other	204	321	310
Total	$1,543	$1,784	$2,013
Percentages:			
U.S. operations	48.3%	43.3%	47.9%
International operations:			
Europe	25.9%	25.6%	22.9%
Asia-Pacific	13.0%	13.2%	13.5%
Other	13.2%	18.0%	15.4%
Total	100.4%	100.1%	99.8%

After-Tax Profits

What are after-tax profits for NTC? (000s)

	Year -3	Year -2	Year -1
Revenues	$21,197	$22,802	$23,512
Cost of products/services	-16,332	-17,600	-17,737
Research and development	-978	-963	-1,122
Selling, general, and administrative	-2,536	-2,651	-2,872
Operating profits	1,351	1,588	1,781
Interest	-275	-244	-221
Pretax income	$1,076	$1,344	$1,560
Income taxes	-384	-464	-523
Minority interests	-107	-130	-131
Net income	$585	$750	$906
Earnings per share	$2.20	$2.85	$3.45

Dividends
How much does NTC pay in dividends?

	Year -3	Year -2	Year -1
Cash dividends	$238	$252	$265
Dividends per share	$0.95	$1.03	$1.10

Retained Earnings
How much does NTC retain for growth? (000s)

	Year -3	Year -2	Year -1
Net income	$585	$750	$906
Minus NTC cash dividends	-238	-252	-265
Retained earnings	$347	$498	$641

Cash from Operations
NTC gets most of its cash from operations. (000s)

	Year -3	Year -2	Year -1
Revenues	$21,197	$22,802	$23,512
Cost of products/services	-16,332	-17,600	-17,737
Depreciation and amortization	840	844	853
Research and development	-978	-963	-1,122
Selling, general, and administrative	-2,536	-2,651	-2,872
Income taxes	-384	-464	-523
Cash flow from operations	$1,807	$1,968	$2,111

NTC uses most of its cash to replace or upgrade assets, pay cash dividends, and repurchase common stock. (000s)

	Year -3	Year -2	Year -1
Capital expenditures	-$759	-$780	-$794
Cash dividends	-238	-252	-265
Repurchase common stock	-270	-221	-459
Other activities or adjustments	-575	-201	-366
Change in cash balance	-$35	$514	$227

Reconcile Cash Flow from Operations to Net Income

	Year -3	Year -2	Year -1
Cash flow from operations	$1,807	$1,968	$2,111
Minus depreciation	-840	-844	-853
Minus interest	-275	-244	-221
Minus minority interest	-107	-130	-131
Equals net income	$585	$750	$906

Assets Held by NTC

What assets are held by NTC? ($ millions)

	Year -2	Year -1
Cash	$900	$1,127
Receivables	3,682	3,717
Inventories	2,954	3,342
Other	1,416	1,425
Current assets total	$8,952	$9,611
Fixed assets	4,420	4,371
Other assets	2.586	2,763
Total Assets	$15,958	$16,745

Which operating units hold the assets? (000s)

	Year -3	Year -2	Year -1
Unit 1	$2,068	$2,613	$2,712
Unit 2	2,776	2,959	3,387
Unit 3	1,818	1,875	1,856
Unit 4	4,221	4,215	4,261
Unit 5	1,720	1,425	1,416
Headquarters and consolidation	3,021	2,871	3,113
Percentages:			
Unit 1	13.2%	16.4%	16.2%
Unit 2	17.8%	18.5%	20.2%
Unit 3	11.6%	11.7%	11.1%
Unit 4	27.0%	26.4%	25.4%
Unit 5	11.0%	8.9%	8.5%
Headquarters and consolidation	19.3%	18.0%	18.6%

Where in the world are the assets located?

	Year -3	Year -2	Year -1
U.S. operations	$7,912	$7,110	$7,252
International operations:			
Europe	2,199	2,540	2,749
Asia-Pacific	1,524	2,078	2,171
Other	1,022	1,357	1,454
Headquarters and consolidation	2,967	2,873	3,119
Total	$15,624	$15,958	$16,745

Financing of Assets
How does NTC finance its assets? (000s)

	Year -2	Year -1
Payables	$2,084	$2,186
Other	4,575	5,204
Current liabilities	$6,659	$7,390
Long-term debt	1,649	1,437
Pension obligations	1,399	1,247
Other liabilities	2,230	2,365
Long-term obligations	$5,278	$5,049
Capital stock	1,081	719
Retained earnings	2,940	3,587
Shareholders' equity	$4,021	$4,306
Total	$15,958	$16,745

Return on Sales
What is the return on sales for NTC?

	Year -3	Year -2	Year -1
Unit 1	9.1%	9.7%	9.4%
Unit 2	5.7%	6.5%	7.1%
Unit 3	6.8%	5.9%	6.1%
Unit 4	6.5%	8.6%	10.3%
Unit 5	8.8%	7.1%	8.8%
Total	7.2%	7.8%	8.5%

Asset Turnover
What is the asset turnover for NTC?

	Year -3	Year -2	Year -1
Unit 1	2.2	2.0	2.1
Unit 2	1.8	1.8	1.8
Unit 3	1.5	1.6	1.7
Unit 4	1.4	1.5	1.5
Unit 5	1.9	2.1	1.9
Total	1.4	1.4	1.4

Return on Investment

What is the return on investment for NTC?

	Year -3	Year -2	Year -1
Unit 1	20.4%	19.6%	19.3%
Unit 2	10.0%	12.0%	12.5%
Unit 3	10.0%	9.6%	10.6%
Unit 4	9.0%	12.6%	14.9%
Unit 5	16.4%	14.7%	16.5%
Total	9.9%	11.2%	12.0%

Index